I0094905

Coaching for Physicians

This edited collection brings together leading voices in the field of medicine and coaching to highlight the growing challenges healthcare professionals face today, providing practical coaching tools and approaches to empower physicians to not only survive but thrive in the 21st century. Combining the knowledge of two professions, healthcare and coaching, the contributors offer a detailed analysis and discussion of the growing issues in the healthcare industry, demonstrating how coaching principles can be implemented to help improve physician leadership, well-being, performance, personal and professional happiness, and positive patient outcomes. Chapters address key topics such as burnout, resilience, emotional intelligence, career coaching, team coaching, and best practice approaches when working with the unique challenges of coaching physicians. Filled with case studies, definitions, summaries, and key points throughout, this book provides solutions to manage the surmounting challenges we are seeing in healthcare across the world today. This book is essential reading for all coaches working with physicians, healthcare executives, nurses, and allied health professionals.

Naim El-Aswad is a fellow of the American College of Physicians and a healthcare professional coach. He has been an internist and emergency room physician for over 20 years. He is the founder and Chief Medical Officer of Vital Signs Vital Skills, a coaching and consulting company that specializes in executive, life, and wellness coaching.

Coaching for Physicians

Empowering Healthcare Professionals in the 21st Century

Edited by
Naim El-Aswad, MD, FACP, ACC

Routledge
Taylor & Francis Group

NEW YORK AND LONDON

Designed cover image: ©juststock @Getty Images

First published 2025
by Routledge
605 Third Avenue, New York, NY 10158

and by Routledge
4 Park Square, Milton Park, Abingdon, Oxon OX14 4RN

Routledge is an imprint of the Taylor & Francis Group, an informa business

Library of Congress Cataloging-in-Publication Data
A catalog record for this title has been requested

ISBN: 978-1-032-58719-6 (hbk)
ISBN: 978-1-032-58903-9 (pbk)
ISBN: 978-1-003-45206-5 (ebk)

DOI: 10.4324/9781003452065

Typeset in Optima
by Taylor & Francis Books

Contents

List of illustrations   ix
Forewords   x
Preface   xiv
Acknowledgement and Gratitude   xvi
List of contributors   xvii

1 Coaching and Perspectives   1
   NAIM EL-ASWAD

2 Coaching Approaches in Healthcare   17
   NAIM EL-ASWAD

3 The Healthcare Environment: The Current State of Affairs   32
   NAIM EL-ASWAD

4 The Uniqueness of the Physicians: Understanding the Mindset
   of Physicians, their Driving Forces, Coachability, and their
   Challenges   46
   NAIM EL-ASWAD

5 Coaching the Physician: Best Practice Guide   56
   RELLY NADLER

6 Coach the Physician, Not the Problem   74
   MARCIA REYNOLDS

7 Coaching the Team in Healthcare   80
   ZEINA GHOSSOUB

8 Burnout and Mental health: A Coaching Approach   90
   NAIM EL-ASWAD

9 Emotional intelligence in Medicine: Impact and Applications   102
   RELLY NADLER

10 Coaching Physician Resilience   119
    CATHY GREENBERG

11 Truly Human-Centered Leadership: Coaching for Physician
    Leadership   144
    CATHY GREENBERG

12 Career Coaching for Physicians   168
    ZEINA GHOSSOUB

13 Female Physicians: Unique Challenges and Coaching
    Approaches   180
    ZEINA GHOSSOUB

14 Legalities, Ethics, and the Business of Coaching   187
    ZEINA GHOSSOUB

15 Challenges of Coaching in the Healthcare Industry   195
    NAIM EL-ASWAD

16 Coaching for Change in the Healthcare Industry   207
    NAIM EL-ASWAD

    Index   212

Illustrations

Figures

4.1 Circles of concern, influence, and focus (Based on Stephen
  Covey's Circle Model)   52
5.1 Ask and Drain Buckets   62
5.2 Strength Balancing Model For Dr. T   69
5.3 Derailer Detector   70
9.1 Levels in Emotional Intelligence Proficiency   110
12.1 Career Competencies Map   175

Tables

1.1 Expert versus Coach's approach   15
4.1 Locus of Control   50
5.1 VIVID Model for Leaders   61
5.2 Fast versus Slow thinking   62
5.3 Eqi results   71
9.2 EQI 2.0 competency   115
12.1 MBTI Preference Scale   170
12.2 Personalities and Specialties   171
12.3 Birkman's Personality Colors   173
16.1 Impact Areas of Coaching   209

Forewords

The professional practice of coaching thrives across borders and contexts because of the focus on humanity and our collective quest for connectedness to flourish. It has been my great privilege to join thousands of volunteer leaders across the globe since 1995, including all five authors of this book. The current constellation of coaching provides evidence-based, scientifically supported methods to continuously produce human development and well-being in any aspect of the human experience. Supported by eleven associations dedicated to moral and ethical quality, people pursue efficacy with the coaching mindset and skill set. Motivated by what the authors quote from Tony Robbins, "the tyranny of how," individuals in every walk of life seek a way to remove what blocks them from sustaining action to fulfill goals set and dreams imagined.

I've walked side-by-side with the five authors who have created this book and the hundreds of professionals that the book curates so that you can appreciate the tremendous breadth and depth of resources available through professional coaching. I've witnessed and experienced the influence of professional coaching's reach globally, including the honor of transferring the skills of coaching to six national health systems and two international health systems. To this day, leaders regularly ask me why the growth of coaching has occurred at this point in history, with the next moment of curiosity that asks, "Why does coaching work?" You will discover your answers to both questions in this book. The authors' direct experience in the health sector as physicians, leaders, physician leaders, and coaches at every level of health systems equips them to inform and impart knowledge and tools for the unique relevance of coaching to transform the business of disease to wellness.

This book delivers rigorous attention to evidence-based research, scientific reasoning, and practice knowledge with a discipline throughout to illustrate the application of coaching to effective leading. Sharing their deep passion, they also anchor this robust compilation in the health industry's reality as it impacts clinicians, system-level leaders, and the patients and communities served. Chapter 5 quotes American psychologist and educator John Dewey, who said: "Provoking people to think about their thinking is the single most powerful antidote to erroneous beliefs and autopilot." Let this book become your antidote to access more resourcefulness and navigate the foundational transformation in the health industry at every level.

The authors set out an aggressive goal to produce a body of work that would stand the test of rigor required for medical curricula, train physicians and clinicians, and equip everyone with methods to thrive personally and professionally in the complex and demanding healthcare industry. Succeeding in their goal is beyond worthy to essential. Physician suicide has skyrocketed to an annual rate of 350–400. Attrition of personnel in health systems due to mental health disorders, substance abuse, and toxic workplace environments drives burnout rates of 35%-50%. This data suggests that the success of this book and the programs that will incorporate it directly affect the viability of health systems everywhere.

Through their extensive and collective experience in various health systems, the authors speak cogently, compassionately, and competently about the suffering in the health professional population. The dire need for support and help understood by this team addresses the pathophysiology of their diseases with the knowledge and skills to apply coaching immediately and sustainably. Ironically, the book offers many answers to the "tyranny of how" with theories, models, processes, and tools, making it clear that the gap in how to change presents uniquely for each person. Why and what to change may be common across health systems, providing a shared aspiration for change. What's uncommon in the pathway of change presents as something very personal for each person to choose in the face of a long-lived life of habits, preferences, assumptions, and biases. As the science would describe, those filters stimulate how a person shows up and interacts quite invisibly or unconsciously.

The intimate partnership that coaching offers motivates the desire to become more self-aware, recognize what limits satisfaction, and imagine what and how to transform the experience of self and engagement with others. Too many believe that change is challenging and requires a lot of time. Coaching supports each person in adopting a more empowering belief in their internal resourcefulness to instantly change thoughts and desires for something better. The coaching dialogue focuses a person's attention on the choices that sustain action to embody the behaviors that fulfill the new thought and desire. Physician leaders, biased toward the earned expert status that their education, training, and positions instill, can present as resistant to coaching. As the authors point out, people providing coaching support must respect this starting point for physician leaders. The strengths used to develop as a physician become the resource to create a balanced humanity; nothing is left behind, and the process integrates everything into a greater wholeness. The opportunity to reconnect with an internal source of wisdom stimulates a new perspective and an ability to ideate new ways to see others as capable and resourceful rather than problems to manage. The transformational promise of coaching is human-centered leadership that begins with leadership of the self. As that change integrates into daily life, leaders see others and the systems they operate within with a wider-angle lens filled with potential and new possibilities.

To be sure you can evoke an aspirational vision from reading this book, the authors conclude with a clear call to action. "We are at a crossroads. A world and an industry are ailing and demanding a new medication/approach for help. In some ways, it has given rise to this ailment, perpetuates its existence, and seeks outside help or internal resources to mitigate and manage this festering reality. In other ways, it holds the key to its own healing approach." Join the team, whether you are a leader, an educator, a policymaker, a physician leader, or a clinician in any form. This book will be a guide and resource you will dog ear, highlight, and reference for a lifetime.

For any reader who picks up this book, read it in a way that's relevant to you. Keep loving your life's work; loving it fuels a flourishing humanity.

Janet M. Harvey
CEO inviteCHANGE and ICD Master Certified Coach

"Hello, Doctor, how are you?" I ask, genuinely concerned. The response, consistently, is a courteous, "I am fine, thank you." However, increasingly, it seems to drift further from the truth.

Physicians find themselves under unparalleled pressure, grappling with mental health disorders, social and familial challenges, and the specter of depression or substance abuse. Burnout, an affliction affecting over one-third of doctors, is an alarming reality. The suicide rate among physicians in the USA is escalating to approximately one per day, and a growing number are opting to leave the healthcare industry.

The root causes of this crisis are manifold, with one constant amidst the chaos—the unrelenting demands imposed upon the healthcare industry. It contends with ever-tightening regulations and intense scrutiny, navigating a landscape rife with conflicting economic, legal, and ethical imperatives. The conditions in which doctors practice medicine are deteriorating, leading to heightened tensions between clinical and non-clinical personnel, exacerbated by a dearth of effective leadership. Consequently, physicians' work-life balance and well-being are in decline, with resilience waning and professional rewards diminishing.

Another critical factor contributing to the accelerated decline in the well-being of healthcare professionals is the lack of holistic support. Unlike other industries, physicians are seldom offered the services of professional coaches. This anomaly can be rectified by integrating proven coaching practices into the healthcare ecosystem, heralding a new era of holistic well-being and higher performance – a "New Frontier".

Coaching serves as a catalyst for clients to improve their self-care and resilience, enhance their communication and leadership skills, and unlock their untapped potential. The International Coaching Federation defines coaching as "partnering with clients in a thought-provoking and creative process that inspires them to maximize their personal and professional potential." It involves discovering, clarifying, and aligning with clients' goals, encouraging self-discovery, eliciting client-generated solutions, and fostering accountability.

A survey by the Ken Blanchard Companies, quoted by the Institute of Coaching, reveals that "coaching positively impacts careers and lives by helping individuals to establish and pursue goals, become more self-reliant, gain job and life satisfaction, contribute effectively to teams and organizations, take responsibility and accountability for actions, and communicate more effectively."

This book, "Coaching Physicians in the Healthcare Industry: A New Frontier," seeks to illuminate the transformative impact of coaching on healthcare and physicians specifically. Tailored for physicians, allied healthcare professionals, and healthcare executives, this compelling read, authored by five renowned experts in coaching and medicine, delves into the science of coaching, its principles, practical applications, and provides evidence-based, scientifically proven approaches to leverage coaching in support of physicians.

The authors' mission is clear: to integrate coaching into medical curricula, physician training, and the personal and professional lives of physicians, so as to empower them to thrive in the complex and demanding healthcare industry. Grounded in scientific research, the authors' approach is robust—a necessity for success given the environment and the stakes involved.

A true measure of success will be when, after benefiting from coaching, my doctor exudes well-being, stamina, and sharpness. At that point, I won't ask, "how are you?" but instead, "Tell me about you, and your secrets to being so well!"

Jean-Francois Cousin, MCC
Global Executive and Team Coach, Speaker and Author
Chairman of the International Coaching Federation Global Board in 2019

Preface

Coaching physicians in healthcare is a new frontier. For over half a century, coaching has been used in various industries. The impact of coaching has been very well documented in the areas of executive leadership, management, self-growth, self-care and wellness, relationships, and families to name a few. Over the past decade, there has been an increase in interest as well as research in the uses and applications of coaching in the healthcare industry. This industry is varied, with multiple moving parts that are as unique as they are complimentary. The clinical and the executive non-clinical side try to form a team that helps navigate the demands of the healthcare industry. Economical, legal, moral, and ethical rules, regulations, and expectations have made this industry one of the most, if not the most scrutinized. One of the healthcare professionals at the heart of this industry is the doctor.

Physicians face unprecedented challenges in the practice of medicine. These challenges range from personal to professional. The landscape of the healthcare industry appears to be shifting towards worsening the factors that have led to the deterioration of the physician's health, wellbeing, ability to practice medicine, and the very essence of their existence. These factors include but are not limited to, tighter regulations and control, worsening of work-life integration, increased scrutiny, decreased professional rewards, lack of proper leadership, and increased uncertainty in both the training and the practice of medicine.

Physicians suffer from some of the worst consequences of any profession ranging from burnout to other mental health disorders, social and family issues/challenges, depression, PTSD, moral injury, substance abuse, and sometimes resulting in the ultimate sacrifice, suicide, at a staggering rate of 350–400 per year, or one per day!

The skills, knowledge, and their applications necessary for physicians to not only survive this hazardous environment but thrive in it are sorely lacking. Recent literature has been focusing on finding ways to remedy that. One of the most promising approaches that is severely underutilized is coaching. The scientific and medical literature provides ample evidence of its benefits, calls for its implementation, and highlights its necessity. The literature also acknowledges the lack of knowledge and expertise in implementing or utilizing coaching in healthcare.

A group of 5 authors, all experts in their respective fields of coaching and medicine, have decided to bring to light the impact of coaching on healthcare in general and physicians in particular. They have authored this book to introduce the science of coaching for physicians, to describe this new frontier, to teach its principles and practical applications, to open the avenue for more research and implementation, and provide evidence-based, scientifically proven, and well-documented approaches to utilize it in support of physicians.

Acknowledgement and Gratitude

There is plenty of time and ink to discuss what this book is all about. Here, I am taking a moment to express my gratitude to God, the Virgin Mary, Zeina, my wife, and our children, my parents, to friends and family, to these amazing co-authors, to the colleagues who have written the forwards and the endorsements, (Mr. Jean-Francois Cousin, Ms. Janet Harvey, Dr. Stephanie Simmons, and Dr. Paul Zak) and to Routledge Publishing; specifically, my supporting editor Ms. Julia Giordano, for making this book a reality. It started as a thought and a dream 4 years ago. Here I am, blessed to be able to publish it.

The inspiration of this book came not only from my personal and professional journey, but from the lessons learned from these world-renowned co-authors, and from all of my colleagues, circumstances, experiences, and from the privilege of being a physician and all the patients, nurses, staff, and administrators that I have encountered in my life.

Last but not least, I am grateful and acknowledge the impact of coaching on my very existence. Coaching has transformed my life. It helped me with the attitude adjustments, mindset shifts and growth, personal awareness, motivational fuel and self-belief. It is through that lens of coaching that I pray this book has the impact on the lives of my fellow colleagues, personally and professionally.

Contributors

Zeina Ghossoub, PhD, MCC, CWC: Zeina Ghossoub, a behaviorist and dietitian, is a master coach whose influence in life and wellness coaching is felt across the executive and healthcare worlds. She is a global figure and a trailblazer for women, especially in the MENA region.

Cathy Greenberg, PhD, PCC: Cathy Greenberg, a best-selling author, is a top 100 coach. Her focus on creating and fostering leadership and emotional brilliance has made her an expert/consultant for Fortune 500 companies, the military, law-enforcement, and the healthcare industry.

Relly Nadler, PsyD, MCC: Relly Nadler, a prolific and best-selling author and psychologist, is an international powerhouse figure in executive coaching, emotional intelligence, educating coaches, and the health-care industry. His work with over 100 companies is researched and studied worldwide.

Marcia Reynolds, PhD, MCC: Marcia Reynolds, a behavioral scientist, is a world-renown highly sought after force in masterful coaching, education, and consulting across the five continents. She is considered the top female coach in the world.

1 Coaching and Perspectives

Naim El-Aswad MD, FACP, ACC

Introduction and Literature Review

The word "coach" originated from the French word *coche* and the Hungarian word *Kocsi*, which means a carriage. In fact, in English literature, the first time the word "coach" was used was to describe a carriage that moves people from one place to another. The first time the word "coach" was used in its current day meaning was in 1861. It was to describe in the athletic/sports world someone who is helping another to train or to provide special instructions for an event or an exam. In 1994, Thomas Leonard created the International Coaching Federation (ICF) and the International Association of Coaching (IAC). These two bodies still exist. In particular, the ICF is the leading accrediting body that certifies coaches and monitors their training, education, and professional compliance and standards. Thomas Leonard was the first to utilize the concept of coaching in the personal realm and not just the sports realm. He believed that utilizing the Socratic method of listening, understanding, and proper questioning would help people realize their potential. He was a firm believer that people are not broken, and that they innately have great abilities and knowledge they can tap into to develop into "better versions" or to realize that potential.

The ICF defines coaching as "partnering with clients in a thought-provoking and creative process that inspires them to maximize their personal and professional potential…". Deiorio et al., 2022, defined coaching as "…the art and science of facilitating positive, sustainable change and growth to realize full potential, including optimal learning, development, performance, and well- being."

The birth of personal coaching led to a revolution in its uses and applications across several professional and personal aspects of people's lives. From the executive and occupational professional world to the personal world, coaching has been diversified into:

- Executive coaching
- Health coaching
- Life coaching

DOI: 10.4324/9781003452065-1

- Relationship coaching
- Parental coaching
- Entrepreneurial coaching
- So much more

It can be argued that there is not a facet of human life that coaching does not touch or cannot impact. If one of the cornerstones of life is to survive and adapt, to be resilient and to advance, then what better way to identify one's abilities and skills, discover their strengths and weaknesses, and maximize the potential to learn or master those skills than coaching? The answer to that question will become evident throughout this book that coaching, applied in the right time and spatial context, may be the best modality of helping individuals, groups, and institutions not only survive, but thrive.

It is difficult to say when coaching arrived on the healthcare scene. However, it is becoming easier to point out its impact. The literature demonstrates numerous studies that have shown the impact of coaching or recommended the need for further understanding the role of coaching in the healthcare industry.

The Science of Coaching

The science of coaching finds its roots in multiple disciplines. These include, but are not limited to (Deiorio et al., 2022): Positive psychology, Self-determination theory, Appreciative inquiry, Nonviolent communication, Motivational interviewing, Emotional intelligence, Flow theory, Social cognitive theory, and Constructive development

These disciplines differ in their meaning and use. Some are modalities of intervention (appreciative inquiry), some reflect abilities and skills (emotional intelligence), some represent a theory or "logic" of existence (self-determination theory), and others represent a method of interaction (nonviolent communication).

Outcomes of coaching

Ultimately, coaching seeks to help individuals change their status quo and move from one point to another. Creating change that is impactful and sustainable requires two necessary parameters, perhaps best explained, or emphasized through two quotes. The first one, by Jay Kimieck, focuses on intrinsic motivation where "…*Intrinsic motivation… is performing a task primarily for its own sake is the most powerful way to change behavior.*" The second one by James Prochaska, highlights the importance of having insight to create long lasting change: "*Overt action without insight is likely to lead to temporary change.*"

Indeed, to create powerful change that is long lasting, one needs to commit based on an intrinsically motivated approach and one needs to know the direction in which they are going. Further, all behaviors have a "frame of mind" that is made up of values, beliefs, identity, and intension.

The key to creating change is to address that frame of mind or else all the change attempted will be brought back and resisted.

Theodore Roosevelt once spoke with his troops. One of his most famous quotes: "Do what you can with what you have where you are."

A simple enough quote and one that seems easy to apply. However, three questions arise from that quote that bely the enormity of its significance when put into perspective in our daily human lives. These questions very few people, if any, can answer. It can be argued that no one can fully answer those questions. The questions are:

- What can you really do?
- What do you have?
- Where are you in your life?

One of the most bewildering yet fascinating events occurs every day throughout humanity. Every day we get up and attempt to move from point A to point B to create change while not being able to answer these questions! If the goal is to move, how can you without knowing your abilities, your strengths, weaknesses, and starting point?

There is another point to consider when trying to create change and reach a goal. Sometimes, we know the starting point, and we know the end point, but the limiting factor or lingering question that must be answered is: How? How do I get to where I want to go? As Anthony Robbins says, the "tyranny of how" frequently stumps people and dissuades them from even attempting or trying to change.

Coaching seeks to help answer these three questions listed above. It also helps the clients to answer or figure out the "How" in their lives. It does so by focusing on several outcomes. These outcomes include increased self-awareness and self-knowledge, increased personal responsibility, acquisition of new knowledge and skills, attainment of personal and professional goals, creating sustainable behavioral change, increased life satisfaction, increased self-efficacy, developed sense of purpose and meaning, and becoming one's best self.

Mechanisms of coaching

For coaching to achieve these outcomes, it relies on four mechanisms of action: Growth promoting relationships. The premises of this relationship are that clients are not broken and need to be fixed. Unlike in therapy where people come in because of symptoms and unresolved issues/problems, coaching focuses on the present and the future, and looks to support the clients, not patients, by helping them determine and outline their goals, focus on their goals, identify their challenges and abilities, and map out ways to achieve them. The value is in the growing process more than the expert opinions of coaches. Most of the growth happens because of neuroplasticity (the brain's ability to grow, change and develop new connections). The second pillar is the eliciting of self-motivation. External motivation is not the fuel that carries the client through. For someone to achieve their goals, stay committed to them, and see them through, one needs internal or autonomous motivation. By helping the clients connect a behavior to something in the future that they value, or the identity that they want to project, they help them identify the motivation behind sustainable results. This motivation taps into a life or energy source that is biologic and intrinsic. The third pillar is building confidence. It is equally important to build confidence and the capacity to sustain motivation. This occurs with effort over time. Coaches try to help clients identify and achieve goals that will build confidence. A little success improves motivation and confidence. Enhancing positive emotions allows for more open-mindedness and creativity as well as resilience. As a result, competence chances increase when people tap into their values, strengths, and talents, and when they see, recognize, and appreciate their results. The final pillar is the structured process of change. Clients will benefit from structured processes and projects. By recognizing that SMART goals (Specific, Measurable, Actionable, Realistic, Time-bound) are available for the clients, they make their targets more achievable. Further, the coach helps to hold the clients accountable, which assists in performance. They do so through regular progress reports, setting milestones, and sometimes having support from other professionals.

Tools for coaching

Coaches have their ways. Much like in the practice of medicine or any other profession, they have "tools of the trade". Some of these tools include, but not limited to, listening, not talking; asking, not telling; reflecting, not commenting; no advising or counseling; being collaborative and co-creative partners and not giving answers, but allowing for self-discovery.

According to Thomas Gordon in 1970, there are 12 ways of approaching in a non-coaching way:

- Ordering, directing, or commanding.
- Warning, cautioning, or threatening.
- Giving advice, making suggestions, or providing solutions
- Persuading with logic, arguing, or lecturing
- Telling people what they should do: Moralizing
- Disagreeing, judging, criticizing, or blaming
- Agreeing, approving, or praising
- Shaming, ridiculing, or labeling
- Interpreting or analyzing

- Reassuring, sympathizing, or consoling
- Questioning or probing
- Withdrawing, distracting, humoring, or changing the subject

These tools of coaching might seem simple, but in effect, are very hard to maintain or practice on a consistent level. And when it comes to the world of healthcare and medicine, these become especially more difficult to achieve. As doctors, or as someone working in the healthcare industry taking care of patients, the usual approach relies on the "expert model approach". Let us explore the difference between that model and the coach's model. (Table 1)

As is clearly identified, the differences are stark. It is important to understand those not just from the physician's perspective as an expert, but from the physician's perspective as either a coach or a client. If one is able to understand the principles of the approach of coaching and the methodology, one is able to better anticipate, expect, and respond to the coaching process.

Methods of delivery

Years of coaching experience, mixed with a pandemic that helped create innovative ways of communication, have demonstrated that coaching works on an individual level, group level, in-person, and remotely through several types of modalities.

From the healthcare literature, remote coaching using telephone coaching (Adams et al., 2013; Fischer et al., 2019) has been shown to be effective. Other modalities, such as internet-based coaching, or e-coaching, became the norm in the Covid era and continues to be a very sought after modality (Passmore et al., 2023). The literature is filled with citations that document its success and impact, (Ribbers & Waringa, 2015; Kamphorst, 2017; Kanatouri, 2020).

Coaching models

There are several coaching models that can be used. Their principles are comparable, but some of the details in the approaches are different. All these models center around a main theme: Help the clients identify their goals, develop their "strengths" and "weaknesses", understand their challenges and opportunities, develop approaches to maximize their strengths, minimize their "weaknesses", and carve out the best possible paths towards achievement of their goals and conquer their challenges, and ultimately gage their success while continuously monitoring their performance and making sure they remain focused on their paths. This is a very dynamic process, a process that allows for discovery and adaptation and change along the way. Here are some of the coaching models:

GROW model

Perhaps the most common model, this was developed in the 1980's by John Whitmore, in conjunction with his friends, Alan Fine and Graham Alexander. GROW stands for:

a   G: Goal(s) being sought. As is expected, the goal is usually addressed at the beginning of the coaching session. Once identified, it is often repeated throughout the sessions. Repeating the goal helps energize the client, helps to focus on the tasks needed to achieve, helps to reconnect to purpose, and helps clarify thought processes. Some common questions for Goal include:

- What is your goal for the session? For the coaching experience?
- What do you hope to reach?
- Where are you on a scale of 1 to 10, and where do you want to be?
- Where do you imagine yourself in a certain period of time?
- Can you articulate your goal in a few words?

b   R: Stands for Realities that need to be considered. Time spent here helps the client better understand their world, what events are occurring, and how that impacts them, the relevant people in their world, and what needs to be considered to achieve the goals. Exploration helps the clients develop different understanding, outlook, and perspectives; a potential 360 degree look at their lives. A key element in this section is to help the client not focus on the past or plan for the future, but to understand the present. Often, coaches and clients are too enthusiastic to try to move forward, try to find solutions, and try to plan. However, if this part is overlooked or not done well, the whole coaching experience could be compromised. Insight and "AHA" moments happen here. The key is to help the clients focus on how what has happened and what they want to happen impacts their now. Most clients, given enough time and with the right questions and approach, can discover better insights and come up with their options and plans. If this step is not done properly, clients will usually state "I don't know", "that's why I am here", and "why don't you tell me". Patience, encouragement, and a relentless curiosity and questioning approach will help the clients reach that insight. Once they do, it will be noticeable by both the client and the coach. It will be a word they say, a movement they make, or a sound they produce. Some of the questions asked here include:

- On a scale of 1 to 10, how would you rank your current situation compared to what you consider would be ideal?
- What have you tried so far?
- Who else is or might be affected?
- What do you believe is working for you now?

- What do you believe is not working for you now?
- What else can you tell me?
- What else have you tried?
- Where do you consider yourself successful?
- Tell me more about what just happened?
- It seems you may have had an "AHA" moment, would you like to share your thoughts?
- What revealed to you now that you did not know before.
- Why not stay in this moment for a bit. Let us explore how this truly affects or impacts you or those around you or your situation.

c   O: Represents options available to reach the goal. With the goal identified, and reality uncovered, the next natural step is to explore options. Some of the approaches/questions here include:

- What are your options?
- What are your thoughts moving forward?
- How would you like to approach your goal?
- What have you done so far? What else can you do?
- Who can help you?
- How can you create a better situation for yourself?

    - The questions are plentiful and are guided by reality and the goals. The important aspect is to help the client discover or consider all possible options. This is the part where they may stumble or focus on certain options while not fully considering all possibilities. It is here that exploration of options with pros and cons and helping the clients pick out the ones that have the highest rates of possible success. Once these open-ended questions are answered, and once the client appears to be drained from answers, the next set of questions could be close ended related to specific dates or times or situations or people. Examples include:

- By when do you anticipate doing this?
- Who can help you?
- What else can you do regarding this particular stumbling block?

d   W: Stands for a couple of things including Will or Way Forward. Discovering the goal, the direction, the path, and the abilities leads to the last question in the GROW model: How? How are the clients going to achieve what they have decided on? The more details in answering the how, the higher the chances of success. In here, the coach explores with the clients the ways they are going to make things work, not in theory, but in practice. Questions here include:

- How are you going to achieve this?
- What can you do differently that you have not done before that will make things work?
- How will you change your schedule? What will you do?

    - If you are going to implement those changes, how will you do that?

The GROW model, much like most models, is a flexible model. The coach and client can start anywhere and oscillate between the different stages.

OSCAR coaching model

This model is a solution-based model. Its primary focus is on solutions, not problems. OSCAR stands for Outcome, Situation, Choices, Action, and Review. The goal of this model was to enhance the GROW model. It was developed by Karen Whittleworth and Andrew Gilbert in 2002. (Gilbert and Whittleworh, 2009) Even though this model can be applied to almost any situation, the literature suggests that its best use comes when there is a focus on long-term outcomes and identifying milestones to be achieved through the action steps.

a   Outcome: As the word suggests, the coach and client discuss the desired outcome of the coaching sessions. Questions that may arise include:

- What are your goals?
- What do you hope to achieve?
- Finish the sentence: At the end of my coaching sessions, I would like to …
- How do you know you have reached or achieved your desired outcome?

b   Situation: This part helps the client focus on their current situation. An analysis of their strengths, obstacles, abilities, and support systems. The coach may ask:

- How do you feel about your current situation?
- Where do you think you are currently?
- If you had to put a number to it, how would you rate your current situation as it pertains to helping you achieve your goal? Why is that?
- What do you need to change your current situation?

c   Choices: Discussion of choices and options follows. Here, the clients are helped to look at the choices they have to get to their goals. Along with these choices the client discovers possible outcomes/ consequences of those choices. Questions here would look like:

- What are some of the options you have?
- What are some of the consequences of these options?
- How will your options impact you? Those around you?
- What else?
- Have you considered all your choices? What else?

d   Action: This part of the conversation focuses on what steps can be taken by the client. These steps need to be SMART (specific, measurable, attainable, realistic, and timely). It is important for the client to have action steps that are doable. Some could be immediate, and others more on the long-term spectrum. Some of the questions would look like:

- What action steps are you thinking of taking now?
- What would help you now?
- What is your timeline?

e   Review: Review helps the client and the coach to look at all the prior steps and ensure that the clients are meeting their goals, managing their choices, and fulfilling their actions. It helps to reestablish, reset, reaffirm, reshuffle, and reassess. Some of the questions asked here include:

- Where are you with respect to your goals?
- What do you need to ensure you are meeting your goals?
- What has worked for you so far?
- What has not worked for you so far?

CLEAR coaching model

Developed by Peter Hawkins, the acronym stands for contract, listen, explore, actions and review. It is a transformational coaching model where individuals are helped to create lasting transformational change based on creating new beliefs, behaviors, and values. It does not only seek to help the clients achieve goals. Often used in executive and leadership coaching, it has found its uses in healthcare as well.

a   Contract: The session often begins with discussing the "rules of engagement" between client and coach. It discusses expectations, outlines responsibilities, sets parameters, and defines agenda. As with all sessions and stages, this is a dynamic process that can be modified or changed anytime. Some of the questions include:

- What would you like to achieve today?
- What would you like to focus on today?
- What will make this session a successful session for you?

b   Listen: Active listening and empathy are an integral part of this stage. Holding the stage well is important for the client, as well as being clear and concise. This is when the coach listens to what is said and not said and develops an understanding of the coachees goals and purpose.

c   Explore: As the name suggests, exploration necessitates asking questions directed at what the clients want to achieve. Probing the client with directed or open-ended questions, the coach tries to elicit as much as possible data and details from the client that would help in the process of goal achieving. The coach tries to help the client understand their connection on a mental, emotional, and physical level with their current state, and the state where they would like to be. This usually satisfies the two parts of this stage: understanding where the clients are and knowing where they want to be.

d   Action: This stage is pretty self-evident at this time with the same coaching approach and questioning as in other coaching models. Similar questions apply here. It is imperative that the coach does not guide or lead the client, and that the questions are left to the client to fully answer and discover.

e   Review: Towards the end of the session, the coach could summarize or ask the client to summarize or review the session as they see it and understand it, its impact, and to discover any further questions or concerns. It helps to focus the client on what has been discovered, the goals identified, and the paths drawn. Review helps develop the trust between the coach and the client. If the end of the session fulfils the contract or what was desired by the client, it further cements the relationship between the two, giving the clients the trust they need to move forward and the coach the confidence that the clients' needs are being met effectively and the session or model is working. The same questions as were discussed before apply here.

f   Perhaps the biggest difference between the CLEAR and the GROW model is this review step. Feedback loops, reassessment, and re-evaluation helps develop a transparent model and define agreements.

STEPPA coaching model

Standing for Subject, Target identification, Emotion, Perception, Plan, Pace, Action/Amend, it was developed by Dr. Angus McLeod. (Mcleod, A. 2004)

a   Subject: By now, what is apparent is the overall approach logic. This model starts with identifying and understand the subject and context of the coaching session. It is important for the coach to help the client clearly identify the subject, and narrowing it down as much as possible. It is important for the topic to stay within the realms of logic and outside the realm of emotions. Further, it is equally important to determine that the subject is within the scope of the coaching contract. For example, if a physician is referred for coaching for "behavioral issues", it is important to keep the subject of coaching within the realm of those issues and not to tackle other issues like growing their own private business.

b   Target identification: Here, the coachee is encouraged to identify a SMART goal (Specific, Measurable, Accurate, Realistic, and Timely).

c   Emotions: No matter the goal, it is hard to strip it of an emotional value. This part of the model focuses on the emotions attached to the goal/target, and to determine if this emotion is a positive (motivator) or a negative (restrictive), and if possible, how it can be used. Sample questions here look like:

- If you achieve your goal, how will that make you feel?
- How important is this goal on a scale of 1–10?
- What does achieving your goal mean to you?
- How motivated are you?

d   Perception: This step aims to help the coachee increase their conscience perception along with a wider understanding of their goals and situation. Questioning and challenge are the tools used here. Some of the questions here might include:

- How will this impact you? Those around you?
- What are your available resources?
- What options have you tried? What have you not tried?

e   Plan: Setting a plan means defining a process, not searching for choices. If choices are still entertained, then the plan is not yet ready to be discussed. Once choices and a path are determined, a plan can be discussed. This is a systematic and stepwise organization of how to move forward.

f   Pace: Setting the pace means to ask for a timeline for certain milestones/goals in the plan or the process. It helps the coachee to date completion of the goals/tasks. Some of the questions include:

- When would you like to complete this step?
- When do you believe you can accomplish this task?
- How comfortable are you with the deadlines you have placed?

g   Action/Amend: Before this step is initiated, the whole STEPPA process needs to be evaluated and re-examined. The coach checks with the coachee if the plan and all the steps appear okay and doable and comfortable and gages the level of comfort. If the coachee gives the green light then the action is initiated and the plan moves forward.

ACHIEVE coaching model

Inspired by the GROW model, as well as the likes of Graham Alexander, Alan Fine, and John Whitmore, it was developed by the Coaching Center formed by Dembkowski and Eldridge, 2003. It stands for Assess current situation, Creative brainstorming, Hone goals, Initiate option generation, Evaluate options, Valid action program design, Encourage momentum. This model is designed to help the clients with increased feedback-reactivity and added flexibility. It goes beyond the walls of the GROW model. This is a cyclical model and approach that is intended to help develop more trust between coach and coachee and to allow for more in-depth understanding of the nuances and steps of coaching, as well as being able to identify and implement more targeted goals and enhanced problem-solving abilities. The steps at this time become self-explanatory as they rely on the same principles and approaches of other models, despite the application being slightly different.

The FUEL Coaching Model

FUEL stands for Frame the conversation, Understand the current state, Explore the desired state, Lay out a success plan. This model stresses that the coach does not ask any leading questions, only open-ended questions to allow for free exploration by the client. This model was developed by Kathleen Stinnet and John Zenger (Zenger & Stinnet, 2010). Some of the questions that are asked include:

a   What do you wish to discuss?
b   Where would you like to start?
c   Can you name some of the things that are working well for you? What is not working well?
d   How would you describe the state you wish to be in?
e   How would it look like for you? How will you know you arrived at your desired state?
f   What are some of the barriers to getting there?
g   What are your action steps to get to your desired state? Where would you like to start?

These questions are asked throughout the 4 stages of the model. Like most coaching models, it is a fluid state of existence and a dynamic one that can oscillate between the different stages.

TIBA coaching model

This was a model developed by our company, Vital Signs Vital Skills. It was based on the different models in the literature. TIBA stands for Target,

Ideas, Barriers, and Actions. Similar to other models, it identifies four phases in the coaching approach for clients. By asking about the person's targets or goals, it attaches them to internal motivation. The ideas elicited are action focused. The clients are forced to think of actionable approaches for them, achievable, and SMART. Barrier identification helps the client identify potential pitfalls and challenges ahead. It allows the clients the space and time to think of all possible scenarios and by doing so, helps them come up with their own solutions that they can achieve. It is a tool that allows for great personalization of goals, abilities, paths, and achievement. We have used this tool multiple times with different clients of various backgrounds, specialties, age groups, ethnicities, races, and gender. They have all bene-fited from the information it provided them and have found its utility in helping them achieve their goals or tackle their challenges with a high suc-cess rate. Below are sample questions for each category of the TIBA.

a   Target - focus for coaching: explore concerns, needs, or goals fully.

- What are your goals?
- What do you want to focus on, VIVID?
- What do you want to change?
- What's on your mind?
- What is the real challenge for you?
- What makes this so important for you?

b   Ideas - what are the clients' thoughts for options or solutions.

- What are your thoughts for a solution?
- What would a 10 on a 1–10 look like for this goal?
- What are some of your options?
- What have you tried?
- What has worked part of the time?
- What strengths have you utilized that you could build on?
- What have others done in this situation that worked?
- How can I help?
- What else?

c   Barriers - what obstacles must be addressed, internal and external.

- Where are you on a 1–10 on this goal now?
- What obstacles do you have to deal with?
- What external challenges do you have?
- What interpersonal challenges do you need to address?
- What internal challenges do you need to address?
- What else?

d   Actions - to address the goals or barriers.

- What is something you can do right away?

- What will you have to say No to?
- How can you bring your strengths more to his goal?
- What resources and support do you have for these actions?
- How will you measure your success on this goal?
- What are other actions to explore to support their goals?
- What advice or best practices do you as coach have for them?
- What is the plan?
- What and when can they commit to for the next steps?
- What was most useful in this conversation?

Like the rest of the coaching models in the literature, TIBA is based on the premise of exploring what the client wants or needs, their ideas to get to their desired goals, their potential barriers and assets, their action steps, and identifying how they will reach their goals.

Conclusions and Recommendations

The science and practice of coaching is being studied extensively in different aspects of human wellness: Emotional, mental, physical, occupational/financial, social, and spiritual. At the heart of this approach is the fundamental belief that human beings, who are mentally well and who do not suffer from mental health disorders, when given the opportunity, are able to not only identify what they need, but possess the knowledge, the expertise, or the potential to achieve their goals. Coaching, through its inquisitive, open-ended, non-judgmental, and growth-promoting approach, was created to help individuals access those innate abilities and utilize them to the best of their potential.

In the healthcare industry, professionals are faced with a multitude of challenges. These challenges share some common points with other professions. They also have some characteristics that are unique to this industry. The literature has shown that among those professionals, physicians are not equipped to take care of themselves nor have the knowledge and know how to navigate the waters of their profession in a safe and productive way to maintain their health and well-being, and to maximize their potential. Teaching, training, curricula, and mentorship have not shown to be the answer to help physicians flourish. In fact, it can be argued that they are some of the major contributing reasons to the demise in the well-being of doctors. Unfortunately, the demands and constraints of healthcare are only getting more challenging. There is a need to help healthcare providers develop the understanding of their current situations, the challenges they face, the impact of their career on their health and well-being, and to discover various approaches that might help them not only survive their profession, but flourish in it.

When it comes to self-determination and self-fulfillment, coaching has been shown to be one of the best approaches in helping human beings in various fields of life, personally and professionally, become the best potential version of who they want to be. This will be the case also in the healthcare industry. Health is not a one-glove fits all. Coaching is one of the cornerstones of helping individuals carve their own "gloves".

Summary and Key Points

- Human beings are not broken and do not need to be fundamentally changed or "fixed".
- Coaching is a partnership between a coach and a coachee/client.
- Coaching can be offered to individuals, couples, families, teams, or groups.
- Coaching relies on multiple theories from various sciences rooted in positive psychology, self-determination theory, appreciative inquiry, and motivational interviewing.
- Coaching is used across different personal and professional fields.
- Coaching does not carry the stigma and professional barriers that are usually associated with therapy. There is a slow transition from seeing coaching as a punitive or corrective measure/approach to a fulfilling and growth-promoting opportunity.
- Coaching is confidential and is governed by certain ethical, moral, and legislative rules and regulations.
- Coaching relies on asking questions that help clients determine their abilities, goals, challenges, strategies, and approaches.
- There are multiple coaching models, but they all follow a similar format of inquiring about goals, understanding obstacles and abilities, outlining a path for reaching the goals, developing ways to bypass the obstacles, and identifying parameters of success.
- Coaching in healthcare is a relatively new approach to help professionals in general, and doctors in particular, deal with their unique and common challenges and to thrive in this ever-increasingly demanding environment.

Table 1.1 Expert versus Coach's approach

Expert Approach	Coach Approach
Authority	Partner
Educator	Facilitator of change
Defines Agenda	Elicits client's agenda
Feels responsible for client's health	Client is responsible for health
Solves problems	Fosters possibilities
Focuses on what's wrong	Focuses on what's right
Has the answers	Co-discovers the answers
Interrupts if off topics	Learns from client's story
Works harder than client	Client works as hard as coach
Wrestles with client	Dances with client

References

Adams, S.R., Goler, N.C., Sanna, R.S., Boccio, M., Bellamy, D.J., Brown, S.D., Neugebauer, R.S., Ferrara, A., Wiley, D.M., Schmittdiel, J.A. (2013) Patient satisfaction and perceived success with a telephonic health coaching program: the Natural Experiments for Translation in Diabetes (NEXT-D) Study, Northern California, 2011. *Preventing Chronic Diseases.* 10:E179. doi:10.5888/pcd10.130116. PMID: 24176083; PMCID: PMC3816609.

Deiorio, N.M., Moore, M., Santen, S.A., Gazelle, G., Dalrymple, J.L., Hammoud, M. (2022) Coaching models, theories, and structures: An overview for teaching faculty in the emergency department and educators in the offices. *AEM Educ Train.* 6(5):e10801. doi:10.1002/aet2.10801. PMID: 36189456; PMCID: PMC9482416.

Dembkowski, S., Eldridge, F. (2003). Beyond GROW: A new coaching model. *The International Journal of Mentoring and Coaching.* 1(1).

Fischer, X., Kreppke, J.N., Zahner, L., Gerber, M., Faude, O., Donath, L. (2019) Telephone-Based Coaching and Prompting for Physical Activity: Short- and Long-Term Findings of a Randomized Controlled Trial (Movingcall). *International Journal of Environmental Research and Public Health.* 16(14):2626. doi:10.3390/ijerph16142626. PMID: 31340528; PMCID: PMC6678542.

Gilbert, A., Whittleworth, K.J. (2009) *OSCAR Coaching Model.* Worth Consulting Ltd; First Edition.

SirJohnWhitmore. (2017) *Coaching for Performance Fifth Edition: The Principles and Practice of Coaching and Leadership.* Nicholas Brealey.

Kamphorst, B.A. (2017) E-coaching systems: What they are, and what they aren't. *Personal and Ubiquitous Computing.* 21: 625–632.

Kanatouri, S. (2020) *The digital coach.* Routledge.

Mcleod, A. (2004) STEPPA Coaching Model. *Anchor Point.* 1, 15–20.

Passmore, J., Liu, Q., Tee, D., Tewald, S. (2023) The impact of COVID-19 on coaching practice: results from a global coach survey. *Coaching: An International Journal of Theory, Research and Practice.* 1–17. doi:10.1080/17521882.2022.2161923.

Ribbers, A., Waringa, A. (2015) *E-coaching: Theory and practice for a new online approach to coaching.* Routledge.

Zenger, J, Stinnett, K. (2010) *The Extraordinary Coach: How the Best Leaders Help Others Grow.* New York: McGraw-Hill.

2 Coaching Approaches in Healthcare

Naim El-Aswad MD, FACP, APP

Introduction and Literature Review

There are many ways to define life, and more specifically, a living organism. No matter the definition, there are a few knowns that can be agreed upon. One of those knowns is change. When change, or the ability to change stops, life ceases to exist. The human body is a perfect example of this phenomenon. On a daily basis, even on a second-by-second basis, there is change happening. On a molecular, cellular, tissue, organ, and organism level, life necessitates us moving from one place to another. The formula then is simple: Locate where you are, identify your goal and where you want to be, and then proceed to go there. Never was such a simple concept more complex.

In the healthcare world, physicians find themselves helping patients identify a clinical or medical problem. Through their training and expertise, they use their tools, history, physical examination, and available tests to confirm the diagnosis. They then proceed to inform the patient of the remedy to their problem. Sometimes, the remedy is dependent solely on the patient, such as purchasing and taking their medications, following a certain diet, doing physical therapy, change of lifestyle, and so on and so forth. The expectation is that the patient will go from point A, the diagnosis, to point B, the solution. Simple, yet so potentially complex. Inherent in this simple formula are two fundamental questions that are a must for meaningful and lasting success to happen: Why and how.

Brown et al state that medication adherence is around 50%, a percentage that decreases with time. It impacts around 40–50% of patients with chronic diseases. (Kleinsinger, 2018). If overall compliance was considered (medication, therapy, diet, appointments...), that rate becomes 25% (Zolnierek & Dimatteo, 2009). This leads to significant morbidity and mortality among patients with a huge economic burden on the health care industry. The reasons for these percentages are multifactorial, but they have in common issues centered on the why and the how. Allow us to elaborate.

DOI: 10.4324/9781003452065-2

One of the problems in the healthcare industry, and perhaps in life in general, is that most change is driven by extrinsic motivation. Either through a reward (a healthier life), or a threat (a diseased life), success rates are not enough to justify this approach, even if at times, the outcome is severe disability or death! So, how do we create long lasting successful change? What are the major factors involved? The literature tells us that purpose, and intrinsic motivation, are necessary to create such a change. (Alfonsson et al., 2017) Based on the Self-Determination Theory (SDT), several factors help promote intrinsic motivation. These include curiosity, control, challenge, competition, recognition, cooperation, and fantasy. Frederick Nietzsche said it best: "He who has a why to live for can bear almost any how".

Another reason why compliance rates could be low is treatment credibility. The lower the credibility, the worse the compliance and the higher the dropout rates. (Gasslander et al., 2021).

Coaching can target these two factors. As we have learned, some of the principles of coaching are based on the SDT. Coaching also relies on theories of positive psychology, appreciative inquiry, nonviolent communication, motivational interviewing, emotional intelligence, flow theory, social cognitive theory, and constructive development. It is the application of coaching and its various components that allows us to be able to help support physicians and other healthcare providers while considering the tremendous variability and uniqueness of individuals and their challenges. In other words, for almost all physicians and health care workers, whatever the problem or issue is, chances are there is a coaching method that would work! We have seen it work with patients and their different ailments, with helping them manage their illnesses and maximizing their health.

Reviewing the literature as it pertains to coaching patients, it has shown that health coaching can improve and have a positive impact on chronic disease interventions (Adams et al., 2013). Life coaching improves self-efficacy and self-empowerment (Ammentorp et al., 2013) Health coaching is essential for changes in health-related behavior (Neuner-Jehle, Schmid & Grüninger, 2013). Coaching works whether in person or remote. Remote coaching using either telephone coaching (Adams et al., 2013; Dennis et al., 2013), as well as internet based coaching (van den berg, Schoones and Vliet Vlieland, 2007) and use of other mobile technologies (Spring et al., 2012) is a cost effective, efficient, and productive way of enhancing physical activity, dieting and maximizing multiple health behavior changes.

The data supports the use of coaching to change lifestyles, follow advice, and find ways to enhance one's health. What if we are able to use those principles to help physicians and other healthcare workers do the same in their personal and professional lives? And what if we use coaching to maximize intrinsic motivation, increase treatment credibility, and help produce better, efficient, and long-lasting desired results? This chapter is about discussing the approaches to help answer that "what if?".

Coaching, unlike counseling, focuses not on a problem/diagnosis, but on a goal or challenge in the present and the future. Life coaching has been defined as *"a dynamic interaction that facilitates the learning, development, and performance of the person being coached"* (Lennard, 2010, p1). Coaching approaches differ, usually based, or influenced by the background of the coach (psychology, health and fitness, management, sports, and others). No matter the background, the goals of coaching remain the same: to help the clients, through a solution-focused approach, reach their goals by maximizing their strengths, minimizing their weaknesses, and navigating their challenges.

Just like in healthcare and medicine, not all approaches are created equal. The argument that the practice of medicine is NOT a one-glove fits all is well known to those who practice it. In fact, the current healthcare system is made to manage and deal with acute and immediate problems. It is not set up for dealing with chronic diseases or issues. As physicians, we are part and parcel of that approach. Most physicians try to deal with immediate problems. They are not able to successfully deal with change within themselves and their outside world (more to be discussed on this matter later). They want to live and be well. Physicians wish they were in control of their health (although some may think they are). The gap between living well and the demands of everyday life is widening. That healthy life includes the personal and the professional parts. There is a need to develop new "life skills". Most people, including health care professionals, do not believe they know the needed skills or know how to master these new "life skills". Most people lack the confidence, stamina, purpose, and focus to lead a healthy life. Each individual needs to develop his or her own approach, philosophy, habits, beliefs, and convictions. There is a shift in healthcare to help people achieve their goals, rather than just imposing their goals on them.

There is another truth in the practice of medicine. Different patients react differently to different medication and different physicians! This sentence underlines the importance of the uniqueness of the patient, the medication given, the therapeutic approach, and the provider. The argument is no different when coaching physicians or anyone for that matter. Different clients respond differently to different approaches and different coaches! Further, each situation/client may necessitate a different kind of coaching style.

The literature does not provide clear, or even vague, guidelines on which coaching approach is to be used with physicians and healthcare providers; with the kind of goals, challenges, or outcomes desired; nor with the situation or environment demands/conditions. The burden of the discovery of what works best lies on the shoulders of the coach and the client. In order to help with making that decision, the following section will review the major types of coaching styles with a discussion on their philosophy, approach, strengths, weaknesses, and applications.

Definitions, Discussions, and Applications

In discussions with one of the VP of ACGME (Accreditation Council for Graduate Medical Education), his ideas and thoughts about coaching were primarily focused on helping clinicians "get well", "get better or healthier", and "support with their burnout". Whereas the impact of coaching in that area is undeniable, as will be discussed later, the scope of application or practice is much wider. The reality is that coaching in healthcare is applied to various situations and at multiple levels: Burnout, wellness and health, resilience, leadership in healthcare, self-leadership, career growth and/or change, management in healthcare, residency and medical school training, personal development, professional development, and other areas.

Coaching has different styles. Each style has its unique advantages and limitations. Where each style is applied depends on the coaching client, the coach, the goals and challenges, and the situation. Never has a "one glove fits all" approach been more nonapplicable! There are several coaching styles or approaches. For the sake of this book, the focus is on the following:

a   Democratic coaching style
b   Autocratic coaching style
c   Laissez-Faire coaching style
d   Holistic coaching style
e   Mindfulness coaching style
f   Intuitive coaching style
g   Transactional coaching style
h   Developmental coaching style
i   Bureaucratic coaching style
j   Transformational coaching style
k   Vision coaching style

Democratic (participative) coaching

As the name suggests, this coaching style considers the interests, desires, thoughts, concerns, and choices of everyone involved. It is often considered the most empowering coaching style. The client is an active participant in designating goals and the coaching approaches to achieve them. Even though the input is vital from the client, the final decision to which method of coaching belongs to the coach. (Amanchukwu et al., 2015). This style depends on or utilizes the client's ability to be inspired, creative, self-efficacious, motivated, empowered, productive, objectively committed, and competently collaborative.

This style of coaching is best used for enhancing decision making and communication skills. It encourages the clients to share their decisions and thoughts, helping to empower them and gives them a sense of control over their situation. This in turn helps them develop their skills. It is best used with clients considering financial coaching, career coaching, and personal growth coaching. However, because this style allows for exploration of different options, it may take longer time to have an impact. So, when considering the client and their situation, along with the time you have with them, this may not be the best option.

Autocratic coaching

On its surface, this kind of coaching may not seem like coaching at all. As the name suggests, this style requires the coach to be the one in control. (Amanchukwu et al., 2015). Contrast to democratic coaching, the client's input is very minimal as to the path to be taken. Sometimes considered as an extreme case of transactional leadership, the coach is the one deciding on the processes and approaches to be taken by the client. The client's mutual understanding is required. This appears to be defeating the purpose of coaching, and its very essence. However, sometimes, circumstances may necessitate this approach. It is also more common when the coach is the one with the expertise in dealing with the issue or matter at hand. This is a prerequisite with the experience of the coach. Sometimes, physicians may appreciate this approach more, especially if the coach is another physician, and even more so if the coach is a physician of the same specialty! This approach focuses on productivity, efficiency, realistic goal attainment, trust in the coach, reduced stress, ambiguity reduction, and learning discipline.

The clinician might resonate with this approach: The "expert" model of getting things done. After all, the focus of this style mimics the focus of the clinician. However, it does defeat the purpose of growth and self-exploration. Some instances where this could be applied include or situations with very limited time, goals needs to be attained very quickly, or there are high stress or urgent situations or topics to be dealt with. Frequently, in the healthcare world, coaches will get physicians referred to them for being a "problem" physician and there is an urgent need to "fix" them else they would lose their job or have some disciplinary actions against them. And frequently, the physician being referred is in a state of mind that is hijacked, burnt out, stressed, or in some other negative state. In those instances, the physician and the situation may necessitate such an approach. It is also used more in military training, physical fitness training, and any area where focus and discipline and structure are needed and part of the culture.

Laissez-Faire (leave alone) coaching

A "hands off" approach to coaching, the belief here is that the clients need little leadership to understand, identify, and reach their goals as they possess the self-efficacy to do so. (Harper, 2012). The coach's role is to be the external leader, and the clients are the primary process owners and drivers. The coach allows the client to come to him or her as the client navigates their own field. This style has been criticized heavily as it attributes almost zero responsibility to the coach, who is required to give some leadership, guidance, and support (Yang, 2015). It has the potential to be negative or positive, depending on the situation in which it is used. It has a greater chance of being a positive experience for the client when the coach provides regular performance feedback and monitoring. (Amanchukwu et al., 2015) Some argue that this approach may be best used in conjunction with other approaches, depending on the situation and the need. This approach helps the clients with their self-management, self-confidence, autonomy, freedom, self-empowerment, decision-making ability, and self-efficacy.

Often regarded as the most "ineffective form of coaching", this approach still has its potential uses. It works best when the clients have a much more knowledgeable base and grasp of what they are facing than the coach does. It is used more in an organizational setting where the coach is more of an observer and allows decision makers to "do their thing" while acting as an external consultant and observer. In the world of healthcare, this kind of coaching may best be suited when decision makers are trying to resolve institutional issues, tackle organizational challenges and goals, or have milestones that need to be reached. It also can be used when your client has certain challenges related to his or her specialty and you as a coach have very little knowledge about their professional lives and its impact on their personal lives. Coaches without a healthcare background my face challenges/questions about their expertise and suitability to the situation from physicians and other healthcare providers due to their lack of knowledge, appreciation, and understanding of the uniqueness of their clients' lives.

Holistic coaching

A coaching style that takes the person as a whole. It focuses on all the aspects of a client's life. The coach needs to provide support and encouragement. The belief here is that to truly help someone grow, the coach has to help them address their entire life. This approach believes in the creation of balance for all the factors that go into decision making. Finding harmony is essential for the clients as coaches here believe that everything in life is connected. Individuals coached with this style often feel more of a sense of purpose as they are allowed to explore all their choices and thoughts. This helps them connect more to who they are, their calling or purpose, and their true nature. It affords them the time to explore themselves on a deep level. They learn relaxation and stress-reduction techniques to help them arrive at better choices and decisions to produce more effective solutions. Only then will the client show true lasting and meaningful change (Whitley, Gould, Wright, & Hayden, 2017). This style of coaching encourages trust in the coach-client relationship, deep exploration of meaning and drives, enhanced well-being of mind, body and soul, solution finding or identification, feeling or being understood, building confidence, and exploration of multiple outcomes, even if one goal is sought.

This coaching approach is best used for the growth of the client as a whole. In the healthcare setting, more and more physicians and other workers are facing existential threats to their purposes, their drives, their professional, and their personal lives. Given the time and space, it is not unusual for the clients to start with one goal in mind but then dive into other aspects of their lives. Frequently, most of them would have never had the time, space, encouragement, or guidance to help them explore their well-being as an entire spectrum and look at the factors that impact their lives and make the necessary connections between them. Providing them with the safe opportunity to do so can and usually will be a life-changing moment for them. Throughout their careers, clinicians find themselves straying more and more from what drove them into medicine and losing themselves into what keeps them in their profession. The humans that enter medical schools exits as the professionals who become the "slaves" or "prisoners" trapped in their profession. When was the last time slaves were happy/safe/healthy/fulfilled in what they were doing? The skills needed to face the moral, ethical, professional, mental, emotional, spiritual, and physical challenges and demands of practicing medicine are never taught nor emphasized. Indeed, many would not know where to start. The power of the holistic coach is help the clients understand that everything is connected, and help them see, discover, understand, transform, and grow towards a meaningful and fulfilling life that highlights and celebrates their humanity!

Mindfulness coaching

According to Jon-Kabat Zinn, mindfulness means "paying attention in a particular way: on purpose, in the present moment, and non-judgmentally." (Kabat-Zinn, 2005) This style of coaching applies those principles. It helps create awareness in the clients of their emotions and thoughts in the moment and most importantly, without judgement. The coaches here must be able to practice mindfulness themselves and suspend all their judgments. Some of the best ways to get the clients to respond is to use guided meditations and positive affirmations. This helps the clients in dealing with stressful and challenging times in a calmer way with more clarity and awareness of themselves. It also helps the clients develop their own resources while navigating their own blocks, perceived or real. It helps the client move from doing to being. Clients usually develop new perceptions and have significant breakthroughs. This may work best with clients who are anxious or lack adequate and necessary control of their emotions to identify and achieve their goals (Blanck, Perleth, & Heidenreich et al., 2018) In this coaching style, clients learn clarity, harmony, peace of mind, acceptance, reduced anxiety, awareness, limiting beliefs and factors, hidden challenges, rewire their brains, and their coping or reaction thought processes and emotions.

Clinicians or physicians are under tremendous stress and pressure. As will be discussed later, stress and pressure have their own unique impact on the prefrontal cortex. That tends to lead to mental health disorders and burnout. One of the hallmarks is anxiety with an inability to think or perform. That anxiety could be debilitating. Whether it is apparent or subclinical, it is there and as more suffer from it, the skills and abilities needed to be able to identify it and deal with it will be that much more important and vital to have. This style of coaching is best suited to help in these kinds of scenarios and situations.

Intuitive coaching

Individuals have their inner voice to listen to. This voice represents perspectives and beliefs, thoughts, conscience, and convictions. This coaching approach encourages clients to listen to their voice and be in tune with it. In 2012, Reimers-Hild discussed intuition and talked about how people can achieve their personal fulfillment through using their intuitions to identify their "musts" in life and make those "musts" essential. These "musts" are the foundation for success, wellbeing, purpose, and survival. Coaches using this style will assist the client in uncovering deeply held motivations, self-efficacy, self-trust, clarity, creativity, and uncovering true passion.

The healthcare industry leaves little room for people working in it to be "reflective". In fact, its demands with their documented clinical, psychosocial, mental, physical, and emotional harmful impacts on the workers have generated considerable discussion on how to change it. As such, the clinicians might not be the ideal persons to use this coaching style with while they are immersed in their professional lives. However, it depends on the clients, where they are in their lives, and how well they can get in touch with their inner voices. People who are seeking deep meaning and fulfillment and are struggling to make their musts come true would benefit from this style of coaching. The coaches need to be aware that their clients are able, ready, knowledgeable, willing, and wanting to go down the path of intuitive self-discovery.

Transactional coaching

Much like the leadership type, this kind of coaching is focused on results. It is focused on actions. The focus here is on the external stimulus and can be a very practical approach in certain situations. The coaches usually support their clients by helping them get to the solution of their problem through an external action that often leads to a shift in performance or doing. This approach relies on extrinsic motivation with set goals or milestones needed to be achieved, usually in a short period of time. (Lennard, 2010). In this approach, clients learn or focus on short-term changes, building competence, clarifying goals, and enhancing problem-solving skills.

This type of coaching is best utilized when short-term goals are needed, or a change in performance is desired. This approach is or could be frequently used in the healthcare industry as it can be driven by the institution, a certain situation that necessitates immediate correction, or the individual seeking immediate change to a well-defined external problem. The change here, however, usually is short lived as the focus is the symptom and not the cause and the fix is immediate and remedial rather than profound and sustainable.

Developmental coaching

In this approach, the coach helps the clients identify a learning opportunity and supports them in their growth. (Lennard, 2010). The client is helped to understand the "what", "why", and "how" of the goals or issues. Frequently, a 360 assessment is used so that the coach can help the clients understand their past experiences and develop a better understanding of where they are in their current state. The client's age, thought process, and mental age is taken into consideration. The goal is usually not to change a behavior. Instead, it is to develop a shift or change in mindset by understanding the root cause of behaviors, thought processes, and actions. This approach helps support the clients by providing them with validation. Through this style of coaching, the clients develop a better understanding of who they are, have an increased awareness, become more aware of their autopilot modes, enhance self-actualization, develop long-term goals, develop greater learning opportunities, and enhance self-growth.

As they grow older, usually between their 40's and 50's, physicians tend to be attracted to different callings. They start to venture outside the medical field and into more of entrepreneurial endeavors. They also start to explore other passions in their lives. That stage is difficult for many as the transition from practicing medicine to doing something else can be daunting on an economic, psychosocial, cognitive, emotional, and physical level. They may also want to explore more growth in their own fields. Developmental coaching is ideal for people who have reached a growth plateau. (Bachkirova, 2011). This approach tends to help them in their journey by finding new meaning, for promoting growth and development, and helping them clarify the "why", "what", and "how" of their next adventure in life.

Bureaucratic coaching

Considered as one of the least flexible coaching styles, this approach is very focused and strict and follows decision-making hierarchies. It is driven by processes and systems. (Amanchukwu et al., 2015) It is intended for a rapid impact intervention and is usually practiced in highly regulated environments where safety is a priority. The focus is less on the individual and more so on a group. Creating a structure for the group to follow helps minimize variability and increases the likelihood of achieving the desired safety and targeted goals. With this style, the individual, but more so the group, learn accountability, consistency, clarity on the job, clear boundaries for job expectations and descriptions, safety, and efficiency.

This style is usually reserved for highly controlled environments, again with safety and processes in mind. Examples would be in construction, the military, sometimes hospital settings especially with safety and hazard training, and public sectors.

Transformational coaching

Sometimes thought of as the most "free-flowing" or "liberal" style of coaching, there is no hierarchy here. The coach focuses on helping the client "transform". This occurs through building a trusting client-coach relationship/alliance with the goals, outcomes, and processes agreed on (Eagly et al., 2003; Lennard, 2010). The coach and client rely on authenticity and candid feedback in a collaborative relationship. The coaches support their clients by building their confidence and helping develop their perspective on their lives, goals, and their methods/approaches. The clients are helped by having them understand how their perceptions, beliefs, and attitudes impact their behaviors. This style is sometimes referred to as life-coaching or perspective coaching. Through this style, clients are usually encouraged to enhance intrinsic motivation, cognitive development, accountability, purpose, collaborative thinking, adaptation skills, and problem-solving abilities.

This kind of coaching is best used with people trying to transform their lives. It is ideal for clients wanting to make life changes. Frequently, this style is used with clinicians who are seeking new meaning or purpose, wanting to go in another direction in their lives, and needing to understand themselves better and how best to support themselves. The goals are more in depth and life-changing with meaning and intrinsic motivation attached to them.

Vision coaching

As the name suggests, this style encourages clients to "visualize" where they need to go. It relies on the power of imagination to be able to "see" where the clients want to be or achieve. (Passarelli, 2015) The coach often relies on these visualizations to help support their clients, remind them of their "reasons", and to help guide them through a positive atmosphere. The coach usually gives directions to the client as well as encouraging objective achievement and remaining focused. In this style, clients are usually encouraged to visualize their goals and destination, develop self-confidence, develop clarity, practice focus, self-reflection, and self-growth.

Clinicians or clients here are usually coached for a short-term goal. In a fast-paced environment, this style works best. It is used in high stress workplaces, jobs, and for clients weighed down by their responsibilities. It can work in a setting in healthcare where results are expected quickly, the client is under tremendous stress, and their job is demanding a change. It can also work with groups to give them a focused goal to achieve.

Summary and Recommendations

"It is more important to know what sort of person has a disease than to know what sort of disease a person has". *Hippocrates.*

The beauty of coaching is the ability to solve a problem, bypass a challenge, or reach a goal through supporting the clients to have a better understanding of who they are. Sometimes, due to circumstances and situations, the focus is on the problem. One of the chapters will focus purely on coaching the clinician, not the problem. The diversity of approaches allows the coach and the clients to benefit in a dynamic and fluid interaction that is the coach-client relationship. There is variability, sometimes within the visit itself. It is great to have a repertoire of approaches that can be used based on the needs, the clients, the coach, and the situation. Mastery is the ability to determine when to use the necessary approach with the right client at the right time for a particular situation!

Highlighting the variability of coaches, clients, coaching approaches, and situations makes it that much more obvious the complexity of challenges and goals and the necessity of individualizing approaches.

Case Studies

Case 1

Presentation

A physician was referred to me who had several complaints about her from staff and other physicians. The complaints were mostly related to "attitude", not performance. As a matter of fact, the physician was a "top performer" in terms of efficiency and outcomes. The referral came from a hospital board and the CEO with the threat of terminating her employment if she "does not shape up".

During my first meeting with the clinician, it was evident that this had caught her by surprise. She just did not understand what the issue was or where it came from. A few things were stressed from the beginning. She stated that she has very little time to correct her actions. She also values her position and her job and wants to do whatever she can to correct the situation so she can keep performing her clinical duties. Lastly, she felt completely unprepared for the entire process, but she was willing to do whatever it takes to "get the job done".

After listening to her, we discussed that there are three issues to consider. She identified them all: Lack of awareness of her "problem attitude", lack of knowledge of how to fix the problem, and lack of time. She also identified the main reasons why she is doing or agreeing to be coached: Keep her job and avoid further complaints.

The situation

With this client, the following was considered:

a   Working in a high stress situation
b   She is under tremendous stress to maintain her job and not to get flagged again
c   She had a short timeline, 4–6 weeks.
d   She was not aware where to start as coaching and changing behavior was foreign to her
e   She asked me to guide her in the process as she did not have time to figure things out, wanted direction and the fastest way to get to her goals

The Approach

In discussing with the client, I spent a good time, even before we started coaching, on the expectations of coaching. We discussed all the possible goals she can reach and how the process would work. I repeatedly asked her to clarify what she wanted, what her hopes were, and how, given the situation, would be the best way to move forward. We went through the different types of approaches and through a joint decision, she decided that the best approach for now would be a combination of transactional with an element of developmental coaching. It was important for her to achieve her goals but at the same time, use the interaction to help her develop on a more profound basis.

The process

We completed four coaching sessions. In the first session, the patient was guided after she asked specific questions. She had no idea how to think about the process or what to do. She wanted to discuss immediate steps she can implement to stop the perceived/real damage. She asked for my input as an expert in the field. The session was a combination of suggestions of how to think and some action steps. In the three sessions that followed, the transition was made from the transactional to the developmental. By the fourth session, it was mostly developmental.

The results

The clinician informed me that she was praised for the immediate action steps. She also felt so much more empowered and aware of her surroundings. She developed a better understanding of who she is and her values. She further realized that the root of the problems perceived Stemmed from the way people Misunderstood her and her attitude, so she decided to work on that after realizing why she behaves the way she does.

This was a great example of where the coach was a fellow "expert" in the field of the client, and where the experience, personal and professional, helped. It was also a great opportunity for the client to learn more about herself and through a process she had never heard before, coaching, develop a better understanding of who she is and what drives her. The client was 72 years old.

Summary and Key Points

a   Change could be one way to define proof of life. All living organisms are constantly moving from one state of existence to another.
b   Creating change is difficult and challenging and most of us falter in the "how".
c   Healthcare is not a one glove fits all. Coaching embodies this philosophy by supporting individuals to create change that is unique to them.
d   There are multiple approaches to coaching. These different styles can be practiced while considering the client and the task/goal/challenge of interest.

References

Adams, S.R., Goler, N.C., Sanna, R.S., Boccio, M., Bellamy, D.J., Brown, S.D., Neugebauer, R.S., Ferrara, A., Wiley, D.M., Schmittdiel, J.A. (2013) Patient satisfaction and perceived success with a telephonic health coaching program: the Natural Experiments for Translation in Diabetes (NEXT-D) Study, Northern California, 2011. *Preventing Chronic Diseases*. 2013 Oct 31; 10:E179. doi:10.5888/pcd10.130116. PMID: 24176083; PMCID: PMC3816609.

Alfonsson, S., Johansson, K., Uddling, J., Hursti, T. (2017) Differences in motivation and adherence to a prescribed assignment after face-to-face and online psychoeducation: an experimental study. *BMC Psychology.* 2017 Jan 26; 5(1):3. doi:10.1186/s40359-017-0172-5. PMID: 28126022; PMCID: PMC5270286.

Amanchukwu, R., Stanley, G., Ololube, N. (2015). A Review of Leadership Theories, Principles and Styles and Their Relevance to Educational Management. *Management.* 2015. 6–14. doi:10.5923/j.mm.20150501.02.

Ammentorp, J., Uhrenfeldt, L., Angel, F., Ehrensvärd, M., Carlsen, E.B., Kofoed, P. E. (2013) Can life coaching improve health outcomes? – A systematic review of intervention studies. *BMC Health Services Research.* 13:428. doi:10.1186/1472-6963-13-428. PMID: 24148189; PMCID: PMC4015179.

Bachkirova, T. (2011). *Developmental coaching: Working with the self.* Open University Press.

Blanck, P., Perleth, S., Heidenreich, T., Kröger, P., Ditzen, B., Bents, H., Mander, J. (2018). Effects of mindfulness exercises as stand-alone intervention on symptoms of anxiety and depression: Systematic review and meta-analysis. *Behaviour Research and Therapy,* 102: 25–35.

Brown, M.T., Bussell, J., Dutta, S., Davis, K., Strong, S., Mathew, S. (2016) Medication Adherence: Truth and Consequences. *American journal of Medical Sciences.* 351(4):387–399. doi:10.1016/j.amjms.2016.01.010. PMID: 27079345.

Dennis, S.M., Harris, M., Lloyd, J., Powell, D.G., Faruqi, N., Zwar, N. (2013) Do people with existing chronic conditions benefit from telephone coaching? A rapid review. *Australian Health Review.* 37(3):381–388. doi:10.1071/AH13005. PMID: 23701944.

Eagly, A., Johannesen-Schmidt, M., van Engen, M. (2003). Transformational, transactional, and laissez-faire leadership styles: A meta-analysis comparing women and men. *Psychological Bulletin,* 129: 569–591.

Gasslander, N., Alfonsson, S., Jackalin, A., Tengberg, C., Håkansson, J., Huotari, L., Buhrman, M. (2021) Predictors of adherence to an internet-based cognitive behavioral therapy program for individuals with chronic pain and comorbid psychological distress. *BMC Psychology.* 9(1):156. doi:10.1186/s40359-021-00663-x. PMID: 34641946; PMCID: PMC8507117.

Harper, S. (2012) The leader coach: A model of multi-style leadership. *Journal of psychiatry consulting.* 4: 22–31.

Kabat-Zinn, J. (2005) *Coming to our senses.* Heprion.

Kleinsinger, F. (2018) The Unmet Challenge of Medication Nonadherence. *The Permanente Journal.* 22:18–33. doi:10.7812/TPP/18-033. PMID: 30005722; PMCID: PMC6045499.

Lennard, D (2010). *Coaching models: A cultural perspective: A guide to model development for practitioners and students of coaching.* Routledge.

Neuner-Jehle, S., Schmid, M., Grüninger, U. (2013) The "Health Coaching" programme: a new patient-centred and visually supported approach for health behaviour change in primary care. *BMC Family Practice.* 14:100. doi:10.1186/1471-2296-14-100. PMID: 23865509; PMCID: PMC3750840.

Passarelli, A.M. (2015) Vision-based coaching: Optimizing resources for leader development. *Frontiers in Psychology.* 6; 412, 1–14.

Reimers-Hild, C. (2012). Coaching for personal innovation: The role of intuition. *Kimmel Education and Research Center – Faculty & Staff Publications,* 17: 1–20. Retrieved from https://digitalcommons.unl.edu/kimmelfacpub/17.

Spring, B., Schneider, K., McFadden, H.G., Vaughn, J., Kozak, A.T., Smith, M., Moller, A.C., Epstein, L.H., Demott, A., Hedeker, D., Siddique, J., Lloyd-Jones, D.M. (2012) Multiple behavior changes in diet and activity: a randomized controlled trial using mobile technology. *Archives of Internal Medicine*. 172 (10):789–796.   doi:10.1001/archinternmed.2012.1044.   PMID: 22636824; PMCID: PMC3402206.

van den Berg, M.H., Schoones, J.W., Vliet Vlieland, T.P.(20017) Internet-based physical activity interventions: a systematic review of the literature. *Journal of Medical Internet Research*. 9(3):e26. doi:10.2196/jmir.9.3.e26. PMID: 17942388; PMCID: PMC2047289.

Whitley, M., Gould, D., Wright, E., Hayden, L. (2017). Barriers to holistic coaching for positive youth development in South Africa. *Sports Coaching Review*. 1–19.

Yang, I. (2015). Positive effects of laissez-faire leadership: a conceptual exploration. *Journal of Management Development*. 34:1246–1262.

Zolnierek, K.B., Dimatteo, M.R. (2009) Physician communication and patient adherence to treatment: a meta-analysis. *Medical Care*. 47(8):826–834. doi:10.1097/MLR.0b013e31819a5acc. PMID: 19584762; PMCID: PMC2728700.

3 The Healthcare Environment
The Current State of Affairs

Naim El-Aswad MD, FACP, ACC

Introduction and Literature Review

This chapter may be best introduced by two quotes. The first, by Walter Cronkite, "America's health care system is neither healthy, caring, nor a system", seems to apply to most of the healthcare systems around the world. The second, by Fr. Robert Barron discussing state of affairs, goes like this: "Go Beyond Your Mind. Change your attitude...your perspective...your angle, your mode of vision. The new state of affairs has arrived, but you are not going to see it unless you change." At the heart of the latter quote are two truths: The first is to have the ability to see things for how they truly are, and the second is to have the ability to change, to conform and not just survive but thrive in the new environment. In both on cases, we are discussing "abilities". These abilities are dependent on and are the responsibility of our pre-frontal cortex. And because we are discussing abilities, we are implying an innate characteristic of our mind to be able to understand, analyze, discover, and enhance these abilities. This chapter will discuss how coaching can be applied on a practical level to help our minds achieve all of that.

To say the healthcare environment is challenging to work in would be an understatement. The narrative and the expectations have changed from thriving to surviving, literally. With the rate of suicide amongst physicians in the USA being 350–400 per year, or roughly one per day, one must pause to fully grasp a landscape that changes the mind of the physician from elation, relief, and jubilee for being accepted into medical school to one that invites suicide and death as a "logical and sensical option". In the words of one of the physicians who committed suicide, as she wrote a letter to her parents, she states, "... the choice of suicide makes sense to me". The challenges that face the physicians and the coach are to not only understand this landscape, but to be able to navigate it to thrive. Surviving is not an option. Thriving is the only acceptable way to live in this blessed profession.

DOI: 10.4324/9781003452065-3

The Journey

So, how do people go from celebrating the day they got accepted into medical school to the day that takes them into an abyss of burnout, depression, and suicide? What changes in the brain must occur to take us on that road? And why are some people susceptible to it while others are not? How does that journey look like? And does it provide us with spatial or temporal opportunities to intervene? And if so, where does coaching fit, and how?

The challenges of the healthcare industry start in medical school. (Slavin et al., 2014). Before medical school, the mental health of medical students was equivalent to that of the general population. At the end of their first year, 57 % had moderate to severe symptoms of anxiety, 27 % had symptoms of depression. It significantly declines after 2 years. And it continues to decline into the training and specialty years. Literature has shown the multitude of reasons why this occurs.

For the past three decades, and in the post Covid era, the findings are best summarized by Harvey et al in 2021. Across the globe, reduced job control, insecurity at work, increased bureaucratic and administrative burdens and responsibilities, a shift in the priorities and age of medical graduates, EMR burden, feeling like cogs in a wheel, and decreased financial rewards have diminished the protective factors of practice that in the past have helped offset the risks of caring for humanity.

Discussions and Applications

In the 1980's Christina Maslach published her book on burnout. She describes three major contributing factors to burnout: Loss of autonomy, unmet expectations, and insufficient rewards. (Maslach, 1982) Fast forward to now, there are 6 other factors that contribute to burnout and mental health of physicians. These include leadership, pressure, personal characteristics, self-care and wellness, and purpose and need. It is at the levels of these factors that coaching can be applied. Before we move forward to the coaching approach, it is best to pause and discuss in detail how each of these factors contributes to burnout, mental health problems, and the overwhelming distress facing physicians. With the discussion of each factor there will be a section that highlights the area of intervention for coaching along with the discussion of potential coaching approaches. Case studies will be given.

- Purpose"Medicine arose out of the ***primal sympathy*** of man with man; out of the ***desire*** to ***help*** those in sorrow, need and sickness."
  Sir William Osler

Science, neuroscience, has proven that empathy and sympathy are primal needs, no different than hunger and thirst. The center for empathy is found in the anterior insular cortex. (X. Gu et al., 2012) Once these needs are fulfilled, they trigger a reward pathway that is rudimentary, and it piggybacks on the mesolimbic pathway. A thank you, a hug, and a life helped and made to feel better is what drives doctors and other health-care professionals. It is that primal sympathy that fuels them to study and go through gruelling years of training to get to the privileged spot in the life of others. But how does that show itself in the practice of medicine?

All human beings interact with each other along three axes: Emotional, cognitive, and behavioral. From a physician-patient relationship view-point, it is expressed/represented through connection, diagnosis, and treatment respectively. There are several ways this relationship is impac-ted negatively through medical training and practice.

- Emotional/connection

For a multitude of reasons, empathy erodes with medical students all the way to residency and specialization training (Laughey et al., 2021; Stratta et al., 2016). The gradual erosion of empathy, along with the training that emphasizes "logical" and non-emotional interaction with patients creates a disturbance in the prefrontal cortex, the wiring that inspired people to becoming doctors and fulfilling their "calling". This disturbance manifests in wiring and neuronal misfiring and malfunction as the brain battles its need for empathy with the external pressure to not only control emotions but subdue them and distance oneself from them. In essence, medical training not only encourages, but also almost demands that emotions be absent from clinical judgement, decision making, and behavior.

- Coaching Focus

Many physicians and healthcare workers have issues with commu-nication and connection with their patients. Look no further than the multitude of interventions that seek to educate physicians on how to communicate and show empathy post training and while in practice. It seems like the medical field created a problem through its education and training and then is forced to fix it through retraining and counseling. This leaves physicians frustrated, and they are exposed to the stress of feeling distant from their patients, developing resentment towards their patients and the institutions, and developing feelings and symptoms of burnout.

Coaching can help physicians not only identify the problems they are facing in this area but help them to connect first with their own emotions and then with others. One of the best approaches used in this arena is Emotional Intelligence. Because emotional intelligence is about under-standing oneself and managing oneself, understanding others and mana-ging others, it is one of the best coaching modalities to help doctors reconnect with their emotions and their primal sympathy, master those emotions, and use them to connect within themselves and others to fulfill their purpose and decrease their burnout.

- Cognitive scarcity

Cognitive scarcity means one head, multiple hats. The brain has a finite amount of energy and abilities. For the physician, the ideal situation is when the brain is free to focus purely on the disease, the patient, and the diagnosis. Instead, what happens, at an increasing rate, is that the doctors are asked to focus on so many tasks such as dealing with insurance company rules and regulations, running their clinics, meeting institutional demands, filling out numerous forms, teach, and problem solve nonclinical issues. This shapes a mind that constantly feels as if it needs to solve problems. Indeed, many physicians cannot turn their "brains" off. Everything to them becomes a problem they need to solve. This exhausts the brain and draws resources to urgent demands. This, in turn, leads to impairments in other domains and functions of the prefrontal cortex such as listening, having patience, having empathy, being able to focus and leads to counterproductive behaviors and mistakes and more primitive responses.

- Behavioral disconnect

At the heart of medicine is the product of its practice and its measure of success: Making others feel/be better/healthier. The outcome desired, improving health and reducing disease, is the focus of training, of passion and purpose, of goals and dedication, of sacrifice and commitment. At the heart of modern healthcare are economics, metrics, customer service, electronic health records, utilization reviews, resource allocations, and risk reduction. The measures of success have shifted. Even though the outcome of "health" among patients is important, it has somehow taken a back seat. Corporations, governments, institutions, and systems have different agendas and items. Consequently, they have tried to shape a physician's behavior to meet those requirements, standards, and outcomes. Even the public's perception of medicine and healthcare has changed. Most studies indicate that the three most valued attributes of physicians are humaneness, patient autonomy respect, and a cooperative approach in decision-making (Dopelt et al., 2021).

The focus in medical training has been about the patient's health and outcome. Further, the training of physicians is now less focused on direct patient interaction. The time spent with their patients on a daily basis among internal medicine residents ranges from 9 to 18 %! (Chaiyachati et al., 2019; Wieler et al., 2020). As physicians' behaviors and purpose get rewarded less and less, and as they are forced to adopt new behaviors and focus on new outcomes, the pathways in their prefrontal cortex get "short circuited", and their reward pathways are not triggered. Not being able to feel "good" about being a physician and having a sense of accomplishment is a direct and straight line towards feeling burned out.

Goethe said: "Treat people as if they are what they ought to be, and you help them to become what they are capable of being". By allowing physicians to focus on what they need to, and providing them the space and time and environment to "behave" accordingly, you help them be engaged and avoid burnout.

- Coaching Focus

Many physicians struggle with their reality and the demands of modern healthcare. Several reports highlight their frustrations and disappointment. One of the main problems in dealing with their reality is that physicians try to "fix" things on their own, using a skill set that works as an "expert" approach. This, as we shall see later also, creates even bigger problems for them. "Fixing" a healthcare industry's changing environment or "adapting" to it through a "doctor's" lens and philosophy does not work. Further, those in the healthcare industry do not understand the impact of their decision making on the professional and personal lives of their doctors. There are several intervention points that coaching can help with, regardless of the approach used:

- Understanding the environment and its "new" demands, and more importantly, coming to terms with them
- Developing the ability and skill set to thrive in the new healthcare industry
- Collaborative work: Turning the "me vs them" argument to "me and them versus the problem" argument. (Case study for illustration to follow)
- Setting realistic expectations
- Developing a "healthy" sense of control
- Reassessing goals and purpose
- Reconnecting with purpose
- Adopting new behaviors and understanding the "why" behind them
- Others including, but not limited to, personal struggles, professional challenges and barriers, institutional constraints to name a few. Any obstacle that is perceived to exist by the doctor could be a focus point of coaching.

- Case study on collaborative work

In a hospital in Texas, our company was hired to help the physician leadership achieve, through its influence on other physicians, certain hospital "metrics" for safety, efficiency, turnover rate, and patient satisfaction. Following our AAA model, "Awareness, Assessment, and Action", we initiated the conversation with the leadership group.

Through discovery, it was evident that one of the issues that are central to not achieving the desired outcomes was the C-suite attitude, expectations, and actions. This led to creating a workshop where we had the c-suite on one side, and the medical leadership on another, literally facing each other as if they were two sparring groups on a reality TV show.

Next up, we went through the challenges of physicians and the challenges of the c-suite according to literature. That experience alone was eye opening for both teams. Misconceptions, misinformation, misunderstandings, resistance, and unrealistic thoughts quickly gave way to empathy, comprehension, collaboration, and acceptance. That became even more evident when each side spoke of their lived experiences and stories, which added a personal and more relatable reality to both sides. The idea of "us versus them" to "us and them versus the problem" became their mantra. The rest of the workshop and what followed was group coaching, team building approach as well as individual coaching.

- Need

The self-determination theory asserts that the three basic human needs are autonomy, relatedness, and competency. One can add purpose or meaning to that trio of needs to help understand why the healthcare industry has contributed so much to the burnout and worsening of physician's mental health. This also helps map out an approach for coaches to help support physicians in their quest to fulfill their needs and manage the burdens of their profession. Physicians need to have clinical competence, empathetic relatedness, and professional autonomy.

Anything that challenges or impedes or disrupts one or all of those needs can and will lead to burnout. Further, one need does not compensate for the other. So being clinically competent without autonomy or relatedness still leads to the same outcome. Physicians are finding it increasingly difficult to fulfill those needs. Add to the problems listed before, physicians are Plagued with less time to connect, perform more duties/chores, being under more intense scrutiny, having less autonomy, and evaluated on non-clinical performances to measure clinical competence.

"He who has a why to live for can bear almost any how".

Nietzsche

The healthcare industry is taking the "why" away from not only doctors, but the rest of its professionals.

- Coaching Focus:

It may be evident now that satisfying those needs, or finding ways to do so and achieving purpose, would be different foci of coaching. That is indeed the case. Physicians do not have the knowledge, expertise, or ability to "survive", let alone "thrive" in this environment. That is a direct result of lack of education, lack of knowledge and experience, lack of preparation, possession of a unique mindset that has been groomed, educated, and evaluated to handle situations in a particular way that can be even more detrimental, lack of support (financial legal, informational, resources, regulatory), lack of overall awareness of the magnitude, pathophysiology, and the extent of the problems, lack of willingness to help, lack of guidelines to help, and lack of time and opportunity to help. So, how does one coach a client to navigate this reality and seemingly insurmountable task? The focus is on two fronts or levels.

•   Mindset intervention coaching

One of the key foci of coaching is to help clients change their internal narrative from "life is what happens to me" to "life is what I make happen". Without that switch, the likelihood of surviving and thriving in this environment becomes very low. If people blame others and wait for others to fix a problem, especially this group of professionals and this type of environment, the worse things will become. As we have seen, the challenges in the healthcare industry are only getting greater, both in quality and quantity. And to be hopeful or reliant on the same group of individuals who seem to contribute to the problem while facing these increasing odds seems almost ludicrous. Yet, this is what most of our clients seem to think and want to believe. The notion that we need to add "more on their plates" while it is someone else's problems sometimes enrages them; and perhaps rightfully so. However, while we await a potential solution from an unlikely source that is contributing to the problem, the truth remains of the demise, destruction, and destitute state of doctors.

It is imperative that we coach or help our clients make that mindset shift to not only get them to accept their reality, but also to succeed in managing it.

Coaching for mindset intervention can and does follow several models. Simplistically, before even diving into solutions to certain challenges, and in the words of one of the authors, and being the focus of one of the chapters, one must coach the "physician", not "the problem".

Case study

An obstetrician, who was in the later stages of her professional life, was referred for coaching by the C-suite. The report on her was that she is rude, disrespectful, dismissive, insensitive, and had several complaints about her from the patients and the staff.

After our first meeting, the client proceeded to tell me her side of the story. With the current "regime" change, and the unrealistic expectations that were placed on her, she felt hopeless. Nothing she did was okay or enough. The nurses were new nurses, as the old crew had left. These new nurses also had unrealistic expectations. They did not know how to Interact a physician, and they were "very sensitive". Patients, too, had unrealistic expectations, they demanded so much time to explain things and even when she did explain, the complaint was that she had not. Patients lost respect for physicians.

She enjoys her profession and loves what she does. Her passion and calling have not diminished one bit. But she is getting dissuaded, dismayed, and discouraged. She is getting bitter and burnt out. So, when asked about what needs to happen, the client went on an hour-long conversation suggesting how everyone needs to change and go back to how things were. Then, when I asked her about what she can do, she stated her sense of defeat and how nothing she does will matter anyway. And what they are asking of her cannot be achieved.

She has been in this hospital for over 30 years. She practically built the department. She does not want to leave but she feels she is being forced to. She stated she was a fighter, a go-get-er, someone who does not give up, and someone who finds a way. This was very difficult for her.

When asked what her challenges are, she stated quite the list. When asked what she has attempted, the list was not quite as long. When asked if she believes there are reasons to think things might get better, the answers became even shorter. When asked if she was ever in a similar situation before, the answer was yes. Comparing the two situations the client started to see the similarities. When asked what the difference was between the two, she stated she believed she could impact the first situation and did; but not this one. When asked what will it take for her to believe she can impact the current situation, she stated she needs to give more input and chances to "drive the conversation, set expectations, and have a say in the overall working environment".

It was then that she was asked what it will take for that to happen... there was a pause.

"I simply have to let them know in a different way; and not quit". It was at that moment when the client went from feeling defeated to feeling hopeful. She no longer felt that she just must "take it and endure", but that she can actually have a say. The switch had happened. The mindset changed. And with that, the attitude, approach, and results.

Challenge-specific coaching

A 52-year-old chief medical officer was discussing with me his challenges of finding time for his personal and professional growth. He enjoys his time at the office and at home. He was getting frustrated at himself and at the working environment for not allowing him the time he needed. Upon further discussion, it became apparent to him that even though he felt okay with where he was, there was something missing in his work-life balance.

During one of the sessions, we went through his week, his times, and his activities. The challenge, like so many physicians or people in the healthcare industry, is lack of time. This point is one of my favorite points to discuss, whether in presentations, workshops, or coaching sessions. Stephen Covey once said: "The key is not to prioritize your schedule, but to schedule your priorities".

With that, I asked the client to list his top 5 priorities in his life. Then, I asked him to list the top 5 things that he prioritizes with his time. He then placed the two lists side by side. It was an "AHA" moment for him. For he had believed the two lists were the same.

When asked what it will take for him to "live" his priority list, his answer was simple yet powerful: The client.

The chief medical officer is a good segway to discuss the next factor that impacts burnout: Leadership.

- Leadership

Frederick Morgeson once declared that "People quit their bosses, not their jobs". In 2017, Tait Shanafelt and his colleagues

> ...demonstrated the importance of front-line leadership on the well-being and professional satisfaction of physicians. For every point upward on a 60-point scale, there was 9% greater staff satisfaction and 3.3% less burnout. At the department and division level, 11% of the variation in burnout and 47% of the variation in satisfaction with the organization was explained by the Leader Index of the chairperson.

These findings have been replicated across multiple studies. Leadership requires a certain set of abilities that are found in self-leadership, emotional intelligence, conflict management, decision-making skills, and communication skills, to name a few.

The 2 main problems with leadership in the healthcare industry are:

- Leaders who are experts in one field leading others who are experts in another field (C-suite executives leading physicians)
- Leaders promoted to lead others based on a set of skills in one area (clinical) that are different from the leadership arena. The mistake that most programs and organizations make lies in the assumption that successful clinicians will make great leaders. One of the main problems in this approach is that physicians get promoted based on their clinical expertise and success into roles that require a totally different set of abilities, desires, and expertise. (Quinn & Perelli, 2016).

- Coaching focus

A group of program directors were undergoing a leadership and burnout workshop. One of their main listed challenges was meeting the expectations of their institutions and their physicians. One of those physicians was having a really hard time amongst her peers and subordinates as well as with the executive leadership of the hospital. She also had to meet the requirements of the ACGME (Accreditation Council for Graduate Medical Education). During her coaching session, she listed her major challenges: Getting people to listen to her.

- Coaching approach: Emotional intelligence.

After administering her EQI, it turns out that one of the lowest scoring skills she has was "assertiveness". She was very surprised to see that. It made sense to her after reflecting as she felt she had to please everyone to "maintain the peace" and "keep her job". It was difficult for her to be able to find the balance between achieving the requirements of her job, being a clinician, satisfying her ACGME role, and leading others. After a few coaching sessions that focused on assertiveness, the impact for her was noticeable. It took a few months to see things turn around. But they did.

- Self-care and wellness:

It is an absolute cliché, but taking care of oneself and maintaining a state of wellness are paramount to avoiding burnout. As it has been shown in numerous publications and studies, self-care and wellness inoculate, help prevent, help support, help combat, and help "cure" physicians from burnout. It is important to highlight the following:

- Self-care: "the **practice** of taking an **active role** in protecting one's own well-being and happiness, in particular during periods of **stress**."
- Wellness: "the state of being in good health, especially as an **actively** pursued goal"

The key issue here is the "active role". One does not gain muscles by going to the gym and standing next to someone else exercising.

Ask a doctor what are some things that drive them mad, and they will tell you the idea that patients want to keep doing the same thing, like smoking, while expecting their diseases to get better.

Hippocrates said it best: "Before you heal someone, ask him if he is willing to give up the things that make him sick."

Would that not apply to the doctors also?

- Coaching focus

Coaching for self-care and wellness can be approached from so many different angles: Time, or lack of (again, priorities), perceived lack of resources, denial, lack of support systems, a culture (medicine) that focuses on helping others at all costs. Other angles include shame, the stigma behind needing to take care of oneself, lack of knowledge, and missing out on the three main requirements at the heart of wellness: Self-love, self-compassion, and self-care. I must point out here to a change in the physician's oath that occurred in 2017. The following statement was added in Geneva: "I will attend to my own health, well-being, and abilities in order to provide care of the highest standard". There has been a shift, albeit on paper, to physicians' well-being and health. The practical aspect of this shift has yet to be realized.

As far as what coaching approach one must adapt, any and all would work.

Case study

A 38-year-old doctor was celebrating his family. He had two children and now has a third. A few months after his third child was born, he was really feeling the impact of the demands of his life and the change in his lifestyle. He had gained around 40 pounds, had last visited the gym 8 months prior to his appointment, and was having body image issues.

Looking at the wellness wheel, he was asked to identify where he was on a scale of 0 to 10 as far as his physical wellness is concerned. It was a 2/10.

Using the TIBA model, he identified one target or goal to achieve. He felt he would become a 5/10 if he went back to exercising regularly, because he was sure his weight loss would follow.

He listed his ideas on how to achieve regular exercise. He looked at his schedule and figured out where he can place his exercise routines. He, through coaching, built his schedule around his priorities. He had to navigate his work, his responsibilities as a provider, a father, a husband, and a doctor. Then, he focused on one activity he can do to achieve his goal. After writing down the anticipated barriers/challenges, he came up with a plan to overcome those barriers. It turned out that for him, waking up 35 minutes before his usual time daily would provide him with the best opportunity and time to exercise.

- Pressure

Pressure is where the outcome is important to you, it is uncertain, and you are accountable and judged for the results. You must deliver the goods or suffer dire consequences. Pressure adversely impacts cognitive success, downgrades behavioral skills. We perform below our capability, is often camouflaged, and is continually increasing. (Weisenger and Pawliw-Fry, 2015). In the healthcare industry, pressure is also accompanied with unrealistic expectations.

In one of the interviews with a physician suffering from burnout, he recalled having his orders over a year's time being reviewed by HR. He had placed a total of around 65000 orders. The expectations were that he would get all these orders appropriately. Not a single mistake was allowed. Such are the expectations from the healthcare industry, the institutions, the academic world, the patients, and us. Who or what on this planet operates like that? Who or what on this planet has a 100 % success and efficiency rate?

- Coaching focus

Dealing with pressure is an innate and learned process. It is an ability that draws on several internal and external resources. The coaching approach to dealing with pressure and the stress it causes, along with the unique mindset of the physician will be discussed in the next chapter.

Conclusions and Recommendations

It is a setup. Not by design, but by outcome. Not by intention, but by necessity. The ideals and dreams of being a doctor and the training and education to become one clash with the realities and nightmares of the healthcare industry. The battleground, the prefrontal cortex, may look like a waste land strewn with detached brain matter, amputated neuronal connections, and dysfunctional holes marking where the impact of the demands and expectations of the healthcare industry hit.

Years after the battles have ended, sometimes we get beautiful fields that grow to cover the brutality of what happened. Sometimes, these fields never grow again and serve as a constant reminder of the charred landscape. We do not have time to wait for fields to regrow, and we need to avoid the burnt-out landscape.

Support comes from the healthcare environment and from us. And while all indications point to a distant, if any, support from the healthcare industry, some might argue even that things will only get worse. There is an immediate opening and opportunity to help doctors and healthcare professionals survive and thrive these battlegrounds. Coaching has become one of the main areas of help and support. It is not a luxury, but a necessity. Time has run out. The battles and wars are here. And the world cannot afford the consequences.

Summary and Key Points

a The demands of the healthcare industry have led to burnout in the healthcare professionals' lives through a multitude of ways.
b The impact of the healthcare industry has left many feeling burned out.
c Burnout is a disease with several contributing factors including:

- Unmet expectations
- Lack of control
- Insufficient rewards
- Leadership
- Healthcare and wellness
- Purpose and need
- Pressure

d Coaching can be applied to any and all of these contributing factors.
e Individual and group coaching help support the physicians.
f Depending on the challenges, different coaching approaches would be applied.
g The healthcare industry's impact may get even worse moving forward.

References

Chaiyachati, K.H., Shea, J.A., Asch, D.A., Liu, M., Bellini, L.M., Dine, C.J., Sternberg, A.L., Gitelman, Y., Yeager, A.M., Asch, J.M., Desai, S.V. (2019) Assessment of Inpatient Time Allocation Among First-Year Internal Medicine Residents Using Time-Motion Observations. *JAMA Intern Medicine.* 179(6):760–767. doi:10.1001/jamainternmed.2019.0095. Erratum in: JAMA Intern Med. 2019 Jul 1;:null. PMID: 30985861; PMCID: PMC8462976.

Dopelt, K., Bachner, Y.G., Urkin, J., Yahav, Z., Davidovitch, N., Barach, P. (2021) Perceptions of Practicing Physicians and Members of the Public on the Attributes of a "Good Doctor". *Healthcare.* 10(1):73. doi:10.3390/healthcare10010073. PMID: 35052237; PMCID: PMC8775310.

Harvey, S.B., Epstein, R.M., Glozier, N., Petrie, K., Strudwick, J., Gayed, A., Dean, K., Henderson, M. (2021) Mental illness and suicide among physicians. *Lancet.* 398(10303):920–930. doi:10.1016/S0140-6736(21)01596-8. PMID: 34481571; PMCID: PMC9618683.

Kirch, D.G. (2021) Physician Mental Health: My Personal Journey and Professional Plea. *Academic Medicine.* 96(5): 618–620. doi:10.1097/ACM.0000000000003942.

Laughey, W.F., Atkinson, J., Craig, A.M., Douglas, L., Brown, M.E., Scott, J.L., Alberti, H., Finn, G.M. (2021) Empathy in Medical Education: Its Nature and Nurture – a Qualitative Study of the Views of Students and Tutors. *Medical Science Educator.* 31(6):1941–1950. doi:10.1007/s40670-021-01430-8. PMID: 34692227; PMCID: PMC8519626.

Maslach, C. (1982). *Burnout: The Cost of Caring.* Englewood Cliffs, NJ: Prentice-Hall.

Quinn, J.F., Perelli, S. (2016) First and foremost, physicians: the clinical versus leadership identities of physician leaders. *Journal of Health Organization and Management.* 20;30(4):711–728. doi:10.1108/JHOM-05-2015-0079. PMID: 27296888.

Shanafelt, T.D., Gorringe, G., Menaker, R., Storz, K.A., Reeves, D., Buskirk, S.J., Sloan, J.A., Swensen, S.J. (2015) Impact of organizational leadership on physician burnout and satisfaction. *Mayo Clinic Proceedings.* 90(4):432–440. doi:10.1016/j.mayocp.2015.01.012. Epub 2015 Mar 18. PMID: 25796117.

Slavin, S.J., Schindler, D.L., Chibnall, J.T. (2014) Medical student mental health 3.0: improving student wellness through curricular changes. *Academic Medicine.* 89 (4):573–577. doi:10.1097/ACM.0000000000000166. PMID: 24556765; PMCID: PMC4885556.

Stratta, E.C., Riding, D.M., Baker, P. (2016) Ethical erosion in newly qualified doctors: perceptions of empathy decline. *International journal of Medical Education.* 7:286–292. doi:10.5116/ijme.57b8.48e4. PMID: 27608488; PMCID: PMC5018358.

Weisenger and Pawliw-Fry. (2015) *Performing Under Pressure.* Crown Currency.

Wieler, J., Lehman, E., Khalid, M., Hennrikus, E. (2020) A Day in the Life of an Internal Medicine Resident – A Time Study: What Is Changed from First to Third Year? *Advances in Medical Education and Practice.* 11:253–258. doi:10.2147/AMEP.S247974. PMID: 32280293; PMCID: PMC7125302.

Gu, X., Gao, Z, Wang, X, Liu, X., Knight, T.R., Hof, P.R., Fan, J. (2012) Anterior insular cortex is necessary for empathetic pain perception. *Brain.* 135(9):2726. doi:10.1093/brain/aws199.

4 The Uniqueness of the Physicians

Understanding the Mindset of Physicians, their Driving Forces, Coachability, and their Challenges

Naim El-Aswad MD, FACP, ACC

Introduction and Literature Review

Allow me to state the obvious: Everyone is different. No two people are alike.

Allow me to question the obvious: Why would healthcare and coaching be delivered in the same way, as a one-glove-fits-all model, to everyone?

Coaching is an approach, a science, a way, and a methodology that has its own rules and regulations. It follows certain steps, algorithms at times, and norms. The coach and the coachee are not the same. This chapter focuses on physicians as clients, and it highlights their mindset, coachability, challenges, and uniqueness.

Mindset

The mindset of the physician has been touched upon in earlier chapters. In general, doctors are doers, experts in their fields, value autonomy, work one-on-one, and in sequence. They are conservative/reactive thinkers, and they are deficit-based thinkers by nature of their education, training, and profession. Physicians are taught to know the normal and identify the abnormal. It is what they focus on: the negative, the missing, the problem. Their approach is to "fix" the problem, "cure" the ailment, and "defeat" the disease. Their success is measured by their ability to problem solve, their relationship with their patients, which is a particular type of expert-person in need relationship, and income generation. This is all great and wonderful when treating a disease. But when physicians live their lives through that same lens and approach, when they approach almost all aspects of their lives, personal, and professional, through that same philosophy, it can produce challenges and problems. Further, a physician is viewed in the eyes of the public, the staff, their working colleagues, and their friends and family through that all-encompassing lens of "being a doctor".

"Atul Gawande describes Western medical practice as "dominated by a single imperative – the quest for machinelike perfection in the delivery of care"... "These ambitious standards for medical practice, while

DOI: 10.4324/9781003452065-4

impossible to satisfy, often seem to bleed over into the expectations for physician behavior beyond the clinical realm."… "society often judges medical professionals on the basis of personal characteristics unrelated to clinical competence." (Sawicki, 2011). This is a practice that keeps happening, and if anything, is increasing in its scrutiny and application.

Asking a doctor to "change" the way they think, or to approach challenges or problems from a non-clinical perspective can sometimes result in a blank stare of bewilderment.

Coachability

Reviewing the factors that impact coachability allows us to have a better idea on the challenges that coaches and physicians as coachees face in this process. It also helps identify areas of intervention or focus during the coaching sessions and process.

A client's readiness for coaching and coachability depend on a number of variables. (Kretzschmar, 2010). This model applies to clients no matter the industry. Looking at it from the physicians' and the healthcare industry's lens is necessary to understand this particular coaching field. According to Kretzchmar, there are six factors that either hinder or enable the client. These categories are culture and class, knowledge about coaching, access to coaching, psychological interpretations, feeling safe, and commitment to change.

Tee et al., in 2022, reviewed thousands of articles and found 47 studies eligible for interpretations after meeting their scientific requirements. There were intrinsic and extrinsic factors that affect willingness to be coached. There were also subjective and objective factors. The list here is not exhaustive by any stretch, but it helps to give an idea of all the factors that impact the coach and the coachee: age and gender, motivation, feedback receptivity, commitment, readiness for change, evaluation of core, openness for change, conscientiousness, willingness to be vulnerable, compassion and patience, western culture norms, self-discipline, cognitive flexibility, and ability to trust.

Coachability has been proven to depend on the coachee as an active rather than passive participant. The coachee is capable of either impeding or enhancing the coaching process. (Weiss & Merrigan, 2021) According to the authors, they define coachability as the coachees "willingness and ability to seek, receive, act on, and change behavior based on feedback provided during coaching interactions". It is coachability that determines willingness to seek, receive, and implement feedback. So important is coachability that organizational experts have identified it as a trait/ability that needs to be explored before hiring individuals. Being non-coachable is behind one of the top reasons for failure in the organization. While this may apply to organizational structures outside the healthcare industry, there is nothing to suggest it does not apply here where, although different in nature, challenges and the need for adaptability are part and parcel of thriving. The authors also highlight similar traits: Increased feedback seeking, receptivity, and implementation of feedback, motive behind coaching, adaptability, and being proactive.

The construct of coachability was described by Cavanaugh et al. in 2021. The authors identified the following factors to assess coachability: Openness, vulnerability, external resources, security, and growth orientation.

These factors allow the coach to measure or assess coachability through various tools and approaches including observations, 360 feedback, interviews, assessment tools (emotional intelligence, personality types, and others), and digital coaching tools. Digital coaching is remote or in person coaching with AI support.

Coachability is looked at as a spectrum that is dynamic. People, even the same person, can be on different parts of the spectrum depending on: Where they are in their life, how they are in their life, when they are in their life, what they are in their life and who they are in their life.

These all apply to their personal and professional lives. It is important to develop an understanding of these situations to help assist in the coaching approach and experience.

Discussions and Applications

Challenges

In the executive world, coaching was first looked at with skepticism, and through a negative lens. Being coached was synonymous with "needing help" and not being good enough. It was between the 1970s and 1980s that the true value of coaching was realized and the business world adopted it where it took off in the 1980s and has not looked back since. In fact, coaching is part and parcel of success and growth within companies. It has become a cornerstone of achievements and a determinant of a company's and its employees' success.

The story is almost duplicating itself in the medical world. Coaching, as of the year 2023, has a mixed outlook and understanding. Some believe in its power, others are sceptical, and some downright hostile. To understand why, let us take a closer look at the coaching challenges in the healthcare industry. More frequently than not, due to financial reasons, time constraints, lack of vision, lack of data, and lack of resources, coaching is mostly used to help "physicians who are in trouble". Physicians usually are referred for coaching for the following negative reasons: They are burned out, they are disruptive, they have communication issues, they are hostile, they have anger and irritability problems, they are about to lose their jobs, they have so many complaints about them, they are making risky clinical decisions, they are unreliable, they have changed in their character and demeanor, they are becoming careless, they are on a performance improvement plan, as well as other reasons.

What ends up happening is that the doctor comes to the coach usually defensive, fixed mindset, uncooperative, angry, resistant to feedback and change, resentful, passive-aggressive, and insulted.

Given the factors that enhance coachability, one can easily see the challenges that coaches face when they are trying to coach the physician. There is one particular challenge that needs to be highlighted as it afflicts all physicians, healthcare professionals, and workers: Burnout.

As was discussed in chapter 3, burnout is a multifactorial pandemic. The end result of burnout is disruption in the neuronal connections and processes in multiple areas in the prefrontal cortex, as well as other parts of the brain. Seeing that coaching targets the prefrontal cortex, the focus will remain on that area. Chapter 3 discussed the different approaches to the varied factors that lead to burnout. With Christina Maslach's definition of burnout and its causative factors (unmet expectations, lack of control, insufficient rewards), chapter 3 discussed the "insufficient rewards" aspect. This chapter will discuss the other two factors from a coaching perspective, and their relationship with each other.

One of the key drivers of burnout is lack of control. In fact, "the degree of control that an animal or human can exert over a stressor has a substantial impact on the emotional, behavioral, neurobiological, and physiological effects of the stressor" (Maier & Seligman, 2016)

Chronic UNCONTROLLED stress in animals can lead to behaviors observed in humans during stress and burnout: "Impaired working memory and attentional flexibility, increased fear in a variety of settings, hypervigilance, decreased water and food intake, reduced social interaction. avoidance of novel objects and reduced exploratory behavior, and learning deficits"

Uncontrolled stress leads to a cascade of chemical events that destroys dendrites, spines, and neuronal connections. These changes manifest as decreased ability to concentrate, plan, make decisions, regulate emotions, resist cravings, and inhibit the stress response.

Now, let us add the impact of control, or lack of, in the physicians' minds, to that list. (Shapiro et al., 2011). "Psychological research has demonstrated that the desire for a 'sense of control,' which we define as 'the ability (or perception that one has the ability) to cause an effect in the intended direction' is a pervasive human experience." Loss of control for physicians comes from disease progression, patient compliance, regulatory requirements, and healthcare industry demands.

The authors found that " ...a healthy sense of control should include not only ways to exercise positive mastery, but also constructive acceptance of lack of control". Controlled stress enhances the PFC's ability to control the limbic system and the brain stem structures that mediate the stress response.

Changing stress from uncontrolled to controlled, and changing the response to the reality of the situation, presents a unique target for coaching. Why do we have to do that? Because we must. As Viktor Frankl once said:

"When we are no longer able to change a situation – we are challenged to change ourselves."

It is an opportune time to talk about the concept of locus of control. Locus of Control refers to an individual's perception about the underlying main causes of events in his/her life. Locus of control sways between external and internal. External locus of control means events or outcomes are determined independent of one's behavior. Internal locus of control refers to outcomes being determined by one's attitudes, hard work, and decisions.

The art of coaching is helping people navigate between the two types of control as it relates to the client, the situation, and the outcome.

Control must involve finding healthy and life-affirming ways to exercise personal mastery and identifying constructive ways to respond to the lack of control that pervades the human condition. The precise nature of this need for control is influenced by factors such as self-efficacy, and personal variability across domains and stages of life. The behaviors and cognitions of individuals can be understood, in part, as an expression of their perceived need to gain, maintain, and/or reestablish a sense of control.

Dealing with stress and control involves active and proactive coping mechanisms. Active coping includes goal-directed behavior, gathering information, acquiring skills, problem solving, and making decisions.

Rotter's theory states that:

- Locus of Control is a perception that is shaped by one's lived experiences with rewards and punishments in response to their actions.
- These same experiences dynamically create beliefs and influence attitudes and behaviors.
- While coaching, it is important to be aware of the client's context and self-perceptions.
- Coaching can be used to target attitudes, beliefs (expectations), behaviors, and emotions.

Table 4.1 Locus of Control

Internal Locus of Control	External Locus of Control
Believe what they've achieved is due to their hard work	Credits luck or timing when they manage to achieve something
Take responsibility for their actions	Put the responsibility on forces outside of their control
Don't believe in "fate"	Feel that they can't change a situation because that's how it's meant to be
Aren't usually as influenced by other people's opinions	Feel hopeless when confronted with a difficult situation
Tend to be driven and motivated to achieve something they want	Believe they'll achieve what they want if the timing is right or if it's meant to be

Let us talk about expectations. As we have seen, one of the key drivers of burnout is unmet expectations. Physicians are set up to have unrealistic expectations that are both internal (self-inflicted) and external (world around us). Let me pause and focus on a very important point that will come up as a challenge when coaching physicians. In general, through their journey, training, profession, and industry, not only do physicians have a difficult time celebrating their own successes, but they also have an even tougher time recognizing them. And when they do, they do not know how to enjoy them, or "sit in them". In one of my workshops, I asked a group of physicians what success means for them. While each gave their own thoughts, they all had one thing in common: A success story usually involved an ambiguous diagnosis, a humungous technical achievement (surgical skill or intervention), or a lifesaving within minutes event, like diagnosing an aortic dissection. When asked how did they recognize and celebrate their achievement, unanimously, they answered, for a few minutes. Because that is the expectation. And then they focused again on trying to help others.

When asked if they ever celebrated treating a middle ear infection, or an infected throat, they all look confused, almost bewildered. Every one of them, and this applies to ten different groups of physicians, did not even recognize this as an achievement. So, when asked if they were ever sick and to describe their state of existence when having a middle ear infection or an infected throat, their overwhelming answer was they felt miserable. Somehow, being able to relief misery and helping people return to their lives, be pain free, feel healthy, and not feel disease is not an achievement!

Physicians, in general, are not able to recognize their achievements, are not trained nor is it in them to celebrate their achievements, and do not know how to fully express them and "sit in them" properly. They, along with their industry, are so focused on sniffing out the mistakes. This becomes a coaching challenge when helping physicians develop a sense of resilience and achievement and manage their expectations. If doctors cannot, do not, and will not recognize success, how could they feel good about themselves when they are successful?

Medicine and its practice are one of the most, if not the most, scrutinized professions. Stress is unmet expectations. There is even an "expectation disease". Expectations disable rather than enable. Disability manifests through 5 types of loss of control: Unmet or excessive need for control, impaired recognition of controllability, misattribution of control, control dissimulation, and fear of loss of control. The manifestations of these control disorders differ in chronicity, rigidity, and intensity. (Frank, 1993).

Jeremy Binns once said: "What screws us most in life is the picture in our heads of how it is supposed to be". Setting realistic expectations and dealing with the pressure of healthcare are challenges that are not easy. It is hard to have an internal conversation about expectations. It is even harder to discuss it with the world around us. Still, we can control only what we can control. And by shifting the focus to control, and mastery of that control, pressure is dealt with in a "healthier way".

From a coaching perspective, how can control and expectations be approached?

A powerful model, first described in 1987 by Stephen Covey, discussed the concepts of circle of concern, circle of influence, and circle of focus. In his book, the author talks about the clients having multiple concerns. He discusses the importance of dividing these concerns, or challenges, into different categories. The first category represents the circle of concern. In that circle, people would place all the concerns or challenges that they have zero control over. No matter what they do or try, they do not have any impact on their outcomes or trajectories. In the second circle, the circle of influence, people would place all the challenges and concerns that they have an impact on. From the circle of influence, the clients are encouraged to bring one concern and place it into their circle of focus. While that challenge is in the circle of focus, the clients will "attack" that challenge and do what it takes within their abilities and capabilities to meet that challenge and resolve that concern. The model looks like this:

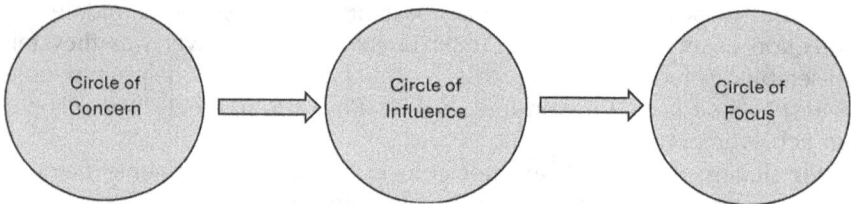

Figure 4.1 Circles of concern, influence, and focus (Based on Stephen Covey's Circle Model)

Coaching can help the clients identify these concerns, dividing these concerns into their respective circles, and developing action steps to meet these concerns.

Case Study

Dr. K wanted to be coached. He was the head of an intensive care group of physicians and was having issues with the group, the cardiologist group, the hospital administration, and the nursing staff. He was hired and tasked to create a team of healthcare providers that would be responsible for all the intensive care units and coordinate the care no matter the specialty or the diagnosis. In his previous job, he was also the director, was very successful, and was managing a smaller group of physicians whom he had known for years. One year into this program, and he is not doing a good job. He is finding resistance from almost everyone, some resentment because he was chosen over a local popular physician, and a lot of pushbacks. Dr. K was convinced he was tasked with an impossible job, and he was set up for failure. He was frustrated, upset, angry, burned out, and doubting himself.

The coaching session(s) focused on the goals he wants to achieve. He listed 4 or 5 goals. The sessions also discussed what he believes are his assets and challenges. Once that list was completed, Dr. K was asked to assess whether he had ever been in a similar situation, both personally and professionally. Realizing that this is a new experience for him, he was asked to list the items in his circle of concern and his circle of influence.

Once the items were listed, some of the sessions focused on how he can manage his expectations with respect to the issues he has no control over. Things like other people's agendas, institutional demands, EMR systems, nursing shortages, supply shortages, and staffing shortages and inexperience were some of the issues listed.

Next, the sessions focused on how to approach the challenges that he does have control over: People's perception of him, his attitude and demeanor, his communication skills, and patient safety and outcomes were some examples. These sessions also dealt with his expectations, managing his sense of control, changing his approach, letting go of his frustrations, turning challenges into opportunities.

This was a year's project. Dr. K was successful in managing himself internally first, managing his expectations, identifying the challenges under his control, and letting go of those that are not. He was able to turn his perceived failures into success stories, and was able to not only manage himself, but understand and manage the expectations of others, and create a team that was not toxic but focused on the common goal of helping the patients and supporting each other.

Conclusions and Recommendations

The mindset of physicians, their training, their environment, their burnout, their expectations, and their need for control create a unique prefrontal cortex that necessitates a deeper look into. Physicians are trained and educated to take care of patients. Their new roles necessitate them developing new skills in management, team leadership, team management, communication, patient expectation management, managing healthcare industry expectations and demands, and adapting to an ever-changing healthcare environment.

Managing expectations and developing a healthy sense of control, while navigating controlled and uncontrolled stress, in one of the most sensitive and scrutinized working environments, while lacking the necessary training and expertise to do so poses a challenge that is different than other industries.

Bridging the gap between what is available (training, mindset, and clinical experience) and what is needed is perhaps best done through coaching. In this arena, there are multiple areas of intervention, both internally within the physicians and externally within their environment. This chapter further illustrates some of these coaching points/areas of intervention.

To best coach your client, it is best to understand them. Many physicians have a skeptical outlook towards coaching, its value, its science and approach, and its application. They especially have an issue with coaches who they believe do not understand them or their unique situation. Further, many physicians have problems understanding themselves and managing themselves and their own expectations. Knowing the background, their work environment, their thought processes, their challenges, and the opportunities for coaching helps the coach create a safe, trustworthy, reliable, and familiar environment where the clients feel they are being heard, their language understood, and are communicated with in an approach that they can relate to.

Summary and Key Points

a   Physicians have a unique mindset that may pose some challenges for coaches unless they understand it.
b   Not all physicians are coachable.
c   Coachability refers to a set of traits, abilities, and circumstances that help hinder or support the physician's response to coaching.
d   Most physicians currently being referred to coaching are "problematic" or are causing potential "harm" to their institution and patients.
e   Control, or the ability to exert a sense of control, is paramount to a physician's health and well-being and is a key coaching point or focus.
f   Managing expectations is also one of the key coaching interventions and challenges that may provide physicians with great comfort and wellness.

References

Cavanaugh, K., Zajac, S. (2021) On Coachability: How Practitioners Determine Whether Someone Can Be Coached. *International Journal of Evidence Based Coaching and Mentoring.* 13(1):1–16.

Covey S. (1989) *The 7 habits of highly effective people: Powerful lessons in personal change.* Free Press.

Frank, S.H. (1993) Expectations disease: a model for understanding stress, control and dependent behaviour. *Family Practice.* 10(1):23–33. doi:10.1093/fampra/10.1.23. PMID: 8477889.

Kretzschmar, I. (2010). Exploring client's readiness for coaching. *International Journal of Evidence Based Coaching and Mentoring.* 4:1–20.

Kylstra, C.D., Kylstra B. (2001) *Restoring the foundations: An integrated approach to healing ministry.* 2nd edition. Proclaiming His Word Inc.

Maier, S.F., Seligman, M.E. (2016) Learned helplessness at fifty: Insights from neuroscience. *Psychology Review.* 123(4):349–367. doi:10.1037/rev0000033. PMID: 27337390; PMCID: PMC4920136.

Rotter, J. B. (1966). Generalized expectancies for internal versus external control of reinforcement. *Psychol. Monogr.* 80:1–28. doi:10.1037/h0092976.

Sawicki, N. (2011) Judging doctors: The person and the professional. 13(10): 718–722. doi:10.1001/virtualmentor.2011.13.10.msoc1-1110.

Shapiro, J., Astin, J., Shapiro, S.L., Robitshek, D., Shapiro, D.H. (2011) Coping with loss of control in the practice of medicine. *Families, Systems, & Health.* 29 (1):15–28. doi:10.1037/a0022921. PMID: 21417521.

Tee, D., Misra, K., Roderique-Davies, G., Shearer, D. (2022) A systematic review of coaching client characteristics. *International Coaching Psychology Review.* 17(1):50–74 doi:10.53841/bpsicpr.2022.17.1.50.

Weiss, J., Merriman, M. (2021) Employee Coachability: New Insights to Increase Employee Adaptability, Performance, and Promotability in Organizations. *International Journal of Evidence Based Coaching and Mentoring.* 19(1):121–136. doi:10.24384/kfmw-ab52.

5 Coaching the Physician
Best Practice Guide

Relly Nadler

Introduction

The origin of coaching and how it is defined by ICF have been discussed in the early chapters. The focus of this chapter is to discuss best practice guidelines for coaching physicians. A coach is a thinking partner for the clients to support them to reach their best version of themselves. There are 3 key components a coach brings to clients:

- Depths of thought to what they think is important and the time dedicated to enhancing the quality of thought and then best actions.
- Resources and tools to reach their goals. These can include assessments, readings, best practices of behavioral interventions and social support.
- Motivation and accountability to what they want to accomplish. Exploring what has worked and why and what to tweak and do more of.

Coaching encourages a "forced focus" on what is most important to the client versus the constant distraction of the urgent that plagues all of us. The majority of us operate out of our habits most of the time. Coaching allows not only time but the strategic and proactive thinking to be one's best at work and in their personal life.

Some of the origins of coaching go back to Tim Gallwey's focus on the Inner Game in Tennis, Skiing, Golf and then business in the 1970's. He focused on the internal barriers to performance. The coaching field then advanced with Thomas Leonard who created Coach University and then the International Coaching Federation (ICF) in 1995. Now ICF is the gold standard in coaching. Today there are over 93,000 certified coaches worldwide in 3 levels of coaching through the ICF. Many organizations today are hiring only certified coaches.

Coaching integrates many disciplines into performance technology. They include applied psychology, adult learning and development theories, positive psychology, neuroscience, peak performance practices, deep listening, wellness, and mindfulness,

DOI: 10.4324/9781003452065-5

There are many types of coaching specialties, such as Executive Coaching, Leadership Coaching, Performance Coaching, Personal Coaching, Life Coaching and delivered through individual, group, and team coaching.

Physician Coaching combines Leadership Coaching, Life and Wellness coaching, and Performance Coaching to focus on the physician leading others, enhancing their wellness, reducing burnout, and enhancing engagement.

The focus is on doing the right things a little more and identifying the behaviors that get in the way to do them a little less. In other words, coaching helps the client know what to "dial up and what to dial down". These don't take a lot of time and one can show their emotional intelligence and brilliance in key relationship moments.

Literature Review: Why Physician Coaching?

In today's world of increased performance demands paired with being busy, most physician leaders are very challenged, don't necessarily have leadership training and consequently are overwhelmed and may underperform.

- In a systematic review on coaching physicians, Boet et al. (2023) found evidence from available randomized controlled trials that suggests coaching for physicians can improve well-being and reduce distress/burnout.
- According to another review and meta-analysis, physicians with burnout are twice as likely to be involved in patient safety incidents, to exhibit low professionalism and to receive low satisfaction ratings from patients (Boet et al., 2023). Burnout is also costly to the healthcare system, with the cost to replace one physician estimated at $500 000, taking into account hiring and training costs as well as productivity losses (Boet et al., 2023). Coaching can save the physician and the organization some of these replacement costs.
- A study on the impact of an online coaching program for medical trainees showed three main themes emerged as benefits to the coaching program from the data: 1) practicing metacognition as a tool for healthy coping 2) building a sense of community, and 3) the value of a customizable experience. The meta cognition focused on burnout, self-compassion, relationship and perfection and imposter syndrome. (Mann et al., 2022)
- In a study of 88 physicians receiving 6 months of coaching, rates of high emotional exhaustion at 5 months decreased by 19.5% in the intervention group and increased by 9.8% in the control group. Absolute rates of overall burnout at 5 months also decreased by 17.1% in the intervention group and increased by 4.9% in the control group. The conclusions and relevance were that professional

coaching may be an effective way to reduce emotional exhaustion and overall burnout as well as improve quality of life and resilience for some physicians. (Dybyre et al., 2019)

- Peer coaching, one physician to another, has proven to be very successful with physicians who are trained in coaching. There is immediate trust and understanding of the physicians' challenges which allows the coaching to progress quickly.
- El-Aswad (et al. 2022) found sustained improvement in performance as measured by patient experience scores of the coached cohort. Clinician retention also outperformed manager estimates, and clinicians were highly satisfied with the process. It was concluded that physician performance can be positively impacted through peer coaching in a process that is satisfying to the client, improves estimated retention and reduces turnover costs. Peer coaching benefits patients, clinicians and hospitals by improving the experience of both patients and clinicians and supporting a stable clinician group.

Physician Coaching helps upgrade their performance by integrating self-skills and developing others skills to be their best in the moment.

Research from Blessing White Consulting found that the top three leadership skills for the future were 1) Communication, 2) Collaboration and 3) Coaching. They stated:

> *"If communication skills are the foundation of a leader's future home, collaboration and coaching create the ground floor. Without a strong foundation of trust and communication, leaders run the risk of directing or deciding instead of collaborating and coaching. Employees will be quick to see this, and despite leaders' good intentions, fail to inspire and empower their teams to the performance they seek."*
>
> (Blessing White, 2018, pg. 25)

a   Why focus coaching on physician leaders and leaders? Their incredible influence on their team and organization.

- The leader/manager has the key role in the hospital or organization. Gallup has found that managers have 70 % influence over the climate of their team. (Gallup, 2023)
- 60% of employees who left their job said the physician leaders or manager were the reason. (Gallup, 2023)
- According to Better Up (2023) insights from over 1,600 teams, effective managers drive 53 % greater team agility, 24 % higher team performance, 20% higher team engagement and 16% greater team resilience.
- Good to Great boost: By increasing the number of high performing leaders the organization gains great strength…it is tempting to

fix low performing leaders, but the greatest gain appears to come by helping more leaders become truly great. Leaders in the top 5% had 76% of their employees highly committed, where leaders at the 90% had 54% of their employees highly committed. (Zenger and Folkman 2020)

So, a physician leader considered top 5% versus top 10%, increases employee commitment 22%. That is huge when many can think top 10% is good enough. Just like in professional sports, physician leaders and corporate leaders can get a boost and be even better with focused time devoted to their craft with executive coaching. Coaching can be the quickest way for physician leaders and managers to manage themselves, the daily complexity, and improve their communication, collaboration, and coaching skills for the future.

Discussions and Applications: What Are the Foundational Principles of a Coach?

Here are some of the foundational principles of coaching. Some have been mentioned earlier.

a   Develops a trusting and confidential relationship with the client.
b   Helps the client create energy and hope to reach their goals.
c   Focuses on their whole person, their future goals, values, thoughts, beliefs, feelings, stories, and commitments and sees them as capable and resourceful.
d   Let's the client set the goal and direction of the conversation. "What would be most beneficial for you to focus on?" "Would you rather focus on …" A or B?
e   Listens deeply and acts as a thinking partner, coaches help them deconstruct their desires, thinking and actions.
f   Co-creates the unfolding of the conversation well as the coach evokes awareness and facilitates growth for new options and actions.
g   Helps the client identify what behaviors to "dial down" and which ones too "dial up" with a plan to address the barriers and resources to achieve success.
h   Focuses more on the person than the problem.
i   Highlights and builds on the client's strengths.
j   Knows the clients are the experts of their situation.
k   Encourages *slow thinking* versus *fast thinking* (Kahneman, 2011) as the client truly needs time to reflect, examine, and scenario play with the coach.
l   Stays present as the conversation unfolds new options, strategies, and plans.

Below are 12 reasons why coaching can be very beneficial for physician leaders and leaders in general. The "You" here is all of us as a leader, physician leader or individual contributor.

a   Coaching works: You will be a better leader. Here is what we know from the research.

- According to the International Coaching Federation (ICF) (2023), 86% of organizations saw an ROI on their Coaching engagements, and 96% of those who had an Executive Coach said they would repeat the process.
- The International Coach Federation (ICF) has presented a body of research demonstrating that coaching tends to generate an ROI of between $4 and $8 for every dollar invested. (Greiner, 2023)
- Better Up a coaching company claims their model conservatively predicts a 3.5X to 5X ROI on an investment. (Better Up, 2023)
- 98% of coaching clients said their coach "provided practical, realistic, and immediately usable input" and helped them "identify specific behaviors that would help me achieve my goals." (Center for Creative Leadership study, 2016)
- 88% of managers said coaching helps them achieve their goals. (Blessing White Consulting, 2015)
- One of the outgrowths of Coaching is to clarify your vision and goals for yourself, your organization and family. It creates the energy or what Dr. Richard Boyatzis calls Positive Emotional Attractor (PEA) to create the path forward and fuel your journey. This is a change in the brain that activates better cognitive functioning, more vision and imagining, all key ingredients for successful coaching. (Boyatzis et al., 2019)

b   You Tell Rather than Ask, as it is quicker and more efficient.

In the desire for speed, efficiency and alignment, physicians and leaders easily fall into telling their direct reports or staff what to do versus asking or dialoguing with them. It is the path of least resistance and ensures more certainty of the leader. We all have a "righting reflex" or fast to fix. Physicians are trained experts and problem solvers coming up with answers, sometimes when an answer isn't wanted like at home or with a colleague. Assessing when an answer is truly wanted or when listening or inquiring is the better response and can help the physician's leadership.

The unexpected results for the employees can be feeling undervalued, insulted, or put down for their ideas. One of Gallup's Q12 questions that lead to more engagement and high performing, is answering, "My opinion seems to count." Assessing when an answer is truly wanted or when listening or inquiring is the better response. When asked in groups employees want validations 70% of the time or more and managers give direction 70% of the time or more automatically.

One coaching tool is the VIVID model to better align which need is requested from the physician leader or manager.

VIVID Tool: Help me help you what do you want?

a   Ask and Drain before you Tell and Fill

Coaches see their clients as resourceful, wise and creative. The direct report has a bucket full of ideas and so do you as the leader. It is best to **Ask and Drain** their bucket of ideas first, second third before you **Tell and Fill** from your bucket. The individuals feel heard, and it gives you more time to think and when they are ready deliver a better solution.

Asking your direct reports their thoughts first builds rapport, enhances the quality of decisions, get more buy-in for the decisions, empowers employees, and trains them to really think.

A coach can help you focus on strategies to ask the right questions and do it in a constructive way that empowers others.

Ask & Drain their bucket, 1st, 2nd, 3rd & then Tell and Fill with your solutions

a   Leadership and Coaching are Slow Thinking: You and we don't think deep or long, and there is a need for more slow thinking.

Reflection is becoming a lost art. Leaders are good at fast thinking, but all need to get better at slow thinking when there is not an emergency. Daniel Kahneman who wrote the book, *Thinking: Fast and Slow* has said, "the reason we don't like to think slow is we are cognitively lazy."

A coach in the coaching session can help you think deeper and longer and can help have better decision making by challenging your thinking. A coach adds clarity to what is your input about yourself and others and thus enhances your output, your decisions, communications, and solutions.

Table 5.1 VIVID Model for Leaders

What a person wants	Leader Misstep
Vent	Hears venting as complaining
Information	Impatience, don't they know that?
Validation	Missing good ideas, more engagement, and opportunities to hear and refine new ideas
Ideation	Missing opportunity to brainstorm with the person
Direction	Jumps in too soon offers advice when they want validation, disempowering, limits new ideas

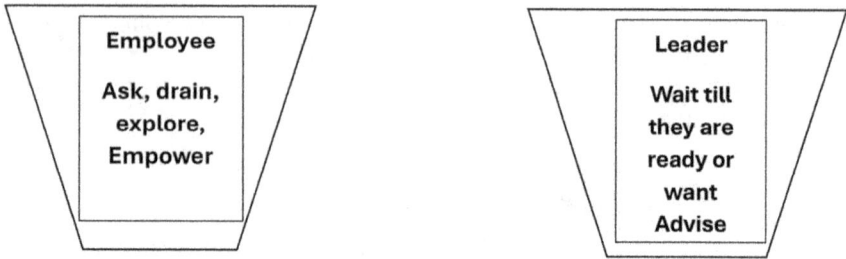

Figure 5.1 Ask and Drain Buckets

Coaching, as leadership, is a slow thinking process, unless there is an emergency. There is always time to check in with your intentions, values, strengths and asking yourself and others powerful questions.

a   You Need to Increase your self-awareness and self-management skills for better performance.

Awareness and self-management are two sides of the coin. How can you manage what you don't see? Coaching helps raise self-awareness and contributes to your self-management and performance toolbox.

Fritz Perls of Gestalt Therapy fame said, "awareness equals responsibility." If you are aware, you have the "ability to respond" in the same way or choose a new behavior.

Tara Eurich in her book *Insight* defines self-awareness as "…the ability to see ourselves clearly – to understand who we are, how others see us and how we fit into this world."

Korn (2022) searched a total of 6,977 self-assessments from professionals at 486 publicly traded companies to identify the "blind spots" in individuals'

Table 5.2 Fast versus Slow thinking

Fast Thinking	Slow Thinking
Impulsive, driven by emotions	Effortful, intentional choices
Involuntary, always on, multi-tasks	Voluntary, will power, deliberate
Intuitive, network of associations	Seat of self-control, concentration
Executor of habitual routines	Learn new models, make plans, orderly steps
Manager of mental models of the world	At times can control automatic responses
Detects hostility, facial expressions	Assessments and comparisons
Automatic = More average performance	Slow, intentional = More exceptional performance
Most frequent process	Only 2–5% of the time

Source: Kahneman, D. 2011.

leadership characteristics. They found poor-performing companies' employees were 79% more likely to have low overall self-awareness than those at firms with robust ROR.

Research shows that focusing on self-awareness enhances well-being, has a positive impact on retention, absenteeism levels, productivity, and overall satisfaction. (Korn, 2021)

A coach helps you master the moment by putting a spotlight on your inputs about yourself and others so your outputs, your decisions, communication, strategies and judgements are the best they can. Often a coaching focus is on accepting yourself more in a friendly and compassionate way rather than a harsh or critical way.

a   You Need to Build and Broaden your strengths and identify derailers.

In coaching, the focus for leaders is to gain more clarity into your strengths first. This is not natural to do on your own. Your coach helps identify your strengths, increase them, use them more, and broaden them to weakness areas.

When employees sit down with their managers, 61% want to talk primarily about their values and strengths and how they can do more work that satisfies them. (GP Strategies, 2023)

A variety of assessments and coaching tools help this process of building your competencies and skills. If a person has some derailers, also called "fatal flaws" those must be addressed first and the coach can help build awareness and management of them. The **Derailer Detector** below can be used to identify your derailers or a person on your team.

a   You have blind spots: We all have them but if you don't know what they are you will continue to undermine your success.

Marshall Goldsmith is one of the top executive coaches with Fortune 100 executives. In his research with executives, he says 70% of people think they are in the top 10%. We all think we are better drivers, cooks, and leaders than we may really be. You don't know that you don't know. In some of the organizational literature this is called "unconscious incompetence".

Executive coaches use validated leadership assessments, 360-degree feedback and interviews with stakeholders to bring to light others' perceptions of you. The gap between your perceptions and others can establish your blind spots.

This can result in some of the hardest conversations for a coach and coachee. A leader says, "I think I have empathy, good problem-solving skills and good interpersonal relations." The coach has data on how other people see them and may say, "that is different than how your boss or direct reports see you, let's look at their perception and talk about the gaps."

I had a leader who was an X-Navy Seal, who took a 360-degree assessment and his self-report had him higher on every competency than did his team or manager. Ouch! That was a challenging conversation to hold the tension and come up with strategies that he could accept and focus on.

a   You get less feedback: The higher up you are in the organization, the less feedback you get.

As leaders move up in their organization they tend to get less feedback from others. Their direct reports are afraid to give honest and direct feedback for fear of retribution and how that impacts their reviews. The leaders' boss has high expectations, and it is common only to give feedback if there was a mistake or complaints.

So, physician leaders and senior leaders don't get the feedback they need to continually improve. A coach can not only give you feedback but help integrate the feedback to specific actions.

a   Change is hard: People want to resist it.

In every organization or hospital, a major challenge is the change process. whether that it is changing a personal behavior or helping your team deal with constant change, or newest technology. Most leaders are inundated in change scenarios. Getting people to accept the change is a leadership challenge.

Coaches can bring best practices on leading change, focusing on behavior changes using neuroscience, psychology of motivation, and performance research to the leader.

a   You are on autopilot.

Most of us operate on autopilot much of the time. We take short cuts rather than thinking hard or long about things. Working on your leadership entails taking a hard look at your capabilities and getting off automatic to be more intentional, have clear focus, and make great decisions.

Researchers tell us we operate out of our habits about 95% of the time. If you had the time what would be your best focus? Coaching is a "forced focus" to stay with the important. There are times I know leaders are not thinking or focusing much on their development or their direct reports unless they are in a coaching conversation. The challenges and fires of the day to put out get the most of our focus. We know that we are interrupted almost every three minutes and 44% of the time we do it to ourselves. (Mark, 2006) We are usually on autopilot and the tyranny of the urgent rule of the day grabs our focus.

Blessingwhite (2018) *Tomorrow's Leaders Today* found the most valued leadership actions are: Communicating Effectively at All levels, coaching and developing the team, developing and executing strategy and building effective relationships with team members.

a   You are the Emotional Thermostat-Enhance your Influence.

Most leaders I have worked with have underestimated their influence. This is because they are focused on their task and results, while their direct reports are focused more on their contribution and recognition. This is a major disconnect in their needs and wants from the conversation.

The leader is the emotional thermostat for the team. Their mood is the most contagious. If they are irritated, stressed and short, other people catch it and will manifest it. If they are optimistic, encouraging, and empathic, so too will their team be.

Dr. Anthony Grant of Australia and a coaching researcher has found his "clients' experience that for every executive coached, hundreds of others are positively affected, including their manager, their peers, their direct reports, and those employees' direct reports as well". This extends to hundreds of people, and even more if one counts customers.

In *Helping People Change* by Richard Boyatzis, Melvin Smith and Ellen van Oosten, (2019) state "…given the role of emotional contagion, being able to effectively manage the emotional tone of the coaching discussion also requires having an awareness of one's own emotions and recognizing the impact that they can have on the person being coached." The goal is to create a positive emotional attractor (PEA) towards the goals that the whole team absorbs and is attracted to.

What are you sending out to your team that they are catching? If you are stressed, impatient and irritated, so will they be. If you are calm, cool and rational, they will be too.

a   Your Sense of Power leads to Less empathy:

Dacher Keltner (2007) a psychology professor at UC Berkeley, speaks and writes about the Power Paradox, once we have it, we lose the capacities we used to gain it. Sukhvinder Obhi, a neuroscientist at McMaster University in Ontario, found a similar phenomenon. (Hogeveen et al., 2014) While Keltner studies behaviors, Obhi studies brains. In his experiments he had people who were powerful and others not so powerful under a transcranial-magnetic-stimulation machine. He found that having power, in fact, impairs a specific neural process, "mirroring," that may be a cornerstone of empathy.

This may explain the neurological basis to what Keltner has termed the "power paradox": Once we have power, we lose some of the capacities we needed to gain it in the first place. Leaders with power end up thinking they know what is needed in almost every situation and don't need to hear from others. They think they are the "smartest person in the room." They value their ideas over all others. Keltner calls this an "empathy deficit." "High-power individuals are more likely to interrupt others, to speak out of turn, and to fail to look at others who are speaking." (2007) This is a hierarchical dynamic we see in hospitals with the power differences between physicians and staff. It is a good topic to focus on when coaching physicians.

a   You are creating your Leadership Legacy:

A coach can help with slow thinking and spending quality time in having developing conversations about the physicians' or leaders' direct reports. This in turn prepares them for quality conversations and coaching with their people. A leader's focus is usually on getting results and having a coach compels them to focus more on developing their team and emerging leaders. This is where the leader can have their greatest legacy. Their best practices of leadership can be passed down to their direct reports and their direct reports after they are long gone. Physician leaders and leaders impact their people, their families and can increase their life quality. A study by Anthony Grant found that executives who received coaching experienced effects that transferred over into the executives' family life, including heightened work–life balance and improved relationships with family members.

If the 3 key leadership skills for the future are communication, collaboration and coaching, an executive coach can help you get better at all these skills quickly. We have found these tools to be effective with physicians and they are explained and used in the case study below.

Success in excess: For peak performers, it is easier to hear that you have a few "overused strengths" than you have deficits or improvement needs. Given most physicians know they are competent and take pride in their accomplishments, a look at how they may be doing a success too much is easier to hear. The tool highlights just the few times, 1–2 times out of 10, to change course or dial down one's strengths. These few times of catching the cues and backing off usually are very encouraging for the client's motivation.

Derailer detector: Identifies the key areas that need to be focused on if these derailers happen too often. It is a diagnostic that labels the behaviors which can lead to poor patients' and colleagues' reviews. Talking about these derailers raises the awareness of these behaviors like symptoms so an intervention can be applied using medical language. The metric of how often a behavior is a derailer is discussed with client and organization as each organization has a different culture to what and how often something is tolerated.

Case Study

Background: Scary Cardiac Surgeon: Dr. T

Dr. T was board certified with the American Board of Surgery. He takes challenging cases others won't, believing he can make a difference.

Saving just one life is tremendous motivation for him and enough to continually work very hard. He regularly does surgery which could take 4–10 hours and is very focused this whole time.

Dr. T. is very passionate about what he does and has high standards.

He will do anything for his patients. He sees the world in very concrete terms.

Dr. T. learned to make decisions quickly in the surgery room but may not serve him as well in relationships.

Situation: Why he came to coaching

Dr. T. yells at people if they are doing something that seems incompetent. He talks very loudly and his intensity scares people.

He gets upset with people just watching him, "if you are not doing anything, get out!" He kicked them out of surgery. There have been many complaints to human resources and the CEO about his behavior not his surgery. Unknowingly Dr T. hurts other people

Dr. T was given the EQi, 2.0 as part of the coaching protocol. His high and low scores are reported below. Definitions for each competency are explained in the Emotional Intelligence chapter.

Emotional Quotient Inventory EQi, 2.O results, where 100 points is average and above 110 high average, under 90 low average:

Table 5.3 Eqi results

Highest Scores	
Social Responsibility	108
Self-Awareness	95
Empathy	94
Self-Actualization	90
Reality Testing	86
Lowest Scores	
Impulse Control	68
Emotional Expression	75
Stress Tolerance	76
Flexibility	80
Independence	86

Examples of EQ questions asked and Dr. T's response:

Impulse: I make rash decisions when I am emotional = Often
Impulse: My impulsiveness creates problems for me = Often

Emotional Expressiveness: It is difficult to show people how I feel about them = Often

Stress: I handle stress without getting too nervous = Occasionally

Flexibility: I need things to be predictable = Often

Flexibility: Change makes me uneasy = Often

Problem Solving: I let my emotions get in the way when making decisions = Sometimes

Coaching Interventions:

Assessments: EQi, 2.0, Derailer Detector
Coaching Goals 1–10, where 10 is high.

1   Awareness of triggers 7
2   Managing trigger with tools 4
3   Relationship with boss 6.5
4   Managing stress 5
5   Develop conflict management skills 4
6   Listening to coordinators and staff 5
7   Listening to patients 8

Success in excess: He was over passionate and too assertive, alienating others.

On the derailer detector he scored a 3 on smartest person in the room, lack of impulse control, drives others too hard, and doesn't ask for feedback, 2's = Lack of insight into others, perfectionism, mistreatment of others.

Coaching Activities

Dr. T took the EQi, 2.0. This led to a raised awareness of triggers. We were able to identify when he crossed over on success in excess tool and what to do differently. We used his strength of social responsibility to help staff along with patients, developed strategies to catch self when he was getting triggered, developed recharging strategies, practiced difficult conversations with intentionality, and reframed people wasting time watching him as possibly being in awe and want to learn from him.

Result

Dr. T was able to become more aware of his triggers and when he felt that way, he exercised more self-control by either walking away for a while or just keeping quiet. He interacted more with staff and got to know and appreciate them more. He took time at the end of the day assessing his behavior on impulse control and building better relationships. The CEO and others noticed the changes he made. There were less complaints about him. Dr. T was more satisfied at work and had better relationships.

Conclusions

This chapter dove into the best practices for coaching physicians. It discusses what coaching is, why it is beneficial and coaching foundational principles. The chapter reviewed some of the best practices and tools used to be effective with this population. A case study with Dr. T highlighted an example of a successful coaching intervention using some of the assessments and tools. Some of the tools included VIVID, Ask and Drain, Success in Excess and the Derailer Detector. These tools and suggestions on how to deal with physicians can be used in coaching engagements in any healthcare organization.

Summary and Key Points

Coaching physicians can be challenging and exhilarating as they are very smart and passionate. Once engaged in the coaching and they take to it, their achievement orientation and self-actualization take over to look for ways to be a better leader in addition to a great physician. This positive emotional attractor (PEA) can create the energy to continue to dial up a few things or dial down some overused strengths. These micro initiatives can create a macro impact for them and the organization.

It is our hope that a coaching approach can continue to grow in healthcare to support performance and more wellbeing with all healthcare workers.

Emotional Intelligence Tools for Coaching Physicians

Success in Excess

In many instances it is very natural to keep using your strengths or successes too much or use them in excess. If you can become aware of the

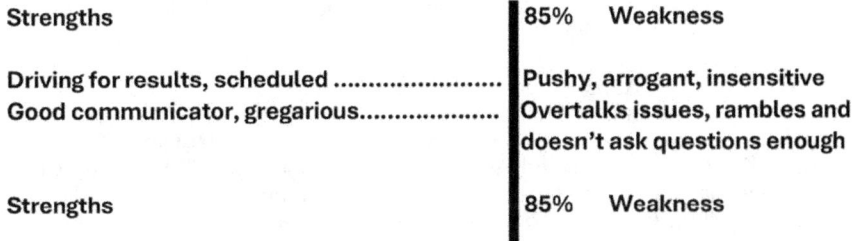

Strengths	85% Weakness
Driving for results, scheduled	Pushy, arrogant, insensitive
Good communicator, gregarious....................	Overtalks issues, rambles and doesn't ask questions enough
Strengths	85% Weakness

Figure 5.2 Strength Balancing Model For Dr. T

Derailer Detector

Rank yourself and a direct report (DR) honestly on these behaviors, 1= Almost never happens, 2 = Happens periodically, 3 = Happens regularly. Decide on each of the time frames. With Dr. T 3 = 2 weeks, 2 = 5 weeks, 1 = 20 weeks

You		DR
☐	1. **Smartest Person in the room syndrome-** Have to be right all the time, married to your own ideas and are not open or distrusts new ideas	☐
☐	2. **Lack of Impulse control –** Emotionally reactive, volatile, abrasive and follow urges to an unhealthy extreme	☐
☐	3. **Drives others too hard –** Micromanage and take over rather than delegate	☐
☐	4. **Perfectionism –** Sets unrealistic goals, Reject criticism	☐
☐	5. **Defensive -** Blame others, inflexible and are argumentative	☐
☐	6. **Risk averse –** Lacks courage to take risks	☐
☐	7. **Failure to learn from mistakes –** Same kind of mistakes show up	☐
☐	8. **Lacks insight into others –** Can't read others' emotions or reactions	☐
☐	9. **Doesn't ask for feedback –** Miss opportunities to include others for better decisions	☐
☐	10. **Self-promotion-** Attention seeking, overlook others accomplishments for own recognition	☐
☐	11. **Lack of Integrity –** "Unhonest" with self and then others, omit and minimize	☐
☐	12. **Fail to adapt to cultural differences –** Do not change your leadership style appropriately	☐

Figure 5.3 Derailer Detector
Count up your number of 2's and 3's
Self -Direct Report
2's = Lack of insight into others, perfectionism, mistreats others
3's = Smartest Person in the Room, Lack of Impulse control, drives others too hard, doesn't ask for feedback
Three or more (2's) = Warning signs for Derailers = Dr. T has 4
Two or more (3's) = At risk to you and the organization = Dr. T has 3
Source: Adapted from Leslie and Van Velsor (1996) A Look at Derailment Today, Center for Creative Leadership, Byram, Smith and Paese (2002) Grow Your Own Leaders, Kaplan (1991) Beyond Ambition, Dotlich and Cairo (2002) Why CEOs Fail, Kellerman (2004) Bad Leadership and Lipman-Blumen (2005) The Allure of Toxic Leadership. Copyright (2011–2023) Relly Nadler, Psy.D., MCC www.drrel lynadler.com.

☐ **13. Indirect with others** – Do not give the hard feedback or make the difficult decisions about people ☐

☐ **14. Approval dependent** – Need too much approval before making decisions ☐

☐ **15. Eccentricity** – Unpredictable and odd in your behavior ☐

☐ **16. Mistreats others** – Callous, demeaning or discounting to others and their needs ☐

☐ **17. Self-Interest** – Acts in self-interest instead of the interest of the whole organization or larger group ☐

☐ **18. Insular** – Disregard of health and welfare of group outside the responsibility of your organization or team ☐

Count up your number of 2's and 3's

2's = Lack of insight into others, perfectionism, mistreats others

3's = Smartest Person in the Room, Lack of Impulse control, drives others too hard, doesn't ask for feedback

Three or more (2's) = Warning signs for Derailers = Dr. T has 4

Two or more (3's) = At risk to you and the organization = Dr. T has 3

Adapted from Leslie and Van Velsor (1996) A Look at Derailment Today, Center for Creative Leadership, Byram, Smith and Paese (2002) Grow Your Own Leaders, Kaplan (1991) Beyond Ambition, Dotlich and Cairo (2002) Why CEOs Fail, Kellerman (2004) Bad Leadership and Lipman-Blumen (2005) The Allure of Toxic Leadership

Figure 5.3b

few times that you have **"crossed over"** the line from strength to weakness, it can help you or others be a top 10% performer.

85% Rule: If you are solid "B" performer you are probably in your strengths 85% of the time. To be an "A" performer consistently it will help to identify when you use them more to **build** and **broaden** or **Dial up** the strength.

Also are you overusing your strengths at times and it has become a weakness. This is usually JUST 1 or 2 times out of 10 to STOP or **Dial Down** doing your strengths, and do something different.

These subtle actions then can give you the 5–7 % change to put you consistently in the top 10%. Below put your top strengths down and then what it **may look like to others** when you are doing it to excess. This is an example:

1. **Dial up Behaviors**: Which strengths can you **Dial up** or broaden? Compassion for patients use the same compassion for coordinators. Use achievement orientation strengths to be better leaders.
2. **Dial down clues:** How will you know you have "crossed over" into the overused, weakness area and need to **Dial down** that behavior. What signal or cues and clues can you use? *Sees colleagues not responding, getting defensive, closing down.*
3. **Action steps:** What specifically do you need to do differently? What support do you need? *Lower voice, ask 4 questions for their input, listen, and explore.*

References

Barna, J. (2023) *Dodcsworking.com*, https://docworking.com/2022/09/14/the-benefits-of-physician-coaching/The Benefits of Physician Coaching.

Better Up (2023) *Why Executive Coaching Works*, www.betterup.com, Austin, Texas.

Blessing White (2018) Tomorrow's Leaders Today. *GP Strategies*. Chatsworth, CA.

Blessing White (2015) *GP Strategies*. Chatsworth, CA.

Boet, S., Etherington, C., Dion, P.M., Desjardins, C., Kaur, M., Ly, V., Denis-LeBlanc, M., Andreas, C., Sriharan, A. I. (2023) Impact of coaching on physician wellness: A systematic review. *PLoS One*. 2023 Feb 7; 18(2): e0281406. doi:10.1371/journal.pone.0281406. PMID: 36749760; PMCID: PMC9904500.

Boyatzis, R., Smith, M., van Oosten, E. (2019) *Helping People Change: Coaching with Compassion for Lifelong Learning and Growth*. Boston, MA.: Harvard Business Review Press.

Clifton, J., Harter, J. (2019) *It's The Manager: Gallup Finds That the Quality of Managers and Team Leaders is the Single Biggest Factor in Your Organization's Long-Term Success*. Washington, D.C.: Gallup Press.

Clifton, J., Harter, J. (2023) *Culture Shock: An Unstoppable Force is Changing How we Work*. Washington, D.C.: Gallup Press.

Dyrbye, L.N., Shanafelt, T.D., Gill, P.R., Satele, D.V., West, C.P. (2019) Effect of a Professional Coaching Intervention on the Well-being and Distress of Physicians: A Pilot Randomized Clinical Trial. *JAMA Intern Medicine*. 179(10):1406–1414. doi:10.1001/jamainternmed.2019.2425. PMID: 31380892; PMCID: PMC6686971.

El-Aswad N., Ghossoub Z., Nadler R. (2017) *Physician Burnout: An Emotionally Malignant Disease*. Create Space Publishing. North Charleston, S.C.

El-Aswad, N., Ghossoub, Z., Nadler, R., Olsen, K., Sigler, S., Simmons, S. (2022). Impact of intensive peer coaching on physician performance. *Management in healthcare*. 6(4): 369–378.

Eurich, T. (2017) *Insight: The Surprising Truth about How Others See Us, How we see Ourselves, and Why the Answers Matter More Than We Think*. New York: Currency.

Gallwey, T. (2018) *The Inner Game of Work: Building Capacity in the Workplace*. Systems Thinker, Leverage Networks, Inc.

Greiner, N. (2018) *Making the Business Case for Coaching. Association or Talent Development*. www.td.org.

Grant, A.M. (2008) *Workplace, Executive and Life Coaching: An Annotated Bibliography from the Behavioural Science Literature*. Coaching Psychology Unit, University of Sydney, Australia.

Goldsmith, M., Reiter, M. (2015) *Triggers: Creating Behavior That Lasts–Becoming the Person You Want to Be*, NY: Crown Publishing Group.

Gallup. Inc (2015) *State of the American Manager Report*. Gallup, Inc. Publishing.

Gallup Report: "*What Separates Great Managers from the Rest*," May 12, 2015 Gallup http://www.gallup.com/businessjournal/183098/report-separates-great-managers-rest.aspx.

Ghossoub Z., Nadler R., El-Aswad N. (2018) Effect of using emotional intelligence, wellness, and leadership training on lived experiences of medical program directors burnout. *Universal Journal of Public Health*. 6(5):298–305. doi:10.13189/ujph.2018.060508.

Ghossoub Z., Nadler R., El-Aswad N. (2018) Targeting Physician Burnout Through Emotional Intelligence, Self-Care Techniques, and Leadership Skills Training: A Qualitative Study. *Mayo Clinic Proceedings: Innovations, Quality & Outcome*. 2(1):78–79. http://www.ncbi.nlm.nih.gov/pmc/articles/6124346.

GP Strategies (2023) *Career Perspectives: A Study in Paradox*. Chatsworth, CA.

Hogeveen, J., Inzlicht, M., Obhi, S.S. (2014) Power changes how the brain responds to others. *Journal of Experimental Psychology: General*. 143(2):755–762. doi:10.1037/a0033477. Epub 2013 Jul 1. PMID: 23815455.

International Coaching Federation (2023) *Global Coaching Study and Future of Coaching*. Lexington, KY.

Kahneman, D. (2011) *Thinking Fast or Slow*. New York: Farrar, Straus and Giroux

Keltner, D., (2007) Power Paradox. *Greater Good Society Magazine*: Berkley, CA.

Korn, F. (2021) *Future of Work in 2022*. www.kornferry.com.

Korn, F. (2023) *Mindful Leadership: Importance of Self-Awareness*. www.kornferry.com.

Mann, A., Fainstad, T., Shah, P., Dieujuste, N., Thurmon, K., Dunbar, K., Jones, C. (2022) "We're all going through it" impact of an online group coaching program for medical trainees: a qualitative analysis. *BMC Medical Education*. 22(1):675. doi:10.1186/s12909-022-03729-5. PMID: 36100880; PMCID: PMC9468533.

Mark, G. (2006) *Gallup Business Journal*, June 8.

McGonagle, A.K., Schwab, L., Yahanda, N., Duskey, H., Gertz, N., Prior, L., Roy, M., Kriegel, G. (2020) Coaching for primary care physician well-being: A randomized trial and follow-up analysis. *Journal of Occupational Health Psychology*. 25 (5):297–314. doi:10.1037/ocp0000180. Epub 2020 Apr 16. PMID: 32297776.

Nadler, R. (2011) *Leading with Emotional Intelligence: Hands on strategies for Building Confidant and Collaborative Star Performers*. NY: McGraw-Hill.

Nadler, R. (2011–2023) *Psychology Today blog*.

Nelson, B (2012) *1501 Ways to Reward Employees*, NY: Workman Publishing.

Stawiski, S., Belzer, M., Saas, R.G. (2016) *Building the Case for Executive Coaching*. Center for Creative Leadership.

Society of Human Resource Management, "Toxic Workplace Cultures Hurt Workers and Company Profits," September, 2019.

Useem, J. (2017) Power Causes Brain Damage. *The Atlantic*.

Zenger, J. and Folkman, J. (2020) *The New Extraordinary Leader: Turning Good Managers Into Great Ones*. New York: McGraw-Hill.

6   Coach the Physician, Not the Problem

Marcia Reynolds

John Dewey once said: "Provoking people to think about their thinking is the single most powerful antidote to erroneous beliefs and autopilot." Coaching sessions generally start with the physician describing a dilemma to explore or naming a topic to discuss. You want to open the conversation easily by asking, "What is on your mind today" so you can hear what is at the source of their frustration or hesitation without the expectation of achieving a specific result too quickly. It's a good place to start but is not the focus of the coaching conversation.

The conversation then moves to what is getting in the way of this smart person from seeing the solution on their own. You seek to discover what they want to create or have that is not happening now, and what needs to be resolved to achieve their desired outcome. Once the barriers are removed, the physician knows what needs to be done without you offering your brilliant advice. The solution is often obvious but they can't see it from the perspective they are stuck in at the moment. Coaching helps them expand their thinking so the next steps that need to be taken, and what they need to make this movement, come into view.

Always keep in mind that the person you are coaching is smart and resourceful. They need you to help them discern what is getting in the way of them knowing what needs to happen next. Are they stuck in an old pattern of thinking, a fear of the worst-case scenario if they aren't 100% sure of success, or paralyzed by what other people are telling them to do that has them doubting their judgement? Your job is to determine with the physician what is keeping them from moving toward their vision of the best-case scenario.

You are not the problem solver; you are their thinking partner

Coaching is *transformational* because it creates insights, shifts perspective, and opens minds. It is not *operational* where you would explore what could work while evaluating risks, which they can do on their own if they weren't doubting themselves or flooded with frustration and resentment. Psychologist Joshua Aronson said, "Fear is the enemy of

DOI: 10.4324/9781003452065-6

curiosity." When the brain closes down to seeing all possibilities, people need someone outside of themselves to help them see through the fog of fear, anger, and burnout.

In 1910, educational reformer John Dewey defined the practice of *reflective inquiry* in his classic book, *How We Think*. (Dewey, 1910) He said teachers using reflective statements so students to hear what they are thinking. Then the teachers ask follow-up questions so students questions what they thought they knew so they were open to expansive learning. Dewey felt that combining the tools that provoke critical thinking with Socratic questioning would prompt a person to think about what they don't know, to confirm or negate inherited but unexamined beliefs, and substantiate the value of a fear or doubt. He said that metaphorically, *reflective inquiry* enables people to climb a tree in their minds to gain a wider view to see connections, faults, and strengths in their thinking. From this perspective, they see new ways of seeing and behaving.

Dewey also said *the most intelligent people need the most help* thinking about their thinking. Smart people are the best rationalizers. They believe their reasoning wholeheartedly and will protect their opinions as solid facts. Telling them to change is a waste of time. Pairing strong reflections with questions is the only way to get smart people – physicians – to question their thoughts.

Because our brains resist questioning how we think when left to our own devices, physicians can navigate daily dilemmas and make better decisions with the coach who coaches using reflective inquiry.

a   How to coach with reflective inquiry

Sometime in the last 20 years, the powerful question was given priority in coaching. Coaching is not just asking questions. Summarizing and paraphrasing what you hear the physician saying and the emotions they are expressing can often be more powerful than a question. You ask what the words mean to them and what is most important for them to create in this moment. Following up the reflection with an invitation to accept or alter what you share prompts the physician to think about what they said. They can then think about their thinking from a more objective point of view.

Reflective statements + questions = reflective inquiry

The intent of *reflective inquiry* is not to find solutions but to provoke critical thinking. This form of inquiry helps the person being coached discern gaps in their logic, evaluate their beliefs, and clarify fears and desires affecting their choices. Solutions emerge when thoughts are rearranged and expanded.

Reflective inquiry also helps the coach feel more competent. The process feels more natural and effortless than trying to remember what questions to use. You don't have to worry about following a formula or be profound. You listen for the key words spoken and offer back what you received.

Political philosopher Hannah Arendt, said, "The need of reason is not inspired by the quest for truth but by the quest for meaning. And truth and meaning are not the same."[2] Reflecting key words and asking what the words mean to the physician and how this meaning relates to what they want to create gives them a greater understanding of themselves. They can then determine what they most want and what they need to do to achieve this. As they see themselves taking positive action, they may start to see who they are becoming in a new light as well.

Instead of thinking what to say, be present, listen, and observe the physician with compassionate curiosity, and then share what you hear and notice to help them think more broadly for themselves. You then become their *thinking partner*, not an expert or healer.

a   Being comfortable with discomfort

Because you are challenging the thinking of a smart person, the conversations may feel uncomfortable, but the outcomes are remarkable. You generate activity in their brains. Insights emerge that could surprise both of you. The changes in their beliefs and behaviors that occur when you focus on their thinking instead of just options and consequences are enduring yet adaptable. The key for the coaching is to maintain their sense of safety no matter what occurs in the conversation. Emotional regulation is important, so the physician feels safe enough to be honest and vulnerable with you as you open their minds.

Many coaches don't feel comfortable shifting focus from the problem to the human. It's more comfortable to focus on the external problem, especially when working with someone who has a strong ego. They may explore the physician's perception of the situation and ask what strengths the physician can use to find a solution, but these approaches are not enough. The conversation feels comfortable but prolongs self-denial and thinking outside of the stories the physician is believing in now.

Physicians with years of experience in their roles like to fall back on what they know, protecting their ideas instead of being open to new ones. They believe their rationalizations for their decisions are truths. They protect their opinions as facts.

To be open to learning, there must be a moment of uncertainty.[3] Doubt prompts people to contemplate their beliefs and motivations. The physician may get defensive, even angry, as they cling to what they know. If you calmly hold the balance of pressure and care in the conversation, they might let go. They may then cautiously step into the space of *not knowing what is true anymore*. What they will then realize is that the discomfort of *not knowing* quickly fades as the fresh perspective becomes clear. Future coaching conversations will be easier for both the physician and coach.

Case Study

I was coaching a physician leader. He was frustrated that his team was not wanting to learn the new software for documenting their patient notes. He said there was one physician in particular who was rebelling so everyone else was following along.

I said I heard two dilemmas to explore. I offered him to choose if he wanted to dig deeper into the motivations of his most difficult physician or look at how he might lead his entire team differently.

He said, "I think I can engage the team if I address the problem with the one ring leader first."

I asked him what he had done to resolve the problem up to now. He said every time they had a conversation, the physician got angry, ranted about being one of the best doctors on their staff, and said he kept notes just fine. The leader then backed down, not wanting to escalate the conflict.

I said, "I hear you don't want to get into a conflict of who is right and wrong. It also sounds as if the physician has a value for good work. In the way he records notes now, is there anything that might be keeping him from getting the best result he is proud of?"

The leaders said, "Right, he does care a lot. I guess his anger is due to his passion. He is also protecting his position. Maybe he is afraid of not being able to use the new software and doesn't want to look foolish. But last month his administrator had trouble reading his hand-written notes. She almost made a mistake that could have hurt a patient. It was resolved but could have been devastating."

I said, "So how can you use this experience as a motivation for change?"

He said, "I think I need to acknowledge his good work for many years, and how dedicated he is. Then I could remind him what happened and ask if he would be interested in knowing how the new software program could help him make his job easier if not better. I could also offer support so the integration to the new software might be easier."

With a sigh of relief, he added, "I just needed a different approach. Actually, this would be a great conversation to have with the entire team."

I closed out the session with asking what having the one-on-one conversation and team conversation looked like. He then committed to the dates he would make this happen. We discussed possibilities if what he hoped for didn't turn out exactly as planned. He said that even having the conversation was a good start. He was happy and confident to have a new approach to counter their resistance. We set our next session to discuss the results and next steps

a   Coaching is a flashlight

When you coach people to see their blocks and biases instead of sorting through problems and options, there is likely a breakthrough awareness that comes to light. It is often more simple than profound, but the clarity shifts their emotions from frustration to relief. Keep coaching the person, not the problem, and the right criteria for making critical decisions and next step actions will become clear.

Coaching the person instead of the problem can be called *awareness-based coaching* to differentiate it from *solution-focused coaching*. The focus of coaching is on identifying beliefs behind opinions and actions, and on fears and conflicting values causing dissonance and confusion.

Coaching is often supportive and encouraging; it can also be uncomfortably disruptive. You must be willing to challenge interpretations, test assumptions, and notice emotional shifts so your clients learn something new instead of just re-ordering the thoughts they already had.

* * *

Three Tips for Focusing on the Physician, Not the Problem

There are times when the physician feels you are more annoying than helpful when trying to shift coaching from the problem to the person. You have to establish psychological safety so they are willing to engage with you. Use the following tips to create the rapport necessary to effectively shift from focusing on the external problem to coaching the person to find a way forward:

a   Set the expectation for coaching

It is important you and the physicians you coach have similar expectations for what coaching sessions will look like. When you first agree to be their coach, let them know you will not be their advisor. You are there to be their thinking partner to sort through what is creating uncertainty or discomfort around handling an issue or deciding a way forward. You might provide facts or ask them about what they have done so far to solve the problem that hasn't worked, but you will act as a confidante to help them explore perceptions and alternatives in the present. You might give reading homework or tasks to complete to aid them between sessions, but they shouldn't expect you to tell them what to do with what they learn.

b   Maintain your belief in the physician's ability to see a new way forward

Your intention for coaching must start with your belief about the physician's potential to solve the problem. You are there to help people see a way forward they couldn't see on their own. You are curious about what they want to achieve and what is stopping them from realizing this outcome. You wonder what is getting in their way and what they need to move forward. You recognize your urge to give advice, and then breathe and let go of this urge as you remember they are creative and resourceful.

When the physician knows you are there to help them discover their best answers, not tell them what to do or fix them, they are more willing to openly admit to their gaps, biases, and fears. Your trust in their ability allows learning to occur.

c Know the right time to shift from clarifying the problem to coaching the person in front of you

Once you clarify a possible outcome for the coaching session – what they want to achieve in your time together – you may ease into coaching by seeking to discover what options are possible, what they have already tried, and what they have considered doing but didn't. Often, exploring what they didn't do will reveal what is at the source of their hesitation. Most likely, the competent person you are speaking to needs to expand their limiting views of what is right and wrong, and what "shoulds" are directing their behavior. They might need to unearth how a fear of failure or a skewed sense of obligation is limiting their perspective. If they are willing to explore what they personally need to resolve, you can shift the focus from the problem to the person. This is when they realize that without the mental distractions, they knew the right thing to do all along.

References

Dewey, J. (1910) *How We Think*. D.C. Heath & Co.

Arendt, H. (1978) *The Life of the Mind*. Harcourt Brace Jovanovich; 1st edition.

Reynolds, M. (2014) *The Discomfort Zone: How Leaders Turn Difficult Conversations into Breakthroughs*. Berrett-Koehler Publishers.

7   Coaching the Team in Healthcare

Zeina Ghossoub

Introduction and Literature Review

Let us begin this chapter with two findings that perhaps summarize the reality of teams in healthcare and the need for their development. The first one by Babiker et al. in 2014, states that "The evolution in health care and a global demand for quality patient care necessitate a parallel health care professional development with a great focus on patient centered teamwork approach." The second one was from 1974, by Wise:

> It is ironic, indeed, to realize that a football team spends 40 hours per week practicing teamwork for those 2 hours on a Sunday afternoon when their teamwork really counts. Teams in [healthcare organizations] seldom spend 2 hours per year practicing, when their ability to function as a team counts 40 hours per week.

The questions beg themselves: Is there a need for a team approach to healthcare? And how do we best create that team? The first question has been undeniably answered with a resounding yes. It is the second one that is the focus of this chapter. In particular, a look at the development of such an effective team through team coaching.

Team coaching is a science or a practice all on its own. It has been thought of in the past that coaching individuals on a team will make them "better" and consequently, benefit the team and make the team "better". We know that is not the case. (Hawkins, 2021). Team coaching relies on three fundamental thought processes or experiences:

- Learning from working with professional teams in high-performance sports
- The newer approaches of coaching
- Traditional consultancy philosophies for the development of teams

This chapter is meant to be an introduction to team coaching. It is beyond the scope of this book to discuss in detail team coaching, its concepts, and its applications. It would be unjust and impossible to do so.

DOI: 10.4324/9781003452065-7

The evolution of team coaching has landed it in an arena that makes use of individuals learning best while on the job and gaining experience. However, experience alone does not guarantee performance as people can continue to be inefficient or not at their best despite performing their task for years. Many companies now look at team development and learning to follow the 70/10/20 rule: 70 % learning on the job; 10% learning from conferences and workshops; and 20 % learning from coaching. There are several limiting assumptions about team coaching. (Hawkins, 2021). Some of these erroneous assumptions include:

- Interest in team building is only when the team is first formed.
- Only when things are difficult will team coaching be needed.
- The sum total of each individual's performance will translate into the total performance of the team.
- Developing teams is about individuals better relating to each other and enjoying better meetings.
- Team development means developing the ability to trust each other.
- Conflict is a bad thing.

According to Castillo and Salas (2023), the healthcare industry suffers from three major problems for their working teams: burnout, lack of psychological safety, and what they describe as "other issues that are a threat to communication". Indeed, a significant number of errors and mistakes occur because of lack of teamwork and communication. Real-live examples, the literature, and personal experiences will tell you that having a group of talented professionals good or even great at what they do does not make a great team. It can lead to a disastrous team. A team is a living organism on its own with its own rules, regulations, expectations, and bond. There are two or three main approaches to team coaching that have developed over the past 2 decades. These will be highlighted.

In 2005, Hackman and Wageman discussed a framework of team coaching and effectiveness. They defined the effectiveness of teams on three levels: Function of effort level by each member, strategy appropriateness used by the team to fulfill their tasks, and the level and amount of knowledge/expertise each individual needs to be able to complete the targeted task. For team coaching to be effective, the authors suggested that four necessary factors or conditions must be present: Time factor, where the intervention needs to be done at the appropriate time; team factor where the focus of the intervention needs to be the team; supportive environment factor and the constraint factor where teams need to be relatively unconstrained by organizational and task requirements. As team coaching is discussed, it would be beneficial to think of it within the contexts of these four factors through the eyes of the healthcare industry and how feasible/challenging this can be.

In the healthcare industry, when questioned, coaches, coachees, and unit leaders agreed that there are four categories that team coaching should focus on: Helping, relationships, context, and technical support. (Godfrey et al., 2014). Each of these categories is a coaching focus on its own that would be looked at through the lens of team coaching approaches.

Just like with individual coaching, team coaching can follow several models. Hawkins (Hawkins, 2021) discusses his CID-CLEAR coaching model. It refers to Contracting-Inquiry-Discovery/Diagnosis and Design-Contracting, Listening, Exploring, Action, Review. He outlines some of the pertinent questions which are similar across the different team coaching models or focus on similar topics. Some of these questions include:
Contracting:

- What is the purpose of this team?
- What is at stake for this team? What is their why?
- What is the purpose of helping this team now?
- Who came up with the idea for this team to be coached? Does everyone agree?
- What do you know about team coaching? What is it for you?
- What are "forbidden" in terms of communication and subjects in this team?
- What are your indicators of success? Your milestones that you want achieved successfully? How will you know you achieved them?

Inquiry:

- Have semi-structured meetings with each individual or stake holder.
- Questionnaires can be sent out to evaluate each individual:

    a   Perception of what the team is or should be.
    b   Send out a team 360-degree feedback tool.

- What sort of team is this?
- Introduce certain tools to measure the team in terms of value, connection, and performance (there are plenty of references and tools available)

Discovery, Diagnosis, and Design

In this section, all the data that has been gathered needs to be analyzed and sorted. Once goals are identified, the coach can create an initial outline co-discovery achieving the goals. That outline gets modified based on co-discovery and co-diagnosis. Meeting with the team allows the coach and the team to agree on targeted goals, proper description of the state of the team, outlining how everyone works together, and mapping the coaching journey.

In 2012, and 2013, and then in 2019, Clutterbuck provided another approach to team coaching. He viewed team coaching as a learning intervention that relies on dialogue for change and reflection. The focus is on behavior, task, and learning as the three key components of teams that are effective.

Teams are deemed successful or effective if their productivity is sustainable over time, they are resilient, and show vitality. (Tannenbaum & Salas, 2021). In the healthcare industry, teams are unique. They can be made up of individuals with the same background and education and specialty, they can be made up of physicians with different specialties, and they can be a hybrid of physicians and non-physicians. They also face tremendous challenges in maintaining their vitality and resilience and productivity for all the reasons discussed earlier about the constraints of this industry on its manpower in general, and physicians in particular.

So, where can we start with team coaching in the healthcare industry?

According to the ICF, "Team coaching empowers teams to work toward continued high performance and ongoing development, requiring innovation, flexibility, adaptability, and goal alignment-all traits that coaching helps support."

Team coaching is an art and a science on its own. Just being a coach does not make one a team coach. Rather, team coaching requires training and certification with certain skills and competencies at its core. Team coaches need to have a broader knowledge base that is significantly greater than individual coaches. Due to the multifaceted nature of teams and individuals,

> they need to have an understanding of how to identify and resolve conflict, recognize power dynamics within the team, understand what is required for high performing teams, know how to build team cohesion, develop rules and norms, encourage participation and contribution by all, and promote team autonomy and sustainability.
>
> (ICF, 2023)

Other features that are highlighted in team coaching more than individual coaching are the need to be more directive to avoid being mired in internal team dynamics, issues, and conflicts. Coaches need to be more careful in shifting modalities of coaching as that shift may not be so obvious or apparent as it is with individual coaching.

The ICF discusses the Team Coaching competencies and uses the term "client" to refer to the team as a single entity that is made up of different individuals. Therefore, this "client" is different in many ways from the individual. It is the realization of the distinction between the two that prompted the creation of these competencies. They will be quoted directly from the ICF website:

a   First competency: Ethical practice.

- Coaching the client as a single entity, not its members individually.
- "Maintains the distinction between team coaching, team building, team training, team consulting, team mentoring, team facilitation, and other team development modalities."
- "Demonstrates the knowledge and skill needed to practice the specific blend of team development modalities that are being offered."
- "Adopts more directive team development modalities only when needed to help the team achieve their goals."
- "Maintains trust, transparency, and clarity when fulfilling multiple roles related to team coaching."

b   Second competency: Maintaining a coaching mindset.

- "Engages in coaching supervision for support, development, and accountability when needed."
- "Remains objective and aware of team dynamics and patterns."

c   Third competency: Establishing and maintaining agreements. This is manifested through:

- "Explains what team coaching is and is not, including how it differs from other team development modalities."
- "Partners with all relevant parties, including the team leader, team members, stakeholders, and any co-coaches to collaboratively create clear agreements about the coaching relationship, processes, plans, development modalities, and goals."
- "Partners with the team leader to determine how ownership of the coaching process will be shared among the coach, leader, and team".

d   Fourth competency: Cultivating safety and trust.

- "Creates and maintains a safe space for open and honest team member interaction."
- "Promotes the team viewing itself as a single entity with a common identity."
- "Fosters expression of individual team members' and the collective team's feelings, perceptions, concerns, beliefs, hopes, and suggestions."
- "Partners with the team to develop, maintain, and reflect on team rules and norms."
- "Promotes effective communication within the team."
- "Partners with the team to identify and resolve internal conflict."

e   Fifth competency: Maintaining presence.

- "Uses one's full range of sensory and perceptual abilities to focus on what is important to the coaching process."

- "Uses a co-coach when agreed to by the team and sponsors and when doing so will allow the team coach to be more present in the team coaching session."
- "Encourages team members to pause and reflect how they are interacting in team coaching sessions."
- "Moves in and out of the team dialogue as appropriate."

f Sixth competency: Active listening.

- "Notices how the perspectives shared by each team member relate to other team members' views and the team dialogue."
- "Notices how each team member impacts the collective team energy, engagement, and focus".
- "Notices verbal and non-verbal communication patterns among team members to identify potential alliances, conflicts, and growth opportunities."
- "Models confident, effective communication and collaboration when working with a co- coach or other experts."
- "Encourages the team to own the dialogue."

g Seventh competency: Evoking awareness.

- "Challenges the team's assumptions, behaviors, and meaning-making processes to enhance their collective awareness or insight."
- "Uses questions and other techniques to foster team development and facilitate the team's ownership of their collective dialogue."

h Eighth competency: Client growth facilitation.

- "Encourages dialogue and reflection to help the team identify their goals and the steps to achieve those goals."

If coaching is at its toddler stages in the healthcare industry, team coaching would be a newborn. The gap between coaching application and team coaching application is wide. If one stops to think about this, it is bewildering, to say the least. The healthcare system, at its core, is a system that thrives on collaboration, communication, clarity, support, trust, and working as a cohesive unit. Yet where, if any, do physicians, or other healthcare providers, learn to work as a team? On the contrary, if anything, physician training emphasizes individuality. Much like with coaching physicians, coaching teams in the healthcare industry is best achieved when the coach understands the healthcare industry! (Castillo & Salas, 2023). The authors advocate for developing an internal team-leader approach to help with making the most of the team while minimizing time and cost burdens. Whether that is the case versus utilizing a third-party vendor remains to be seen.

In 2020, Taylor et al. developed a concept of team coaching that begins with the team-leader. They divided the approach into two paths. The first path, the training interventions, dealt with the ad hoc team and the leader and it focused on team competencies and team training along with leader qualities and leadership training. The second path, the process intervention, dealt with the intact team. It focuses on developing or targeting two aspects of the team: Interpersonal processes through team building and team processes through team debriefing. All of these steps were followed by team coaching.

Incorporating team coaching into the TDI interventions literature. Based on Lacerenza et al. (2018), p. 520.

Each process or step requires its own approach, philosophy, and coaching technique. This could be a viable option for the healthcare industry to implement.

Conclusions and Recommendations

Some of the available studies have shown the positive impact of team coaching on developing interprofessional teams in healthcare. (Carney et al., 2021). For others, the jury may still be out when it comes to the effectiveness and the impact of team coaching on the health care industry. Some argue, due to its lack of consistency, definitions, responsibilities, and clearly defined applications, that the results are not there, unreliable, and questionable. (Castillo & Salas, 2023). But that may not be a function of the lack of effectiveness of team coaching, and more a function of the lack of its appropriate application, lack of time and expertise, lack of proper data, and inherent resistance to coaching with unrealistic expectations. Conceptually, team coaching works. Realistically, it has: In sports, in the executive worlds, and in other industries outside the healthcare world. These industries have a multitude of advantages including acceptance of the discipline, even relying on it as the major approach to success (sports), enough data for analysis, proper applications, and time for growing pains.

One cannot deny the truth that the future of healthcare depends on the effectiveness of its teams. That has already been proven. And while debates arise on how to best cultivate those teams, another truth exists that points to the lack of availability of "well-oiled" teams, and a paucity of viable approaches to remedy that. Borrowing from other industries and looking at the limited yet promising research from the healthcare industry, team coaching deserves a closer, more thorough, and fairer look. Let me add to the word "deserve", emphasizing necessarily so. Can we afford not to do so?

Case Study

A hospital in Texas hired us for workshops on coaching and group coaching benefits as well as implementation of tools and skills to deal with personal and professional challenges. Each coach had two to three departments to handle. One of those departments, the anaesthesia department, had a problem with "teaming" rather than being a "team". These are two distinct entities. Their issue was that they were able to team up for a certain task, but overall, were not able to operate as a team in the department.

A team coaching approach was undertaken.

- The first step was to introduce the group to the nature of team coaching and what it entails. A description of how it was different from group and individual coaching followed.
- Next, the stake holders were identified. These were the physicians and the nurses.
- Once the stakeholders were identified, a detailed description of the hierarchy and the organization of the department/team followed.
- Next, the following questions were asked:

    a   What did the medical director want and hope to achieve from their team? What are their thoughts and goals?
    b   What would a successful team look like for them?
    c   How would they need to work together to avoid continuous team coaching?

- Next, the team were coached on the following topics:

    a   Agreeing on their commission
    b   Mission statement clarification, including defining the purpose of the team, their core values, strategies, and a vision for the future over a certain time frame. In this group, they were hoping to expand and develop a residency/training program. They had a limited time to fulfill all their requirements and then to apply for accreditation.
    c   Protocols for teamwork
    d   Acceptable behaviors: What they wanted to encourage in each other.
    e   Unacceptable behaviors: What they wanted to discourage in each other.
    f   Defining the roles and responsibilities of everyone and identifying each other's lanes of operation and responsibility.
    g   Developing signals for discomfort and encouragement.

- After roles were defined, and goals agreed upon, the physicians decided to divide themselves into "mini teams" of 2 to 3 to help focus on their designated tasks which varied from developing curricula to creating safety measures and work environment to designating roles and responsibilities of faculty to creating courses, curricula, and presentation models. Some were responsible to be program directors, liaisons with accreditation bodies, developing wellness committees, and the handling of the financial aspects of the residency program.

- Once each mini-team finalized their roles and approaches, they met again and the discussion followed on how each mini-team will interact with the other, when their scheduled meetings would occur, gave updates on their positions, challenges, approaches, and requirements. They each discussed what they need from the other team and how they can help the other teams. They identified best forms of communications, accountability measures, benchmarks, and follow ups.This team, with their mini teams, quickly became a functioning unit where people felt safe, heard, and felt they operate in a fair, positive, and encouraging environment.

References

Babiker, A., El Husseini, M., Al Nemri, A., Al Frayh, A., Al Juryyan, N., Faki, M.O., Assiri, A., Al Saadi, M., Shaikh, F., Al Zami, I. F. (2014) Health care professional development: Working as a team to improve patient care. *Sudan Journal of Paediatrics.* 14(2):9–16. PMID: 27493399; PMCID: PMC4949805.

Carney, P.A., Dickinson, W.P., Fetter, J., Warm, E.J., Zierler, B., Patton, J., Kirschner, G., Crane, S.D., Shrader, S., Eiff, M.P. (2021) An Exploratory Mixed Methods Study of Experiences of Interprofessional Teams Who Received Coaching to Simultaneously Redesign Primary Care Education and Clinical Practice. *Journal of Primary Care Community Health.* 12:21501327211023716. doi:10.1177/21501327211023716. PMID: 34109864; PMCID: PMC8202267.

Clutterbuck, D. (2012). Coaching the team. In D. Brennan & K. Gortz (Eds.), *The philosophy and practice of coaching: Insights and issues for a new era* (pp. 219–238). Wiley.

Clutterbuck, D. (2013). Time to focus coaching on the team. *Industrial and Commercial Training*, 45(1):18–22. doi:10.1108/ 00197851311296665.

Clutterbuck, D. (2019). Towards a pragmatic model of team function and dysfunction. In D. Clutterbuck, J. Gannon, S. Hays, I. Iordanou, K. Lowe, & D. MacKie (Eds.), *The Practitioner's Handbook of Team Coaching* (pp. 150–160). Routledge.

Castillo, F., G., Salas, E. (2023) Can team coaching provide healthcare the remedy it needs? *Journal of Interprofessional Care.* 1–11. doi:10.1080/ 13561820.2023.2285030. Epub ahead of print. PMID: 38019103.

Godfrey, M.M., Andersson-Gare, B., Nelson, E.C., Nilsson, M., Ahlstrom, G. (2014) Coaching interprofessional health care improvement teams: the coachee, the coach and the leader perspectives. *Journal of Nursing Management.* 22(4):452–464. doi:10.1111/jonm.12068. Epub 2013 Jun 20. PMID: 23782339.

Hackman, J. R., & Wageman, R. (2005). A theory of team coaching. *The Academy of Management Review*, 30(2):269–287. doi:10.5465/AMR.2005.16387885.

Hawkins, P. (2021) *Leadership Team Coaching*. Kogan Page Limited. 4th edition.

ICF Team Coaching Competencies – International Coaching Federation.

Lacerenza, C.N., Marlow, S.L., Tannenbaum, S.I., Salas, E. (2018) Team development interventions: Evidence-based approaches for improving teamwork. *The American Psychologist*, 73(4):517–531. doi:10.1037/amp0000295. PMID: 29792465.

Tannenbaum, S.I., & Salas, E. (2021). *Teams that work: The seven drivers of team effectiveness*. Oxford University Press.

Wise, H. (1974). *Making health teams work*. Ballinger Publishing Company.

8 Burnout and Mental health

A Coaching Approach

Naim El-Aswad MD, FACP, ACC

Introduction and Literature Review

In the previous chapters, the discussions focused on not only identifying and understanding the causes of burnout and stress in the healthcare industry, but also the impact and ways and avenues available for coaching. This chapter will discuss coaching approaches for the different factors that impact burnout, coaching approaches for burnout and their applications, and using coaching for prevention.

To recap, burnout is caused by a multitude of factors including lack of control, unmet expectations, insufficient rewards, leadership (or lack of), pressure, personal characteristics, well-being and wellness, and an inability to connect to purpose and need. Most individuals are referred for coaching because of the consequences of burnout on their mental, physical, and emotional health with the corresponding behaviors that result from them. Unfortunately, coaching, and the research surrounding it, has focused mostly on its use in these situations. As data emerges on the use of coaching in prevention, in education, in preparation, and in adaptation, we will find that the full spectrum of coaching can accompany the full spectrum of emotional, mental, and physical wellbeing. Perhaps, in the process, we are able to truly appreciate the impact of coaching on the individual doctor, personally and professionally, and consequently, on the healthcare industry in general.

The WHO has described burnout as a *"Syndrome conceptualized as resulting from chronic workplace stress that has not been successfully managed."* Burnout is an occupational phenomenon. The thought process is that when the individual is removed from their stressful environment, their burnout ceases to exist. However, the impact of burnout is sometimes much more permanent and profound.

Let us take a closer look at the stressed/burned out brain. According to multiple authors, the effects of stress on the prefrontal cortex reveal the following (Haines & Arnsten (2008; McEwen, Gray, and Nasca (2015)):

DOI: 10.4324/9781003452065-8

- Dysregulated prefrontal cortex control over the amygdala which is one of the underlying pathogenetic factors of psychiatric diseases including depression and anxiety.
- Chronic stress leads to worsening of these effects that can last past the stressful event or time.
- Additional architectural changes occur with chronic stress which further exaggerate the switch from highly evolved to more primitive brain circuits.

On an organic level, from neuroimaging, the prefrontal cortex starts to lose neuronal connections and the architecture of the brain changes. What ends up developing are a series of functional holes that represent areas of severe brain dysfunction. The brain will look like "Swiss Cheese". Both shape, integrity, and function are altered and/or compromised. These changes are used to explain the increase in PTSD, anxiety, depression, burnout, moral illness, and even bipolar disorders (Walton, Murray, and Christian, (2020); Davis et al, (2017)).

Understanding your clients is paramount to enhancing your ability to coach them. When dealing with burnout, care must be taken to make sure there are no mental health issues such as depression or anxiety or bipolar. These will need to be referred to appropriate care and management with a psychologist or psychiatrist or counselor.

Discussions and Applications

Coaching as prevention

For more details on the pathophysiology of burnout, please refer to chapter 3. Physicians will be the first to tell you that one of the things that drives them mad is the idea that patients can continue doing the same that causes them disease and expect to get better. People continue to smoke, gain weight, not take their medication, and hope their overall health improves. Hippocrates said it best:

> Before you heal someone, ask him if he is willing to give up the things that made him sick.
>
> *Hippocrates*

In discussing burnout prevention, it is understood that the 21st century doctors need certain skills and abilities that are absent from their training, education, and job description. Prevention can occur or start in medical schools, in residency and fellowship, or in practice. The challenges that will face the doctors are known by now and have been discussed. An argument can be made to help physicians understand their situation, develop their goals, and be coached towards achieving their goals. Some common goals of all physicians include, but are not limited to, having a work-life integration, being professionally satisfied, getting adequate rest and remaining in good health, taking care of their families and loved ones, and minimizing errors while maximizing their impact. By understanding their challenges and their unique situations, and by developing a sense of understanding of their abilities, capabilities, support systems, options, and needed skills, physicians can be helped to develop these necessary skills, be supported in carving their way to their goals, and coached into achieving their purpose. Here are some examples:

Coaching for engagement

The opposite state of burnout is sometimes referred to as engagement. How, then, do you help someone go from being burned out to being engaged? Here are some guidelines and practices in coaching.

- Connect to purpose: Coaching your clients to reconnect to their purpose helps them to become engaged. Some of the approaches/questions would include:

    a   Why are you a healthcare provider?
    b   What gives you the greatest pleasure in your work?
    c   What describes success at work for you?
    d   What boosts you the most in your work?
    e   What helps you to fulfill your purpose?
    f   How do you stay connected to your purpose/work?
    g   What interferes with that connection?
    h   What have you done in the past to help you bypass that interference?
    i   What else can you do?

- Prepare for the day: Burnout is on the same disease spectrum at PTSD. It is no wonder that some of the doctors, if not all, dread certain days or assignments. They feel the angst and the stress of the coming events/days before even starting them. Here are some of the coaching approaches to help clients prepare for their day:

    a   Before going to work:

        - It is said that the "start of the day is the rudder of that day". What are some activities/action steps you take to ensure you will have a good day, or to prepare you for your day?
        - How can you view your stress as a challenge?
        - These questions can also occur in a group coaching session, and they can be very powerful as people volunteer or suggest what works for them.

b   If you visualize your day, what do you see?
c   How can you make your day better even before it starts?
d   What are some of the challenges you foresee?
e   Have you been successful in the past to bypass or avoid or manage those challenges?
f   What can get in your way in managing these challenges?
g   What can you do to bypass your obstacles?
h   One of the topics of coaching, especially for physicians, is "Re-attachment".

- Rebuilding a mental connection to work
- If people consciously take a few minutes to mentally reattach to their work by reflecting on their goals and priorities, they will experience "a cascade of positive experiences during the day."
- They will be more engaged, less burned out, more satisfied with their work, and feeling more inspired. (Sonnentag et al., 2019)
- Questions to be asked:
- Why does the work I do matter to me? How does my work impact the lives of others?
- Who are the people – both at work and in my personal life – who support me and my professional success?
- What would I like to focus on today?

- During your workday:

a   What are your negative triggers? Positive triggers?
b   Why are they negative triggers?
c   Why are they positive triggers?
d   How much do these triggers affect you? On a scale of 1–10, how much do your negative triggers affect you. (If the client gives a number, say 5, this may be followed up with: What do you need to do to make it a 3?) Quantifying helps clients, especially doctors, create a reachable quantitative goal that they can measure and assess and use as a reference. The same approach can be done for the positive triggers. In this case, the question would be how the clients can increase the number to enhance their positive triggers.
e   We know that connections build resilience and help with supporting against burnout. Some questions directed at connection include:

- Do you feel less burned out if you are connected with others at work? If the answer is yes;
- Who do you connect with at work?

- Are you able to increase/enhance that connection? If yes, how? What would you do? What works for you?
- What can you do to ensure you are able to increase that connection? What would get in your way? How can you bypass that?
- The same approach can be utilized for other behaviors. Two important contributors to burnout include personal boundaries and personal standards. When these two are compromised, burnout and stress increase.
- Personal standards: You hold yourself to. When people in general, and doctors in particular, sacrifice their standards, especially professionally, moral injury can occur. "Moral injury refers to an injury to an individual's moral conscience and values resulting from an act of perceived moral transgression, which produces profound emotional guilt and shame, and in some cases also a sense of betrayal, anger and profound 'moral disorientation'" *Stephanie Frost*. This occurred frequently during the Covid era when doctors were forced to practice medicine outside the norm and guidelines. The unacceptable became acceptable, like managing the patients without physically examining them. This led to burnout and significant trauma. Coaching doctors to identify their standards and maintaining them helps alleviate their burnout symptoms and even mitigate the whole process. During coaching sessions, physicians may express their anger or frustration or sense of defeat. They may question their own existence and relevance. One client of mine told me that while covering the ICU in the height of the covid era, she never felt so needed and so useless at the same time. When a client expresses their loss of standards or being forced to operate outside of them, and this might happen frequently due to budget cuts, institutional demands, and other reasons, some of the approaches/questions that can be used include:

  - How are your standards being compromised?
  - How does that make you feel?
  - Why is it important for you?
  - What would be ideal for you?
  - What have you tried to tackle/fix the situation?
  - What has worked? What has not?
  - What can you do differently about it?
  - Who can help you? Do you need help and support?
  - What would get in your way?

- Personal boundaries: You hold others to
  - Are made up of imaginary lines that are meant to hold others at a safe distance.
  - They cannot be seen by others if you do not show them and make them known and recognized.
  - They are essential to keep unwanted and damaging behavior away from you.
  - These boundaries are essential and necessary for self-care.
  - Coaching for maintenance of boundaries would tackle the following:

f   Others may not yell at me.
g   Others may not speak to me rudely.
h   Others may not enter my office without knocking.
i   Others may not call me at home to discuss office matters.
j   Others may not gossip in my presence.

- Steps to enforce your boundaries:

k   Inform others.
l   Make a request.
m   Give a warning.
n   Follow through with the stated consequence.
o   Let go of the outcome.

- Coaching for these steps involves asking the clients similar questions to their "standards" questions.

- After you leave: One of the key practices that help doctors decrease their risk of burnout is detachment. Just as it is important to reattach to one's work and purpose, it is equally important to detach. Detachment is difficult for multiple reasons:

a   Not enough hours at work to finish the job, so work travels home with the doctors. There is a saying: Physicians' date night is Saturday night between 6 pm and 2 am. That is when there is the highest use of EMR's and medical charting happens!
b   Electronics and the ability to be reached outside of work.
c   The impact of the processes that lead to burnout on the brain as has been detailed in the earlier chapters makes it very hard for the doctors to disconnect. Their minds are always in "solving problems mode".
d   Some of the coaching approaches used help to:

- Increase awareness of the physician's mindset or state of mind when they leave.
- Help physicians identify or realize the importance of detachment and the impact of not being able to detach.

- Help physicians identify their emotions and their states after work.
- Help physicians identify ways to detach. Discussion of successful activities/action steps taken in the past.

e   One of the main activities that helps physicians to detangle and close those functional holes in their brains is mindfulness. Mention mindfulness and one would get a lot of eye rolling. Doctors have heard enough about mindfulness that it makes them nauseated at times. But why stress it? Mindfulness, as defined by Jon Kabat-Zinn, "means paying attention, in a particular way, on purpose, in the present moment and non-judgementally." In his book, "Leading well from within", Dr. Daniel Friedland discusses the importance of mindfulness on the plasticity of the brain. This phenomenon has been shown through neuroimaging with the brain recovering from those functional holes and calming down, not being hijacked, and leading to a calmer existence that helps combat stress and pressure. It is even more needed due to the hyperconnectivity of our age and how that has led us to disconnect from ourselves. The new challenges of the healthcare industry require doctors to be more self-aware and emotionally intelligent.

Coaching for burnout

Coaching for burnout can be direct and indirect. It can have immediate and long-term effects. It can target burnout the disease, its factors, the individual, the surroundings, and the industry. Reviewing the literature shows that coaching has been linked to improving physician well-being, enhancing resilience, reducing burnout symptoms, and improving quality of life (Dyrbye et al. (2019); Boet et al. (2023)). The burned-out mind is its own beast to tackle. Coaching works best when both coach and client are present, are aware, feel safe, are engaged, focused, and connected, to state a few requirements. Consider the burned-out brain from the descriptions thus far and you can see how it is less likely to exist in that desired space. If you add on top of that that most coaching has been used for remedial purposes, you arrive at the inescapable conclusion that coaching the burned-out mind is not only less than ideal but has its own challenges that necessitate paying attention to.

During my training in internal medicine, my chairman, Dr. Donald O Castell used to say, "Assumption is the mother of all evils". This is brought up because when coach meats client, there is a certain assumption, or assumptions: That the client is willing and able, that the client has the support and freedom, that the client is enthused and ready, that the client is positive and engaged. Often, with the burned-out brain, this is not the case. So where does one start? There are different approaches to coaching the client who is burned out.

- Enhance the awareness: As discussed before, most clients/doctors are referred for remedial purposes. Most of them do not know what coaching is and view it through a negative lens. They may feel offended, angry, disgusted, aggressive, and downright hostile at times. An introductory session that goes over:

  a   What coaching is and what it is not.
  b   The reason for the client to be there.
  c   Their expectations.
  d   Discussion of their views, thoughts, reservations, and ideas.
  e   Defining their goals.
  f   Discussing the ethics of coaching and the privacy laws and how these laws protect the clients.
  g   Making sure they understand the relationship between you and them and how referring groups, institutions, or other authorities have no input or say in the coaching sessions, nor are they allowed to know what goes on in the sessions.
  h   During training, physicians learn that the approach to a patient complaint is referred to as the SOAP approach (Subjective, Objective, Assessment, plan). This same mnemonic can be used to explain to the physicians the coaching sessions and approach.

    - Subjective: What are your perceived signs and symptoms?
    - Objective: What are others telling you? Friends, colleagues, supervisors, and family.
    - Assessment and what those entail (Discussed later)
    - Plan: Discuss how a plan of action looks like.

- Assessments: Assessments here are not only directed at burnout, but also at finding out the abilities of the client.

  a   Assessing burnout could be done through multiple tools, paid or free, online or in person. Most assessments are through third party companies. Having you and the client go over their burnout scores and profiles affords you both the opportunity to understand where the client is and have a better picture or idea of their abilities. Sometimes, before the coaching even starts, addressing the severity of the burnout may necessitate psychological or psychiatric referrals.
  b   Well-being: Understanding the well-being of the client creates a better understanding of mental, physical, and emotional abilities. Again, several online and in-person assessments are available, each with their own interpretation scores and approaches.

    c   Emotional Intelligence: As has been discussed before, this is a tremendous tool that looks at 15 different abilities that the client may have. Identifying these abilities and their roles as they pertain to the different goals and challenges can be paramount in setting the agenda for the coaching sessions.

    d   Personality types: This follows the same pattern of having you and the client better understand what and who you are dealing with. Different personalities respond differently to coaching. It is beyond the scope of this chapter to discuss these. Suffice to say, the more you and the client know about who they are and what they are able to do and not do, the better the coaching outcomes.

- Coaching: The burned-out brain, like other coachable brains, needs to be challenged. Coaching is the approach that does so. Coaching is meant, through its processes, to examine fixed thought processes and thoughts. (Gazelle et al, 2015). As has been discussed, clients need to examine their own assumptions, thought processes, perceptions, and beliefs. By altering perspectives, clients can turn a seemingly impossible out of their control situation to a controllable or partially controllable situation. This can be achieved through a series of approaches/questions:

    a   Are you comfortable? Do you feel safe? Do you have any other questions?

    b   At the end of the coaching session, what would you like to happen? What are some of your goals? Finish this statement: "At the end of the session, I would like …"

    c   Are you able to better understand yourself and your brain when it is burned out? When is it engaged?

    d   Are you ready to proceed?

    e   What do you need to be ready?

    f   Once the clients express their willingness and readiness, coaching can proceed. This is extremely important, again, for the reasons listed and discussed ad nauseum. More often than not, doctors are unwilling participants. Getting them to be willing would dramatically and drastically improve the rates of success.

Conclusions and Recommendations

Throughout this book, much has been made on the uniqueness of the physician's mind, especially when it is burned out. The coaching experience in the healthcare industry is young and still being discovered. Although robust data maybe lacking to fully demonstrate its impact, and although this industry is especially reliant on objective and reproducible data, the argument has been made that there is a need for coaching, and that it maybe, at time, the only conduit for helping and supporting the burned-out physician. Burned-out physicians face a multitude of challenges to be able to maintain their personal and professional lives. Coaching has emerged as a viable approach to help and support them. Since it is not counseling or a psychiatric intervention, physicians are more likely to accept it and give it a try, if only to avoid the negative outcomes of maintaining the way they are acting professionally. (More on that in chapter 15).

Too much is asked of the 21st century physician outside of their designated professional roles that they have sculpted through medical school and residency training. The expectations are unfair and unrealistic. The industry asks of the physicians to never be wrong, and to operate as a skilled doctor, leader, manager, teacher, and business owner as well as mastering the ever-changing landscape of rules, regulations, and demands by legal, economical, and third party (insurance and pharmaceutical) establishments.

This is not an impossible task to master, but probably very close to it. And make no mistake, it is all about mastering, not just getting by. To do so, physicians must learn new skills and techniques, deal with the demands of their own professions, and be able to navigate a burned-out brain that is continuously being harassed by the environment in which it operates. Coaching may be the best option for them to become those masters.

Summary and Key Points

- The 21st century physicians are more than just medical doctors. Their increased and varied roles, as well as the demands of their profession have made them susceptible to burnout.
- Burnout is extremely prevalent among physicians. It has deleterious effects on physicians and patients alike.
- There is a need to help support and protect the physicians while allowing them to thrive in the healthcare industry.
- Burned-out physicians have a unique brain that necessitates coaching within rules and regulations that may only apply to this industry and this target population.
- Coaching can be used in prevention, as well as enhancing engagement and managing/mitigating/conquering burnout.
- Approaching the physicians through increasing their awareness about the process of coaching, assessment of their burn-out status, their abilities, and their skills, and then helping them to develop the necessary tools, thought process, and approaches is part and parcel of the science of coaching.

Case Study

A 52-year-old physician was referred for coaching by his supervisors. The physician had issues with communication skills. He was a brilliant clinician, very reliable and dependable. His main issue is how he comes across as rude, aloof, sometimes obnoxious, and "scary". He is a heavy-set man who is tall, so he has an imposing figure. His culture and his upbringing have helped him develop his communication style and approaches. Upon our first interaction, he proceeded to let me know that I know nothing of him, not to patronize him, that he does not know why he is here, and that if he does not do these coaching sessions he will be fired. So, in his words, we just need to get on with it and be done.

The client was angry, felt insulted, dismissive, and not interested. He was also confused as to the nature of the interaction, the process, and what is asked of him. This is very common. Clients often do not know why they are referred and are told very little. This despite me telling the referring leadership group that it is very important to communicate with the client why he is referred and what to expect and what is expected of him.

First session: This session was spent talking to the client. The whole process of coaching was explained: What it is, what to expect, why he is here, and why he thinks he is here. Connection was made based on similar backgrounds as he made it a point to let me know that because I too was a physician and have practiced for as many years as he has, that I get the small benefit of the doubt. He wanted to know my story and why I am a coach and why my interest in burnout. Halfway through the conversation, he changed. He understood that this is a safe, non-judgmental, secure, and supportive environment that is meant and focused on helping him, no matter his goals. He also understood that even though he was referred to be coached, that it is his best interest and his personal and professional life that is at the center of the sessions and not the referring group.

Second session: The client had the insight to understand that his communication skills were the problem. He has spent enough time in the USA to figure out that he impacts people negatively at times. As the coaching session proceeded, the patient made the comment that he feels he is burned out. At that moment, the conversation shifted. I asked why he feels he is burned out, and he proceeded to tell me. He definitely had the symptoms of burnout, and it was impacting his personal and professional life. As a coach, one needs to be able to pivot based on the client's needs. In this case, the communication issues clearly became less important than the suffering the physician was having. Further, it was part and parcel of the issues that were plaguing him and it was evident that it would not be affected or impacted or improved as long as burnout is the prevailing state of existence. This is when the approach now switched to focusing on burnout. Assessment of his burnout, along with his emotional intelligence and well-being were made. The three aspects of burnout, emotional exhaustion, depersonalization, and reduced personal accomplishments, were targeted. Even though he was only allotted 6 sessions by the group, the change that they started seeing in him, and the change he was feeling and experiencing, got them to extend to 12 sessions.

References

Boet, S., Etherington, C., Dion, P.M., Desjardins, C., Kaur, M., Ly, V., Denis-LeBlanc, M., Andreas, C., Sriharan, A. (2023) Impact of coaching on physician wellness: A systematic review. *PLoS One*. 18(2):e0281406. doi:10.1371/journal.pone.0281406. PMID: 36749760; PMCID: PMC9904500.

Davis, M.T., Holmes, S.E., Pietrzak, R.H., Esterlis, I. (2017) Neurobiology of Chronic Stress-Related Psychiatric Disorders: Evidence from Molecular Imaging Studies. *Chronic Stress (Thousand Oaks)*. 1:2470547017710916. doi:10.1177/2470547017710916.

Dyrbye, L.N., Shanafelt, T.D., Gill, P.R., Satele, D.V., West, C.P. (2019) Effect of a Professional Coaching Intervention on the Well-being and Distress of Physicians: A Pilot Randomized Clinical Trial. *JAMA Internal Medicine*. 179 (10):1406–1414. doi:10.1001/jamainternmed.2019.2425. PMID: 31380892; PMCID: PMC6686971.

Friedland, D. (2016). *Leading well from within: A neuroscience and mindfulness based framework for conscious leadership*. Super Smart Health. 1st edition.

Gazelle, G., Liebschutz, J.M., Riess, H. (2015) Physician burnout: coaching a way out. *Journal of General Internal Medicine*. 30(4):508–513. doi:10.1007/s11606-014-3144-y. Epub 2014 Dec 20. PMID: 25527340; PMCID: PMC4371007.

Hains, A.B., Arnsten, A.F. (2008) Molecular mechanisms of stress-induced prefrontal cortical impairment: implications for mental illness. *Learning & Memory*. 15(8):551–564. doi:10.1101/lm.921708. PMID: 18685145.

McEwen, B.S., Gray, J., Nasca, C. (2015) Recognizing Resilience: Learning from the Effects of Stress on the Brain. *Neurobiology Stress*. 1:1–11. doi:10.1016/j.ynstr.2014.09.001.

Sonnentag, S., Eck, K., Fritz, C. (2019) Morning Reattachment to work and work engagement during the day: A look at day-level mediators. *Journal of Management*. doi:10.1177/0149206319829823.

Walton, M., Murray, E., Christian, M.D. (2020) Mental health care for medical staff and affiliated healthcare workers during the COVID-19 pandemic. *European Heart Journal of Acute Cardiovasc Care*. 9(3):241–247. doi:10.1177/2048872620922795.

9 Emotional intelligence in Medicine

Impact and Applications

Relly Nadler PsyD, MCC

Introduction

This chapter will define emotional intelligence. It will highlight the impact of emotional intelligence and emotional quotient (EI and EQ respectively) in personal and professional lives in general, and in medicine and healthcare in particular. The chapter will identify why coaching physicians to improve their EI is vital and discuss the potential impact of the coaching process using EI. It will discuss the different competencies of EI, the ways to test and measure it, and the different approaches to impacting it. It will end with some case scenarios.

Definitions

The term *social intelligence* was first used by psychologist Edward Thorndike in 1920. Decades later, in 1983, another psychologist, Howard Gardner, wrote about seven types of intelligences in *Frames of Mind*. Two of the seven types were intrapersonal intelligence and interpersonal intelligence, the core of today's EI models.

In 1985, Dr. Reuven Bar-On first coined the term *emotional quotient*, or EQ. He saw EQ as a set of emotional and social skills that influence the way we: Perceive and express ourselves; develop and maintain social relationships; cope with challenges; and use emotional information in an effective and meaningful way.

In 1990, Salovey and Mayer first used the term *emotional intelligence* in a research paper, stating that "our framework for *emotional intelligence, is* a set of skills hypothesized to contribute to the accurate appraisal and expression of emotion in oneself and in others, the effective regulation of emotion in self and others, and the use of feelings to motivate, plan and achieve in one's life."

Dr. Daniel Goleman then popularized the term with his books *Emotional Intelligence* (1995) and *Working with Emotional Intelligence* (2000). The simple definition we have adopted for emotional intelligence is, understanding and managing yourself and understanding and managing others.

DOI: 10.4324/9781003452065-9

Six Seconds is a leading EI provider globally, they define Emotional Intelligence as: The capacity to blend thinking and feeling to make optimal decisions. It's being smarter with feelings. They break down into 3 pursuits:

- Self-Awareness: Be more aware, by clearly seeing what you feel and do
- Choice: Be more intentional, by doing what you mean to do
- Purpose: Be more purposeful, by doing it for a reason

Literature Review

Organizational Research from Six Seconds.org (2023). Why do organizations need Emotional Intelligence?

- What separates exceptional leaders? It's emotional intelligence.
- Leaders who are high in emotional intelligence are 7x as likely to be high in leadership performance outcomes.
- Employee engagement is the lifeblood of organizational performance – but only 21% of global employees are engaged.
- Emotional Intelligence is a key driver of engagement, accounting for as much as 70% of the variation in engagement.
- A healthy organizational climate matters, yet hybrid and remote work adds emotional and logistical complexity. Organizations that prioritize EQ are 22x as likely to be high performing.
- Companies with higher emotional intelligence build better relationships with customers, which strengthens trust, which drives loyalty. A 5% increase in customer loyalty results in 25% increase in profit.
- High emotional intelligence is a strong predictor of performance and profitability for leaders, teams, and entire organizations.

How much is low emotional intelligence costing your organization?
From Six Seconds.org (2023)
Organizations prosper with more focus on Emotional Intelligence, as we see above. Without EI there is a broad negative impact.

Low emotional intelligence ultimately results in lost productivity, higher turnover, and lower revenue.

Here's how to calculate the costs – and break the cycle.
What's happening: Companies are wasting money in an endless cycle of poor communication, broken trust, and low employee engagement. Globally, only 21% of employees are engaged. A massive 60% of people are emotionally detached at work and nearly 1 in 5 are miserable, per Gallup. Even worse: These numbers have declined in the last 20 years.... even as organizations have invested more time and effort than ever to improve them.

Why it matters: There are massive financial implications: Employees who are not engaged or who are actively disengaged cost the world $7.8 trillion in lost productivity; 11% of global GDP. The costs fall into 3 broad categories: lost talent, lost productivity, and lost customer loyalty. Organizations who get it right have a massive competitive advantage – more important than ever as we face uncertain economic conditions and a tight labor market.

How to respond: Invest in emotional intelligence training for leaders and employees. It's strongly correlated with employee engagement, which fuels a wide range of critical business outcomes, including retention and customer loyalty. (2023) Six Seconds.org.

Emotional Intelligence in Medicine

There has been a lot of research validating the power of EI in medicine from peer reviewed articles, doctorate dissertations and hospital-based research. We have selected some of the more current studies below.

Wasfie T, Kirkpatrick H, Barber K, Hella JR, Anderson T, Vogel M. (2023) did a longitudinal study of Emotional Intelligence, Well-being, and Burnout of Surgical and Medical Residents in their first year of residency.

At the end of the first year, they found:

- 46% increase in exhaustion ($P < .001$),
- 48% increase in depersonalization ($P < .001$),
- 11% decrease in personal achievement ($P < .001$).
- Physician wellness domains also changed significantly.
- 12% decrease in career purpose ($P < .001$),
- 30% increase in distress ($P < .001$),
- 6% decrease in cognitive flexibility ($P < .001$).
- Each burnout domain and physician wellness domain were highly correlated with emotional quotient (EQ). Emotional quotient was independently assessed with each domain at baseline and with changes overtime.
- The lowest EQ group reported their distress increased significantly over time ($P = .003$) and a decline in career purpose ($P < .001$) and cognitive flexibility ($P = .04$).

Their final conclusion was that emotional intelligence (EI) is associated with well-being and burnout in individual residents; therefore, it is important to identify those who require increased support during residency in order to succeed.

McNulty & Politis (2023) studied empathy, emotional intelligence and interprofessional skills in healthcare education. They found that EI is closely linked with the provision of quality psychological, emotional, and physiological care to patients by healthcare professionals. This more holistic approach to health care can be positively associated with social support, resilience, and empathy and negatively associated with burnout. These can directly or indirectly help sustain the caring behavior of health professionals and thus lead to increased levels of EI. Lower levels of EI were linked to increased stress while higher EI levels were linked to self-compassion and job. One of the major implication of high EI skill levels is more positive outcomes in client-professional interaction. Therefore, EI is valued in healthcare professions because of its relevance to interactions and patient needs.

In 2023, Abi-Jaoude et al. reviewed 4435 articles. 37 articles satisfied their criteria. Studies varied in surgical specialties, settings, and outcome measurements. The authors found that EI has been demonstrated to be beneficial in terms of overall well-being and job satisfaction while also protecting against burnout. They concluded that EI skills may provide a promising interventional target to help achieve outcomes that are desirable for both the surgeon and the patient (Abi-Jaoudé et al., 2022).

In an extensive review of the literature, Sharp, Bourke, and Rickard (2020) found that

> high EI is positively associated with leadership skills in surgeons, non-technical skills, reduction in surgeon stress, burnout and increased job satisfaction, all of which translate to better patient relationships and care. Future implications of EI have been postulated as a measure of performance, a selection tool for training positions and a marker of burnout. EI should be an explicit part of contemporary surgical education and training.

In looking at the Contribution of emotional intelligence and burnout, Sanchez-Gomez and Breso (2020) found

> the results demonstrated a positive relationship between EI and performance, and a negative relationship with burnout, which has a mediator effect in the relationship between EI and work performance. Professionals with high levels of EI and low burnout reported the highest performance. These findings demonstrate the importance of burnout in understanding work performance and emphasize the role of EI as a protective variable which can prevent the development or chronic progression of workers' burnout.

Discussions and Applications

Below are 10 reasons physicians need Emotional Intelligence (EI) training and coaching to combat burnout. (Nadler, 2018)a

Burnout: The National Academy of Medicine noted that more than half of U.S. physicians exhibited signs of burnout, a syndrome marked by "a high degree of emotional exhaustion…and a low sense of personal accomplishment." They cited links between doctors' disaffection and the care they gave patients, with studies suggesting "a significant effect on quality and risk of malpractice suits." 68% of physicians have said burnout has negatively affected their relationships. (Kane, 2022) We know physician burnout is a root cause of medical errors, malpractice lawsuits, and patient complaints, as well as physician depression/drug use/suicide and so much more. Although the main focus here is on physicians, studies of nurses report a similarly high prevalence of burnout and depression. Since the COVID-19 pandemic began, nurse burnout has increased to over 70%. What's more, the repetitive and constant exposure to trauma and death in the workplace leaves nurses at risk for developing PTSD. (BCEN, 2023)

b   Pressure: Physicians are making life and death decisions be all day long. This is a lot of pressure where vital decisions have to be made in the moment. A mistake can mean death or disability. In most professions, a mistake doesn't have these severe consequences. There are only a few other professions with as much in-the-moment pressure, such as the armed service, policemen, firemen, air traffic controller, and pilots.

c   Underdeveloped EI: To be in the top 1 % year after year in school and get into medical school and then residency programs, students have to focus on their cognitive development, such as memorizing, studying causes and effects, and building associative skills. There is very little time to focus on emotional development such as self-awareness, knowing your patterns and triggers, emotional regulation, managing difficult conversations and building their empathy.

d   Blind Spots: We all have blind spots but if you don't know what they are, they will continue to undermine your success. Marshall Goldsmith, one of the top executive coaches with Fortune 100 executives, says from his experience: 70 % of people think they are in the top 10 percent. This is a major blind spot. Using EI coaching, assessments, 360-degree feedback and interviews you can establish what your blind spots are and begin to shed light on them.

e   Hero Complex: To become a physician, individuals had to make significant self-sacrifices over the years. The average physician has had up to 10–12 years of schooling and residency. They have had to be in the top 1 % of their class throughout schooling and are used to being the smartest person in the room. They take pride in being very smart and confident about their intelligence and problem-solving. Consequently, it is hard to feel fallible and examine their assumptions and decisions. It is easier to assume that their decisions are the right decisions. Reinforced during the school years that their answers are usually the correct answers. When operating from burnout though, they may no longer be the smartest in the room at those critical moments.

f Disillusionment and Cynicism: A crushing identity crisis (CIC) usually occurs for physicians in their forties. After delaying gratification, fun and socializing for decades for their idealized career; the reality of the day-to-day existence is depressing. Add to that less time with their family and the resulting rising family tensions leads to dissatisfaction and questioning, "Is that what I signed up for?"

g Old School Training: The training for physicians has not incorporated new learning and neuroscience research, where people learn best when they take breaks, are not sleep deprived, and focusing on how they best recharge. A program director from a well-respected resident's program stated: "We have a beat down environment." Physician's mentors have had to tough it out with long hours, limited sleep, and expect their new residents to tough it out just like they did. Lunch is eaten on the elevator ride to a meeting or meeting patients. An hour or two should be a sufficient amount of sleep if on call. Physician training is just starting to see some changes where some residencies are learning about emotional intelligence and resilience strategies.

h Environmental Factors and Pajama Time: Today, with electronic records, physicians are putting in 60–90 minutes of extra time after hours completing their records. They get automatic tardy notes if they are late with their notes. One surgeon said 18 hours after surgery he was getting multiple notifications to complete his records.

In Physician Burnout, El-Aswad, Nadler, and Ghossoub (2017) present the top environmental factors that physicians have identified, and rated them on a scale of 1–5 with 5 being the most important below:

Having too many bureaucratic responsibilities (4.96)
Spending too many hours at work (4.29)
Income not high enough (4.04)
Feeling like just another cog in the wheel (3.96)
Increasing computerization of practice (3.81)
Too many difficult patients (3.74)
Too many patient appointments in the day (3.64)

a Physician as the Team's "Emotional Thermostat": The physician's mood and temperament influence everyone on the team more than can be imagined. Gallup (2023) has found that managers account for up 70 % of the variance in employee engagement surveys. Research has shown from the Korn Ferry Hay Group that the leader has 50–70% over the climate of the team. If they are calm and collegial, so is the team; if they are impatient, stressed, and irritable, so is the team. In the hospital hierarchy, the physician may even have higher influence over the climate of the surgery team, or in the emergency room. The physician's mood is the most contagious mood with others.

b   Decision Fatigue: You will make better decisions: In today's world we are all "crazy busy." Some people call this a VUCA environment, which means Volatile, Uncertain, Complex, and Ambiguous. To be outstanding, an individual needs to be able to make effective decisions in the moment with as much information and knowledge as they can gain. It is a matter of getting accurate input to improve the output. The EI input is knowing about yourself and assessing others quickly so the decisions can be better. This kind of strategic intelligence is highly valued by the military. It is also a critical skill for any executive that is making thousands of decisions a day. To be a top performer you must quickly assess and adjust in this VUCA environment.

c   Emotional Intelligence Formula: Our formula for top performance that we share with physicians and leaders is:

Empathy X Insight X Clarity = Top 10 % Performance.

Whether it is training or coaching the focus is to gain more clarity into your strengths and weakness and those of your direct reports or your teams.

Making micro-initiatives about yourself and others can have a macro-impact and help make great decisions in the moment.

Empathy includes an individual's observable signs as well as invisible feelings of others. We use this information or input to make decisions and adjustments, like during a typical day of seeing patients. The more clarity and knowledge we have about these signs, the less potential risks and better decisions or output we will make. Spending time with patients and co-workers to truly understand them incorporates listening carefully, asking follow-up questions, and respecting their feelings and opinions.

The *insight* part of the equation is also invisible and often overlooked as a means of obtaining information (or input) and knowledge. The ability to know our biases, strengths, and weaknesses, and emotional triggers that lower our impulse control and impair communication is vital to optimal patient interactions and medical decision making.

When we are interacting with others – patients and co-workers – what emotional intelligence are we exhibiting? What is our external awareness, and can we make the appropriate adjustments? And what is our internal awareness, and can we make the appropriate adjustments?

Clarity is acquiring the nuisance data about yourself and others. You can increase this clarity with coaching, training and reading, Coaching is one of the best ways as it can be tailored for your specific interests and concerns.

What we know about Emotional Intelligence Interventions

Research has shown promise in advocating the use of EI-based education systems to develop and improve the art of professional development and communication skills. (Cherry et al., 2014) A study of 2,800 physician "star performers" showed that 75% of a high-achiever's success is a function of emotional intelligence; only 25% of success reflects technical competency (El-Aswad, Nadler, Ghossoub, 2017). In a critical review of the literature performed by Arora et al. the authors identified a total of 485 articles that have looked at EI in medicine. The authors discussed the importance of EI with respect to the six core competencies of the Accreditation Council for Graduate Medical Education (ACGME). They noted the EI is inherently linked to empathy, effective communication, leadership, stress management, teamwork, and academic performance. EI's inherent characteristics are such that they warrant further research.

In a study with colleagues Dr. El-Aswad and Dr. Ghossoub with program advisors, we found that: Training directors using the unique combination of emotional intelligence, self-care techniques and leadership skills may be an effective intervention against combating burnout in residency programs. It was sustained for 9 months after the intervention.

Main Pillars of EI

There are two main pillars of emotional intelligence: The first is its application and relevance to burnout, and the second is its ability to be modified and enhanced to produce change in oneself that leads to a decrease in burnout rates and severities, and ultimately better clinical outcomes. To illustrate this, let's focus on one of the ACGME competencies: communication skills.

Measuring the EQ of a physician will highlight their strengths and weaknesses in areas that are needed for better communication skills. One of these areas is the realm of self- expression. Physicians who are inferior communicators score poorly in the self-expression realm. The relevance of the EQ test is that it outlines these deficiencies and points them out in a quantifiable manner. Once deficiencies are identified, intervention processes follow.

The intervention process has seven steps:

- Assess the physician's EQ competencies.
- Decide which competencies are best to improve and do more of, considering the physician's results, position, and ACGME competencies.
- Identify key tools to improve these EQ competencies.
- Create a plan for improvement.
- Practice these competencies.
- Reevaluate competency level.
- Make a follow-up plan to maintain the progress.

Emotional intelligence can be learned and improved, unlike IQ, which is static. Interventions are less developed than the assessment of EQ at this point. Like medical training, there is a process to becoming skilled in emotional intelligence competencies.

Exposure: Awareness, assessment, and identification of which competencies to improve		Practice: Development plan for continual practice of the new skills		Proficiency: Ability to be effective at the new skills		Mastery: Expert at the identified EQ competencies and teach others
	→		→		→	

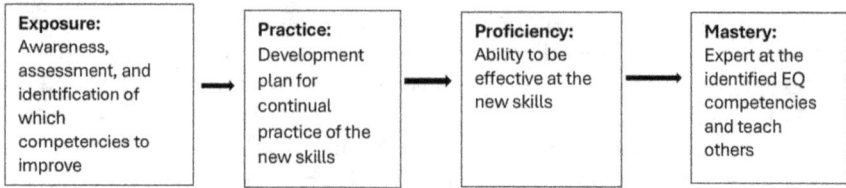

Figure 9.1 Levels in Emotional Intelligence Proficiency

Measuring EI

In 1991, Dr. Goleman collaborated with his colleague Dr. Richard Boyatzis and the Hay Group to come up with the Emotional Competence Inventory (ECI). One version has eighteen competencies, and another has twelve competencies, and both are a 360-degree assessment. A wealth of research on the ECI competencies has been promoted by the Hay Group over the last thirty years, based on four clusters areas: Understanding Yourself, Managing Yourself, Understanding Others, and Managing Others. Both the EQ-i and ECI are considered a mixed focus on both traits and abilities.

The last test we will look at is more of an abilities measure: the Mayer-Salovey-Caruso Emotional Intelligence Test, or MSCEIT. It includes the ability to label emotions, understand the relationships between words and feelings, distinguish between authentic and non-authentic emotional expressions, and manage emotions by strengthening positive and reducing negative ones.

Measuring EQ is important, but more essential is having a development plan to enhance strengths and minimize weaknesses. So how do we do that? By understanding the five realms of emotional intelligence with their competencies. Our abilities – our emotional intelligence – can be scientifically measured in a valid and reliable methodology, and that is significant because when something is measurable, it is quantifiable, observable, and, perhaps most important of all, modifiable.

Finding Your Emotional Intelligence Balance

We will now go more into depth about the EQ-i 2.0. Both competencies and clusters will be explored along with some case studies to help elucidate the interplay and balance of the competencies. All of these work together in a systematic way, like the body, to impact emotional and social functioning and overall performance. Some competencies may need to be improved, or "dialed up," and some competencies may need to be "dialed down." The result can be a prevention of burnout and an intervention to lessen physician burnout and dissatisfaction. Presented here is an introductory overview. There are 5 clusters: Self-perception, Self-Expression, Interpersonal, Decision-Making, Stress Management.

Self-Perception Cluster

The self-perception cluster involves the inner self and is made up of self-regard, self-actualization, and emotional self-awareness. It is "designed to assess feelings of inner strength and confidence, persistence in the pursuit of personally relevant and meaningful goals while understanding what, when, why and how different emotions impact thoughts and actions."

This translates to the following questions:

How confident am I?
Am I constantly trying to get better?
How aware am I of how my emotions affect me and others?

This cluster is the most important place to start and to master. Knowing yourself well give you information and data that not only helps manage yourself, but also shows you what to change, adjust, or manage. It incorporates the insight and clarity part of our top 10 % equation. As Socrates said, "The unexamined life is not worth living." And according to Benjamin Franklin, "There are three things extremely hard: steel, a diamond, and to know oneself."

- *Self-regard* is knowing and accepting your strengths and is often associated with self-confidence. Do you accept yourself and feel good about yourself?
- *Self-actualization* is striving to be better, being driven to achieve, being self-motivated, and living a meaningful life. Self-improvement and continuous learning are examples of this competency.
- *Emotional self-awareness* is being knowledgeable about your emotions, understanding which ones contribute to your performing at peak, which ones get in your way, how your emotions influence others, and how your emotions impact your decision making. We all have blind spots; it's just that good leaders and top performers have fewer of them.

In a *Forbes* magazine article, a study of 6,977 self-assessments from professionals at 486 publicly traded companies identified the "blind spots" – defined disparities between self-reported skills and peer ratings – present. They found that "poor performing companies' employees were 79 % more likely to have low overall self-awareness than those at firms with robust return on revenue. Stock performance was tracked over thirty months, from July 2010 through January 2013. During that period the companies with the greater percentage of self-aware employees consistently outperformed those with a lower percentage." In 2010, the Hay Group found leaders with higher self-awareness also had heightening of many of the other EI/EQ competencies. This was to a degree more than they expected.

Self-Expression Cluster

This self-expression cluster involves the outward expressions or action components of the internal perceptions from the cluster above – in other words, openly expressing thoughts and feelings in a constructive way. It includes emotional expression, assertiveness, and independence. This translates to the following questions:

Can I speak appropriately about the uncomfortable experiences and emotions that arise during the workday?

Can I defend my points of view in a non-offensive manner?

Can I make decisions autonomously?

- Emotional expression is openly expressing your feelings verbally and nonverbally. Given the variety of emotions experienced during the day, from anger to disappointment to sadness and regret, can you express these effectively, so people know what is happening to you?
- Assertiveness is expressing your opinions and recommendations and defending your personal rights in an appropriate and inoffensive manner.
- Independence is making decisions without dependency on others and making the appropriate call autonomously.

The ACGME competencies of communication, interpersonal skills, and patient care will be impacted by a professional who scores high in these self-expression competencies.

Interpersonal Cluster

The interpersonal cluster involves developing good relations based on trust and compassion. It is understanding others and showing concern for others. This cluster includes interpersonal relations, empathy, and social responsibilities. This translates to the following questions:

Do patients and co-workers trust and want to work with me?

Do they feel that I really get them and their concerns?

Am I a helpful member of the community?

- *Interpersonal relationships* is your ability to make good relationships, and have people want to confide in you and feel comfortable talking to you about their issues. An important part of this competency would be your bedside manner.
- *Empathy* is being sensitive to others' feelings and being able to anticipate their reactions.
- *Social Responsibility* is being socially conscious and making efforts to be a contributing member of your organization and society in general.

Decision Making Cluster

The decision-making cluster is about your understanding of how emotions and biases may affect your decision making and help delay your impulses. It includes problem solving, reality testing, and impulse control. This cluster is the most outward representation of your emotional intelligence and can impact the medical risk of professionals. This translates to the following questions:

Am I able to manage my impulses and reactions in what I say and do?
Can I find good solutions when my emotions are aroused?
Can I stay objective in spite of the situation?

- *Impulse control* is the ability to stay calm, composed, and patient when there is emotionality in a situation.
- *Problem solving* is the ability to understand how emotions impact decision making and is a systematic way to solve problems.
- *Reality testing* is recognizing when emotions or personal bias can cause you to be less objective. You have limited biases that cloud your decision making.

Stress Management Cluster

The stress management cluster is about how well you can cope with the emotions associated with change, unfamiliar and unpredictable circumstances, while remaining hopeful about the future and resilient in the face of setbacks and obstacles. This cluster includes flexibility, stress tolerance, and optimism, all of which directly influence burnout.

This translates to the following questions:
How adaptable am I?
How much stress can I handle?
What is my attitude when there are difficult circumstances?

- *Flexibility* is effectively adapting your emotions, thoughts, and behaviors to changing circumstances and conditions, and being open to new viewpoints.
- *Stress tolerance* is having effective coping strategies and believing you can manage or influence dynamic situations in a stable and relaxed manner.
- *Optimism* is remaining hopeful and resilient despite occasional setbacks, while remaining hopeful and confident about the future.

Case Study

The following is an adapted assessment tool that can be used by coaches on their clients. It takes you through the conversation you might have with your client.

Where are You?

Your EQi, 2.0 Adapted Assessment

EQi Competencies: For each one below, rank yourself on a 1–10, where 10 is high and you consistently do this behavior, and it is a definite strength. A 5 would be you do it and are fair at it, a 1 this would need a lot of improvement. An 8 signifies that you regularly and consistently do this competency about 80% of the time. Use this as a self-assessment and you could also use the other column to rate a direct report or have a stakeholder rate you.

Action Plan

Look at your assessment and note which 2–3 competencies are the most important for your position now? Put a check and next to them now. How did you rate yourself on them?

What strengths are the 8 and 9's, and could you use to move these key competencies up 1–2 numbers? Now look at which 2–3 competencies you are at a 6 or 7, your "almost". How can you do them a bit more to reach an 8?

Think of who is good at what you want to improve on, what do they do and ask them about their ideas. Use your support system to get new ideas and hold you accountable. There are other chapters on Coaching, Resiliency and Change that can give you more tools, behaviors, and skills to focus on.

Case Studies

Let's now look at a few examples of burnout and EI in medical practice. This will help integrate the competencies in real world applications.

Case 1: Poor Decision Making

Dr. F. storms into the next operating room after performing a long surgery. He glances briefly at the chart and remembers the patient's name and situation. He then asks for the scalpel to begin the surgery. The operating nurse, JS, meekly asks a clarifying question about the surgery. Dr. F interrupts and barks an order for the next instrument. JS doesn't inquire again as Dr. F performs surgery on the wrong leg.

In which two competencies does Dr. F need to be coached to dial down this behavior?

Table 9.2 EQI 2.0 competency

EQi 2.0 Competency	Self	Other
Self-Perception Composite		
Self-Regard respecting yourself; confidence		
Self-Actualization pursuit of meaning; self-improvement		
Emotional Self-Awareness understanding your emotions		
Self-Expression Composite		
Emotional Expression constructive expression of emotions		
Assertiveness communicating feelings, beliefs and ideas; in a non-offensive manner		
Independence self-directed; free from emotional dependency		
Decision Making Composite		
Problem Solving find solutions when emotions are involved		
Reality Testing objective; see things as they really are		
Impulse Control resist or delay impulse to act		
Interpersonal Composite		
Interpersonal Relationships mutually satisfying relationships		
Empathy understanding, appreciating how others feel		
Social Responsibility social consciousness; helpful		
Stress Management Composite		
Flexibility adapting emotions, thoughts and behaviors		
Stress Tolerance coping with stressful situations		
Optimism positive attitude and outlook on life		

Source: Adapted from Multi-Health systems Inc. Copyright © 2011, All rights reserved. Based on the original BarOn EQ-i authored by Reuven Bar-On, Copyright 1997.

Note: Number of areas of strengths = an 8 or above

- Problem solving
- Assertiveness
- Empathy
- Independence

In which two competencies does JS need to be coached to improve?

- Self-regard
- Intrapersonal relations
- Assertiveness
- Optimism

Case 2: Dissatisfied and Overwhelmed

JH, Senior Vice President, is in charge of the electronic records initiative. His deliverable is to go live on September 1, and he has been working on it nonstop for the last six weeks, until ten o'clock every night and on almost every weekend. He has been unable to get key stakeholders to make his meeting critical to get buy-in from Dr. P and his team, who are necessary for the implementation. Dr. P had promised that they would have representatives attend, but they missed the last two meetings. JH now realizes there are not enough hours or resources to meet the deadline. Dr. P apologizes, stating he had an emergency come up at the time of the last two meetings. JH is stressed and wondering if this is the right position for him. He has to report to the oversight committee tomorrow and is anxious and unable to sleep, thinking about what he will say.

In which two competencies does JH need to be coached to improve?

- Assertiveness
- Impulse control
- Self-actualization
- Expressiveness

In which two competencies does Dr. P need to be coached to dial up his behavior?

- Intrapersonal relations
- Emotional self-awareness
- Empathy
- Optimism

Summary and Recommendations

All emotional intelligence starts with your self-awareness, identifying what you want to get better at and then try out new behaviors. They can be small, as micro-initiatives can create a macro impact. Get feedback from others, listen to podcasts, read books and blogs and be a learner for small improvements, Try to be 1% better in each of your identified areas. Its maybe just doing them more regularly.

There are other chapters in this book, such as On Coaching, Resiliency and Change, that can give you more tools, behaviors, and skills to focus on.

In summary you have seen how EI is needed by physicians and healthcare workers to reduce burnout, increase retention, productivity, engagement, and your overall well-being.

You were able to evaluate yourself and others on your EI and start on your EI development plan for you and your direct reports.

References

Abi-Jaoudé, J.G., Kennedy-Metz, L.R., Dias, R.D., Yule, S.J., Zenati, M.A. (2022) Measuring and Improving Emotional Intelligence in Surgery: A Systematic Review. *Annals of Surgery.* 275(2):e353–e360. doi:10.1097/SLA.0000000000005022. PMID: 34171871; PMCID: PMC8683575.

Arora, S., Ashrafian, H., Davis, R., Athansiou, T., Darzi, A., Sevdalis, N. (2010) Emotional Intelligence in medicine: a systematic review through the context of the ACGME competencies. *Medial Education.* 44:749–764.

Balch, C.M., Freischlag, J.A., Shanafelt, T.D. (2009) Stress and burnout among surgeons: Understanding and managing the syndrome and avoiding the adverse consequences. *Archives of Surgery.* 144(4):371–376. doi:10.1001/archsurg.2008.575.

Board of Certification for Emergency Nursing (2023). https://bcen.org/nursing.

Cherry, M.G., Fletcher, I., O'Sullivan, H., Dornan, T. (2014) Emotional intelligence in medical education: a critical review. *Medical Education.* 48(5):468–478.

Clifton, J., Harter, J. (2023) *Culture Shock: An Unstoppable Force is Changing how we Work and Live.* Washington, DC: Gallup Press.

Codier, E., Kooker, B.M., Shoultz, J. (2008) Measuring the emotional intelligence of clinical staff nurses: an approach for improving the clinical care environment. *Nursing Administration.* 32(1):8–14.

Dyrbye, L.N., Shanafelt, T.D., Sinsky, C.A., Cipriano, P.F., Bhatt, J., Ommaya, A., West, C.P., Meyers, D. (2017) Burnout among health care professionals: a call to explore and address this underrecognized threat to safe, high-quality care. *NAM Perspectives.* 1–11. doi:10.31478/201707b.

EQi 2.0 User's Handbook (2011) Toronto Canada: Multi Health System.

El-Aswad N., Ghossoub Z., Nadler R. (2017) *Physician Burnout: An Emotionally Malignant Disease.* Create Space Publishing. North Charleston, S.C.

Ghossoub Z., Nadler R., El-Aswad N. (2018) Effect of using emotional intelligence, wellness, and leadership training on lived experiences of medical program directors burnout. *Universal Journal of Public Health.* 6(5):298–305. doi:10.13189/ujph.2018.060508.

Ghossoub Z., Nadler R., El-Aswad N. (2018) Targeting Physician Burnout Through Emotional Intelligence, Self-Care Techniques, and Leadership Skills Training: A Qualitative Study. *Mayo Clinic Proceedings: Innovations, Quality & Outcome.* 2(1):78–79. http://www.ncbi.nlm.nih.gov/pmc/articles/6124346.

Gardner H. (1983) *Frames of Mind.* New York: Basic Books.

Goleman D. (1995) *Emotional intelligence: Why it can matter more than IQ.* Bloomsbury; 12.2.1995 edition.

Goleman D. (2000) *Working with Emotional Intelligence.* Bantam; Reprint edition. https://www.kornferry.com/institute/647-a-better-return-on-self-awareness https://atrium.haygroup.com/downloads/marketingps/nz/ESCI_research_findings_2010.pdf.

Kane, L. (2022) *Physician Burnout & Depression Report 2022: Stress, Anxiety, and Anger.* Medscape. https://www.medscape.com/slideshow/2022-lifestyle-burnout-6014664#1.

McHugh, M.D., Kutney-Lee, A., Cimiotti, J.P., Sloane, D.M., Aiken, L.H. (2011) Nurses' widespread job dissatisfaction, burnout, and frustration with health benefits signal problems for patient care. *Health Affairs.* 30:202–210.

McNulty, J.P., Politis Y. (2023) Empathy, emotional intelligence and interprofessional skills in healthcare education. *Journal of Medical Images and Radiation*

Sciences. 54(2):238–246. doi:10.1016/j.jmir.2023.02.014. Epub 2023 Apr 8. PMID: 37032263.

Nadler, R.S. (2011) *Leading with Emotional Intelligence: Hands on Strategies for Confident and Collaborative Star Performers.* New York: McGraw-Hill.

Nadler, R.S. (2018) 10 Reasons We Need Emotional Intelligence Now. Psychology Today. *Leading with Emotional Intelligence blog.*

Salovey P., Mayer J. D. (1990). Emotional intelligence. *Imagination, Cognition, and Personality.* 9:185–211. doi:0.2190/DUGG-P24E-52WK-6CDG.

Sanchez-Gomez, M., Breso, E. (2020) In Pursuit of Work Performance: Testing the Contribution of Emotional Intelligence and Burnout. *International Journal of Environmental Research and Public Health.* 17(15):5373. doi:10.3390/ijerph17155373. PMID: 32722557; PMCID: PMC7432932.

Sharp, G., Bourke, L., Rickard, M.J.F.X. (2020) Review of emotional intelligence in health care: an introduction to emotional intelligence for surgeons. *ANZ Journal of Surgery.* 90(4):433–440. doi:10.1111/ans.15671. Epub 2020 Jan 21. PMID: 31965690.

Six Seconds (2023) *Definition of Emotional Intelligence,* https://www.6seconds.org/emotional-intelligence/.

Wasfie, T., Kirkpatrick, H., Barber, K., Hella, J.R., Anderson, T., Vogel, M. (2023) Longitudinal Study of Emotional Intelligence, Well-being, and Burnout of Surgical and Medical Residents. *The American SurgeonTM.* 89(7):3077–3083. doi:10.1177/00031348231157813.

10 Coaching Physician Resilience

Cathy Greenberg

Key Concepts (Monti et al., 2018)

❖ The neural circuitry associated with experiencing emotional pleasure such as from spiritual fulfillment, happiness or love is likely the same or closely replicated by the neural circuitry associated with experiencing physical pleasure such as from sex, music, or warmth. We can strengthen these pathways over time through attention to them.

❖ The neural circuitry associated with experiencing physical pain such as from a headache, injury or disease is likely the same or closely replicated by the neural circuitry associated with experiencing emotional pain such as social rejection, depression, or self-criticism. We can also strengthen these pathways and increase "stressors" that impact our flexibility for responses through imbalanced attention to these negative issues.

Neural circuitry that influences the plasticity of the brain to support experiencing these associated emotional and physiological processes can also have an impact on how we respond, known as resilience.

Emotional and physiological responses to resilience are strongly associated with three innate psychological needs considered as universal necessities: competence; dealing effectively with our environment, and relatedness; having close, affectionate relationships to others, and autonomy; feeling in control of our life. (Martin et al., 2017)

These authors add *purpose* to this well-established theory; *the cumulative effect of meaningful goals consisting of the central and motivating aims for your life*. Together these four innate psychological needs create the foundations for staying motivated when things get tough, to enable meeting short term and long-term goals which allow us to feel like we are making a positive difference in the world.

❖ Attention management to these innate psychological needs is essential for developing happiness and satisfaction required for resilience, while the opposite, attention mismanagement, is a catalyst for unhappiness or dissatisfaction which reduces overall capacities for resilience.

DOI: 10.4324/9781003452065-10

Supporting Concepts

❖ Happiness is believed to have a set point in each person – a base level in a similar way that each person has a foundational level of intelligence – and by all indications this set point can be enhanced through deliberate and supportive constructs.

❖ "Being on your side", is a resilience construct based on a daily approach to self-awareness through attention management focused on a positive mindset. This practice proves to be a more balanced, rational, realistic, and self-caring approach to our foundations of psychological motivation for achievement. Such practices can yield more sustainable degrees of happiness, resilience and satisfaction than does "being on your case". Together, these collective concepts and positive approaches build upon existing "set points" to improve performance through adaptive coaching strategies over time known as resilience.

Resilience requires the ability to adapt, overcome and improve the way we think and respond to challenges in our lives to build upon these positive self-awareness constructs.

Introduction: Setting a Context for "Resilience Strategies"

Our knowledge of the brain and behavior, including its impact on overall life satisfaction, health, wellness, and its ability to underscore peak performance is evolving greatly. The Self Determination Theory (SDL) is a social-psychological framework that explains how different types of motivation affect our day-to-day wellbeing and decision making (Martin et al., 2017). SDL proposes that there are three fundamental psychological needs essential for human flourishing: autonomy, relatedness, and competence (ARC). We include a fourth psychological need, *purpose*, to this theory to support the goal orientation required to enact these elements in a productive, outcomes-based manner. Current research suggests that resilience is a combination of these factors which provides the flexibility needed to "bounce forward" during or after times of struggle or crisis.

Bouncing forward is a concept defined as the ability to come back stronger, better positioned for the future, rather than back to baseline. Professor Patricia Longstaff, Syracuse University, is attributed with its first use in the published record by D. Borenstein, 2014 *Bouncing Forward: Why "Resilience" Is Important and Needs a Definition.*

Despite the need for physicians to be resilient coaches, for themselves as well as for others, research in the general population indicates most people are not equipped with the *competencies* to do so. A recent study (Scoular & Scoular, 2019) had non-physicians assess their coaching effectiveness, and then these assessment findings were paired against what their direct reports said. 24% of participants significantly over-estimated their coaching abilities, rating themselves above average, while others ranked them in the bottom third of the group. While this is an obvious overestimate of one's capabilities in the general population it also demonstrates how "realistic" we think we are when it comes to understanding how competence, and a mindset for coaching, as a resilience strategy itself is seen as important.

From the time physicians decided to become a part of the medical profession they were tasked with both their own self-awareness on the *competence* required to achieve this milestone, and the *purpose* for that endeavor. Here is a quick synopsis. Their psychological motivations for *autonomy* in this life choice were probably quickly met. This autonomy soon shifted from the joy of independence to the increased needs for interdependences or *relatedness*. Relatedness intensified due to their coursework and higher mental and energy resource output required to achieve the goal. These resources, both for the effort dedicated to their education and the sustained energy resources as they increased, were met by increased *competence* and the resilient flexibility needed to meet the immediate needs of the *purpose* or goals. Therefore, while their decision to be a medical professional supported their autonomy and purpose, their competence needs may have increased significantly, while their relatedness may have felt inadequate at times.

Resilience, as a wellbeing strategy, requires constant monitoring in all the domains outlined here as self-determination theory (SDT). Physicians also require other self-awareness considerations like reality checking, and rebalancing with a focus on their emotional, social, physical, mental and relationship needs which will normally shift throughout their daily routine. Some of them may also require a spiritual aspect to this rebalancing. These ebbs and flows are the normal rhythm of life's daily challenges including how we rebalance or bounce forward during and after struggle.

Each of us will respond differently to these ebbs and flows based on our experiences, knowledge, and more importantly attention to our self-awareness throughout our daily rhythm. While some people are motivated by the challenges of acquiring competence in their field (eustress), others may feel depleted by it (destress). While some of them are motivated by the intrinsic value of autonomy for long term success in their career endeavors, they also have needs for interconnectedness with others in the delivery of their purpose as a physician. This required relatedness among members of the medical profession may have different levels of emotional qualities that sustain or drain them in the delivery of their purpose. Understanding these psychological needs through self-awareness with a positive mindset or "being on our side" is critical. The risks of ignoring these intrinsic needs not only include burnout, or error in medical treatment, they can, if unchecked, far outweigh the motivational drivers for long term success. This can turn into psychological states often attributed to burnout which can turn into stages of maladaptive behaviors that hinder one from adapting to or coping with situations or stressors in a healthy way. Examples include self-isolation due to anxiety, sleeping too much due to depression, and lashing out at others when overwhelmed or angry.

To ensure we are actually "great" coaches for all our people, we need the opportunity to first build our own knowledge and self-awareness skills. Only then can we build on how to coach and develop others, or embrace the techniques required for building resilience, as part of an overall skillset which can be acquired through training. However, the most valuable step in the development process is understanding our own capacity for resilience: A focused self-awareness to examine our daily responses to setbacks, challenges, and conflicts (commonly referred to in the literature as struggle).

a   Where to Begin: Understanding Self Before Others

While many self-assessments exist to reveal our current capacities for resilience, there are a few ways coaches can approach this topic. A focus on our self is key. While I won't go into depth on how to take action on self-awareness, other authors in this volume can support you. One of the best ways to do this is using "nondirective" self-coaching techniques or the "dialogue model". GROW is a nice example because it's simple to follow ourselves, as well as with others. (See chapter 2) In Chapter 11 we take a deeper dive into using GROW with others. To help us focus on our resilience we can also apply GROW as a self-awareness model. It involves four basic action steps; the letters give the model its name. It's easy to grasp but a little harder to practice than you imagine because it requires training yourself to think, observe, and withhold judgement, or opinion, in new ways.

The four basic action steps are an ideal starting point because they're easy to remember. In this example of the application of GROW, we will focus on "ourselves" before moving to how we can apply it to others in the next Chapter as a leadership practice. You will notice in the examples provided here; it takes the original non-directive question developed by Whitemore coupled with an adaptation for self-awareness applications. For example, if the question was intended as "What do you want when you …. today? We swap the I for you; "What do I want when I …. today? or What are the key things you need to know"; to "What are the key things I need to know? "

Goal-**R**eality-**O**ptions-**W**ill

a   Goal: To start we usually ask something like "What do you want when you walk out the door now? To apply this to yourself – try this: 'What is my immediate need right now?'"

b   Reality: With the "goal" above established, ask questions rooted in "reality checking" for *what, when, where,* and *who,* which forces us to focus on specific action steps and facts. You'll notice that we didn't include *why*. That's because asking why demands that people explore reasons and motivations rather than facts. *Why* can carry overtones of judgment, or trigger attempts at self-justification, both of which can be seen as a challenge to the ego and may derail the discussion.

Helpful Coach Questions include:

- "What are the key things I need to know?" Attend carefully to the response.
- Am I missing something important?
- Am I talking about "operational issues" but forgetting the human side of the equation?
- Am I talking about the "human issues" but forgetting the "operational side" of the equation? The underlined words indicate a "fill in the blank" scenario.

When you ask yourself or other people to slow down and think in this way, it often requires a pause for "reflection" due to the task of contemplation – and then, often, a light comes on, and off you go, engaging with the problem with new energy and a fresh perspective. That's a great self-coaching experience because you create both the opportunity for relationship, good reflection, reality checking, problem solving, flexibility, and the added benefit of "building" an increased capacity for resilience through wading through the aspects of the struggle to a level of better awareness and eventually success. Often this engages our struggle for a basic need for autonomy, or competence in pursuit of our purpose. All contributing to resilience.

This last step, "engaging with new energy", is critical because your job here is to raise the right questions, engage more "energy", motivate, inspire, and then get out of your own way. Learning to recognize you have control over your response to issues takes some grace. Here is where being on your side really matters, which brings greater rewards. Especially when you see the benefits of creating psychological safety for yourself.

a   Options: When your inner voice feels stuck it sounds like this:

- "There's nothing I can do,"
- Or "I have only one real option."
- Or "I'm torn between A and B."

At this point you need empathy for your situation and "flexibility" to reflect more deeply. That requires "a higher step towards understanding resilience" and how it works. Most importantly for yourself. To broaden someone's view we must bend some boundaries. Press refresh on the "mind" and possibly the heart.

Using questions like "If I had a magic wand, what would I do?" may sound a little "out there" but when we can help remove the usual boundaries as a visual exercise to get the ideas flowing, You'd be surprised how we respond to freeing the block to using imagination and how quickly we can start being funny, or sarcastic, which also helps engage different parts of the brain for a more productive way forward. Once your perspective changes, your job is to prompt ideas by encouraging exploration of both the upside, or the downside, of the responses and the potential benefits or risks of the options joked about. Somewhere in there is the right answer for either through laughter, or struggle. Another option is to reflect on when you've felt this way in the past and what you did to change that, and the impact it had on who you were when you had reflected on these issues. It never hurts to have an accountability partner to help you see beyond the boundaries of your mindset.

a   Will: The Will step has two parts, each involving a different sense of the word *will*.

What will you do? Encourages us to review the specific action plan that has emerged from the prior conversation. If it's gone well, we have a clearer understanding. If not, you'll need to cycle back through the earlier steps of the GROW process and help redefine how to attack the problem another way. Act, Assess, Adjust. Using a standard learning loop is always an easy way to continue the process until you believe in your progress.

Here are some questions to help open further a GROW dialogue about resilience. You will find similar questions in Chapter 11 on Leadership focused on using this set of questions as a coaching tool with your direct reports, or others you may have a professional relationship with within your career. We simply change the "me" focus to a "we focus".

- Is the current state of resilience in my workplace serving me and the people well?
- Are my/our current levels of engagement, performance, and satisfaction where I want them to be?
- What support might my/our people need to navigate their biggest struggles with resilience?
- Do my /our people have the Wellbeing ENABLER levels they need to individually and collectively experiment with intelligent and creative ways to care for their resilience?
- How can I/we help all workers overcome the barriers to caring for their resilience and wellbeing?

- Are my/our people seeking help when they are struggling with their resilience from the people that are best equipped to support them?
- How am I/we encouraging and supporting your leaders to create a resilience work environment?
- Are my/our people experiencing the benefits of thriving, regardless of their levels of struggle? (Resilience is the result of "thriving beyond the struggle" and as needed creatively continue to evolve these traits over time)
- Which factors and Workplace Wellbeing Factors are making the biggest positive difference for my/our people who are successfully thriving over time, to both demonstrate and foster resilience, in themselves and their direct reports/teams?

In any case, you have revealed three key elements of any human connection for resilience.

Even a connection with ourselves: How to **connect;** how to **reveal;** how to **empower.**

a   What is Happiness vs Resilience?

Happiness is difficult to quantify though the field of study is gaining tools to better assess emotion. The Positive and Negative Affect Scale (PANAS), Oxford Happiness Inventory, Subjective Happiness Scale, and Satisfaction with Life Scale are among the most recognizable batteries. Along with those are subdivision measurements including the Fordyce Emotions Questionnaire which measures current happiness and the Subjective Happiness Scale which measures happiness relative to changing variables.

Just as important to understanding happiness itself, is the study of unhappiness. Research reveals the role that regret plays in a sense of happiness as well as unhappiness – most notably the greater feelings of regret the more miserable a person feels for a longer period of time (Tversky & Kahneman, 1992; Kahneman, 2011). Thus, the natural tendency toward an avoidance of pain offers comfort and a subjective feeling of happiness. A patient who suffers from chronic arthritis will feel a sense of relief if they have a good day with minimized pain. That relief, however, may be experienced as happiness. An employee passed over for a promotion may feel vindicated if the winning candidate eventually goes on to fail in their new position. This vindication however may be experienced as happiness too. In each of these two examples, a diminishment of pain can be misconstrued to be an increase in happiness. Whereas most healthcare providers define authentic happiness as being based more on character traits such as those advanced by the positive psychology movement's three dimensions of happiness: positive emotion, engagement, and meaning (Seligman & Csikszentmihalyi, 2014). Indeed, beyond the positive psychology model, these same tenets for true happiness are taught by spiritual leaders, career counselors, families, and applied in coaching for performance through resilience techniques.

Brain imaging studies further show that the neural circuitry associated with experiencing physical pain such as from a headache, injury or disease is likely the same or closely replicative of the neural circuitry associated with experiencing emotional pain such as social rejection, depression, or self-criticism (Eisenberger, 2015). A potential corollary to this is research that additionally shows the neural circuity of the brain is likely replicative or the same too in regard to emotional pleasure such as from spiritual fulfillment, happiness and love, and physical pleasure such as from sex, music and warmth. (Ferguson et al., 2016)

In our own work with leadership training for private sector CEOs, federal and state government administrators, and military and paramilitary officers, the application of happiness theory is directly related to priming peak performance through fostering a conscious shift from ordinary thought processing to an inspired one. The bridge between the two is often characterized as "flow" (Csikszentmihalyi, 1990). We believe the same tenants for resilience, and its impacts on peak performance apply to healthcare providers.

The primary objective of this work is to help individuals maximize their opportunities for resilience. Though much of our effort is directed at leadership development in a traditional sense, a broader application is emerging for us in developing models for greater personal fulfillment through self-leadership (Neck, 2006), and since the publication of the original manuscript in 2018, I believe it is also the result of a combination of "self-leadership" and "resilience due to wellbeing and self-care" in the delivery of these leadership roles that make the biggest impact. Especially in healthcare. Thus, this Chapter and the Chapter on Leadership in Healthcare will overlap to some degree.

The foundation for our original efforts (Monti and Newberg, Integrative Psychiatry and Brain Health, Oxford Univ. Press Feb, 2018) is constructed on improving each individual's self-awareness, or in colloquial terms, their Emotional and Social Intelligences (Goleman, 1995). We broadened this well researched idea to extend to "Emotional Brilliance" with the publication of a co-authored work by the same title in 2020 and 2021 respectively (Greenberg & Nadler, 2020).

Being emotionally brilliant is "being well received in the moment", any moment, and really making the best decision, or saying just the right thing to enhance your relationships, both under stress as well as in a relaxed setting. With this approach individuals can more deeply understand their decision making and attention-focusing processes. This includes making conscious decisions, versus being on autopilot, and thus reduces unconscious biases, self-delusions, and errors in judgement due in large part to heightened emotional intelligence (EI) behaviors such as reality testing, impulse control, flexibility and most importantly self-empathy as measured by emotional intelligence assessments. Other benefits of such attention include an overall measure of wellbeing through the integration of positive interactions of key behaviors associated with interpersonal relationships, self-regard, self-awareness, and optimism.

The focus here reflects on the importance of resilience for self-care, self-empathy and self-awareness. With the goal of offering individuals, as leaders or team members, more choices in pursuit of resilience-based leadership behaviors resulting in a greater potential to develop into better listeners, with more compassion for themselves, among other aspirations, particularly in the workplace, and hopefully to be more attuned to respond with greater effectiveness to both colleagues, administrators, and those they serve, as well as to potential adversaries across healthcare. In addition, they are better attuned to the experiences of all four brain hemispheres. In particular, taking into account the regions responsible for empathy, creativity, and intuition, and not just the more frequented domains controlling cognition and concepts associated with higher order thought functioning such as logic related to problem solving (Goleman & Boyatzis, 2008) so critical to peak performance under pressure throughout the healthcare industry.

Striking this balance between feeling and thinking is potentially one of the greatest opportunities to advance not only leaders as individuals and the organizations they serve, but society. It is through this advancement that compassion and empathy, reason, and analysis, can bring both resilience and the science of happiness to greater numbers of leaders and their people. The validity of this claim is supported by Functional MRI illustrating the effects this integration has on the brain as does pioneer work in the new field named interpersonal neurobiology (Siegel, 2012).

Recent research from Marie Taryn Stejskal, Chief Resilience Officer at the Resilience Leadership Institute, who served as the Head of Executive Leadership Development and Talent Strategy at Nike and Head of global Leadership Development at Cigna also supports such advances. Considered an international expert on resilience, mental health and wellbeing in leadership and life, I interviewed her specifically for her up to date perspective on leadership, resilience as it may apply to healthcare for this Chapter.

With expert interviews on resilience, our work on emotional brilliance, and combined experiences across healthcare this chapter explores methods on how to create that delicate balance between self-awareness, self-care, and resilience across any industry, but specifically in the highly personal delivery of healthcare. This process has, as its end goal, the creation of happiness and satisfaction; both measured in terms of awareness and attention management and a genuine well-being with a "bounce forward" mindset. While greater wealth or influence may result, these are by-products of the conscientious lifestyle we advocate for healthcare providers. More central than these externalities, are the internal personal transformations such as self-compassion and self-forgiveness – both of which lead to greater fulfillment that results in peak performance from an increased inner-resilience in the workplace and at home. To master the human needs of self-awareness for resilience we need one more piece of the formula for success: Attentional deployment with a positive mindset.

a   Conscious attentional deployment

In a major review of 128 studies on positive interventions looking at emotional regulation strategies, attentional deployment before, during and after an event revealed strong empirical support for it being at the center of many positive interventions (Quoidbach et al., 2015). These researchers define attentional deployment as "the way we direct our attention within a situation can powerfully influence our emotional experience."

In support of this attentional deployment hypothesis is Robert Cialdini, PhD., author of the classic book *Influence: The Psychology of Persuasion*. In his subsequent book, *Pre-Suasion: A Revolutionary Way to Influence and Persuade*, he outlines the importance of pre-framing or priming in a conscious manner. Cialdini states that, "Channeled attention leads to pre-suasion: the human tendency to assign undue levels of importance to an idea as soon as one's attention is turned to it." (Cialdini, 2016).

Additionally, we have adapted some constructive pre-suasion strategies in our own work titled *Emotional Brilliance: Living A Stress Less, Fear Less Life* that were originally developed by Sonya Lyubomirsky, PhD (Lyubo-mirsky, 2013) such as:

- Starting the day with gratitude using a dedicated focus on what's good in your life.
- Contemplating how you can grow from all situations, even unfortunate ones. ("bounce forward" rather than "bounce back").
- Mitigating negative self-talk by deliberately limiting the time allowed for it (a mindful approach to learning self-care through self-awareness by practicing compassion for "being on your side rather than being on your case").
- Recognizing your "go to" emotions for "emotional brilliance" using:

    - *NAME* as a coaching model: (Greenberg and Nadler, 2020): Notice and declare or name your emotions; Accept your emotions – allow them to pass through you; Manage your emotions in the moment as they arise for better expression as appropriate; Express your emotions in balance with your desired outcomes using the emotional audit:
    - What am I thinking? What am I feeling? What do I want as a result of this interaction?
    - What am I doing that is getting in my way?

Attention management thus facilitates a path toward happiness and satisfaction across leadership behaviors. *Attention mismanagement* can lead to unhappiness and dissatisfaction which can lead to physical symptoms euphemistically referred to as "pain in the brain." Furthermore, Naomi I. Eisenberger, PhD suggests that there may be an "overlap in the neural circuitry underlying experiences of physical pain and 'social pain' – the painful feelings following social rejection or social loss" (Eisenberger, 2012). However, usually with physical pain individuals mediate it, for example by resting the injured body part. But with social or emotional pain, individuals often engage in self-beratement, self-punishment and a general lack of self-compassion, among other unhealthy coping mechanisms. This mismanagement of attention then is in effect re-injuring. Additionally, the way an individual soothes or agitates their emotional pain shares similarities with how they cope with their physical pain. Thus, by increasing self-awareness of overall painful experiences, individuals can advance their ability to apply conscious attention to grieving, healing, and resurrecting.

In both cases, the neurological overlap and the coping responses, the often-cyclical nature of many unconscious behaviors is revealed. Furthermore, studies also reveal that through reframing, individuals can shift from experiencing a situation as negative to one being viewed as positive – or at least from the negative to a point of acceptance where pain is mitigated (Butler et al., 2006). The natural tendency to avoid this emotional pain triggers defense mechanisms, some of which are associated with theories on an individual's awareness of rational and irrational choices (Tversky & Kahneman, 1986) as well as theories on reframing negative experiences to be viewed more positively (Zettle, 2005). In regard to chronic physical pain such as from backaches, degenerative diseases and arthritis, advances in the treatment of these conditions include similar techniques as those applied to emotional pain. Guided imagery, positive self-talk, and self-compassion all play vital roles in helping patients cope (Turk et al., 2008).

According to the American Academy of Pain Medicine, an estimated 100 million Americans suffer from chronic pain. Thus, there is a great opportunity to apply this model of conscious attention management to bring relief, and in turn, greater degrees of happiness and satisfaction.

The following illustrates feedback "loops"; one constructive through attention management and the other harmful through attention mismanagement. It provides an opportunity for coaching intervention to help change and shift the focus along each step of those loops.

The first loop: Attention Management Loop. Five steps in that loop:

Attention management-conscious and positive-self compassion-gratitude-happiness and satisfied... and that loops back into attention management.

The second loop: Attention Mismanagement Loop. Five steps into that loop:

Attention mismanagement-Unconscious and negative-self-critical-pain in the brain-unhappy and dissatisfied... and that loops back into attention mismanagement.

The Happiness Focus

This concept of attention management has found further support from Greenberg's own research beginning with that conducted on behalf of the Institute for Strategic Change (Robertson & Greenberg-Walt, 1998–2003). A result of this longitudinal study was the determination that "personal mastery," or understanding oneself, was essential for effective leadership. Other key leadership behaviors identified included technological savvy, embracing diversity of style and a networked approach to leadership. (Goldsmith et al., 2003) An outgrowth of that study was an extensive synthesis of original and existing research from behavioral sciences, anthropology, neuroscience, leadership development and positive psychology including the subsets of emotional and social intelligence, to reveal an emergence of three themes: Personal Mastery, Happiness Traps, and Happiness Tips (Baker, et al., 2006). In total, this year-long research conducted across four continents, with two generations of leaders and future leaders – representatives from two generations; Group 1: leaders in the succession plan within a 2 to 5 year period and Group 2: leaders in the succession plan within a 5 to 10 year period – from a range of industries established a baseline for the application of personal mastery and to date is still the most comprehensive research on the subject.

These findings later were included in research conducted across the top Fortune 100 Companies which resulted in the H.A.P.I.E. model – **H**eartfelt, **A**daptive, **P**rofit with People, **I**nnovate, **E**ngage Community Partners, as well as proved instrumental in forming foundations for iterations directed at the educated layperson such as popular literature on emotional and social intelligence in a number of bestselling books including *FOCUS* by Daniel Goleman, and *What Got You Here Won't Get You There, MOJO, and Triggers* by Marshall Goldsmith, among others. The research is also utilized broadly across studies on attention management and mindfulness. We apply these findings in our own present-day work with our clients/patients toward attention management, increased productivity, leadership development, satisfaction, and happiness.

Based on the original formula for happiness as defined by psychologist Daniel Gilbert – frequent positive feelings accompanied by an overall sense that one's life has meaning – 50 % of happiness is genetically postulated with the remaining 50 % broken into two key elements as follows: 40 % focused on our individual habits of mind and body while 10 % remained outside of our immediate control such as mortgage rates, taxes, and cures for the common cold (Gilbert, 2007).

Happiness is therefore deemed to have a *set point* in a similar way that each person has a foundational level of intelligence, and by all indications this set point can be enhanced through deliberate and supportive constructs including reciting positive affirmations, talking about feelings, expressing gratitude, giving of oneself through compassion and kindness, and adopting behaviors that reduce anxiety. (Brickman et al., 1978). Expressions of gratitude are particularly fertile areas of study today in relation to happiness theory development (Krakauer, 2017). These practices and others focused on growing happiness have been shown to have a direct correlation to an overall sense of wellbeing. (Easterlin, 2005). Further research evaluates L. W. Sumner's views on an individual's sense of wellness being tied to their authentic autonomous self, as opposed to the inauthenticity one experiences when feeling manipulated and controlled, with authentic happiness. (Habron, 2008).

Thus, when awareness about happiness is understood to be influenced largely by individual choices, those variables can be incorporated into daily practices for sustained happiness and wellbeing. Yet, when those choices are ignored or withheld, happiness and its influence on wellbeing can become diminished thereby setting up a domino effect through which overall life satisfaction can decrease as well (Kushlev et al., 2017).

Therefore, focus and deliberate action become an important component of happiness. This conclusion is at the core of the ground swelling present day interest in mindfulness as an outgrowth of pioneering work by Jon Kabat-Zinn, PhD; in particular his founding of mindfulness-based stress reduction (MBSR). Mindfulness, as a separate and distinct science, adds yet another critical component to the science of happiness and overall life satisfaction (Carmody & Baer, 2008).

When individuals are focused on the present or on being in the moment, the ability to leverage that ever-important 40% of habits related to mind and body as defined by Gilbert becomes vital to our ability to remain optimistic and brave in the face of adversity and to consequently maintain ongoing feelings of happiness. This positive outlook is generally covered by the term "resilience" and refers to steadily recovering from the continual energy drains from daily challenges.

When resilience is coupled with courage and confidence individuals can more effectively engage in mindfulness to achieve a greater capacity for higher order thinking or consciousness (Greenberg & North, 2014). Further studies show that those with a higher level of overall happiness and satisfaction are also more resilient due to their propensity for a homeostatic system that supports wellbeing – this includes a readiness to circulate "feel good" neurotransmitters such as endorphins and dopamine (Cohn, 2008).

Taken in total, this homeostasis promotes both self-awareness to resolve subconscious barriers to happiness and satisfaction, as well as supports rapid behavioral changes to adapt to the demands of society and the realities of human limitations and vulnerabilities (Connor & Davidson, 2003; Taryn Marie Stejskal, 2023)

Happiness, mindfulness, and resilience have become *de rigueur* of popular psychology as evidenced by the currently available thousands of books, studies, workshops and more for both professionals as well as for lay people seeking a means to greater fulfillment. Yet, there is also a growing skepticism about some of the motivations behind the happiness movement – one weakness characterizes it as being fueled by behavioral economists and their big business underwriters seeking new ways to stimulate individuals to buy more of their products (Davies, 2015). Among these stimulants is the encouragement of a "keeping up with the Joneses" rat race that awards happiness only if you measure up favorably to others. This is a significant concern because it can adulterate the reception to well-intentioned findings such as those that show there are indeed economic factors at play. Namely, that individual personal transformations leading to more happiness and satisfaction are linked to higher performance levels in the workplace thus generating more opportunities for prosperity (Baker et al., 2007), along with how an individual spends their money – particularly through generosity that enhances the lives of others – fuels greater degrees of happiness and satisfaction (Dunn et al., 2011).

Return on Investment

The economic benefits of happiness are bolstering a societal movement toward income equality which can then help stabilize national economies (Schneider, 2016). Further research indicates that companies engaging in more employee happiness expenditures trend toward having a return on investment (ROI) to be as much as three times greater than companies which do not engage in more employee happiness expenditures. Other research suggests that happiness is tied to job satisfaction by as much as 93 % (Pryce-Jones, 2010). Additionally, a theory long-held to be central in philosophical teachings dating back to thousands of years ago (Plato, 380 BCE) is also making its way into modern day boardrooms: happiness creates success rather than the traditional thinking that success creates happiness – furthermore, happy employees engage more in organizational enterprises, are more productive and are viewed by supervisors as being more trustworthy than those who display unhappiness (Achor, 2010). Though happiness is typically thought of as an intangible, these findings reveal a measurable correlation with financial reward.

Being on Your Side Versus Being on Your Case

Self-evaluations of happiness with our clients as the test population, including self-evaluations correlating to financial reward, reveal that more than half of these individuals demonstrate unreliable self-evaluations. And this is not just in one or two instances per individual. It is instead a pervasive, rigid pattern. Specifically, they most often rate themselves as having performed unsatisfactorily even when they have been quantifiably measured to have been successful. This may be linked to what is termed "the impostor syndrome" because individuals fear they will be discovered as incompetent and thus may push themselves mercilessly to establish their own sense of competency, as well as it may be linked to these individuals identifying themselves as feeling low in confidence because of unrealistic expectations and hyper self-criticism. This syndrome is pervasive and present, more often than expressed, in the healthcare industry, regardless of the specialty. However, the more the specialty demands perfectionism, say surgery for example, the more the prevalence. It is also found more among females and the younger practitioners. (Medline et al., 2022).

Yet, many of our clients view this distorted impression as a positive as they claim their self-criticalness motivates them to drive for greater success. Oftentimes, however, these same individuals acknowledge an equally harmful result because their self-criticalness can lead to feelings of torturing themselves and eventually this "motivator" becomes burdensome, even disruptive, as they continually try harder only to fall short in their own eyes. They scold themselves for failing to live up to their abilities. One client described it as: "I take out the whip and start whipping myself into shape." *How could I be so stupid? When am I going to finally learn? What is wrong with me?* For them, a better effort, a larger result, a faster delivery is a panacea where nothing will be good enough to earn their self-praise. Adding insult to injury is operating in a world where praise is rarely given, as the expectation is that one should be perfect, and frequently, the feedback that physicians receive is mostly negative. The words, "hey, remember that patient..." illicit feelings of angst and despair. There is a constant review of physicians' work with scrutiny and reprimanding or advising as the usual outcomes. Physicians have peer review rounds and morbidity, and mortality rounds not to celebrate their success, but to magnify or highlight the failures.

These individuals readily admit they are hard on themselves. However, for many "the stick" rather than "the carrot" has given them their best performance and so they are reluctant, in their view, to "fix what isn't broken." Yet, to the observant eye, their system is indeed in need of repair. Specifically, we observe three major unintended consequences of this behavior:

- Damaged self-esteem associated with a lack of empathy for themselves.
- Pervasive tension, unhappiness, and a deepening sense of disappointment.
- Unconscious harsh treatment of others similarly to how they treat themselves.

We have found that breaking through to such individuals requires a coaching process that applies the same direct, strong communications, as well as engaging them in the habitual type of critical thinking, risk versus reward assessment, and data analysis that they apply in pushing themselves to greater heights. We simply advocate tuning up their lack of empathy for themselves by a counter measure that balances their overly pessimistic, or negative view, to one focused on the education and knowledge as a result of their effort. This mindfulness on their effort over accomplishment and ego can then be applied in their future endeavors.

An approach that we have frequently used, successfully, is known as "being on your side versus being on your case." Confidence is the trust in oneself and one's abilities and is the core of reaching one's potential. To build one's confidence, it is important for physicians, or anyone, to be on their side, not on their case. On their case means they are overly critical, negative, and rarely satisfied with their performance. On their side means they are more patient, rationale, realistic, and encourage learning from their mistakes rather than browbeating themselves in the process. To become more adept at being on their side it is vital to focus on the experience and what was gained or discovered from the time invested over continuing to internally beat themselves up.

The neurological component to this approach is illustrated in the research findings from Long, O. et al.:

> Self-criticism was associated with activity in lateral prefrontal cortex (PFC) regions and dorsal anterior cingulate (dAC), therefore linking self-critical thinking to error processing and resolution, and also behavioral inhibition. Self-reassurance was associated with left temporal pole and insula activation, suggesting that efforts to be self-reassuring engage similar regions to expressing compassion and empathy towards others. Additionally, we found a dorsal/ventral PFC divide between an individual's tendency to be self-critical or self-reassuring.

Resilience Tools to Encourage Being on Your Side

In light of these findings on the dominating roles of self-criticism and its opposite, self-compassion, a variety of evaluative assessments can be administered to bring more clarity to an individual's behavioral patterns in regard to happiness. Among the most recognizable of these tools are The Positive and Negative Affect Scale (PANAS), Oxford Happiness Inventory, Subjective Happiness Scale, and Satisfaction with Life Scale. Along with those are subdivision measurements including the Fordyce Emotions Questionnaire which measures current happiness and the Subjective Happiness Scale which measures happiness relative to changing variables.

We have also developed our own tools to help individuals become more aware of their unconscious patterns of hyper self-critique, as well as hyper-vigilance in looking for errors. Through "redirection" in particular, or often referred to as reframing, individuals can evolve to being more compassionate toward themselves and others. An important part of the coaching plan is to track, on a weekly basis, the amount of time they spend being on their case as well as the time they spend curtailing that behavior and redirecting their self-talk to being on their side.

We have determined anecdotally from our own work that the most effective way to change from "being on your case" to "being on your side" is first take notice of and then nonjudgmentally observe the self-disparaging, which we refer to as whipping, and next turn that awareness into a constructive action plan. This observant-self theory is supported by extensive scholarly research most often based on the benefits of mindfulness (Rolnick, 2016) as well as through more accessible popular books directed toward the educated layperson such as *Super Brain: Unleashing the Explosive Power of Your Mind to Maximize Health, Happiness, and Spiritual Well-Being* by Rudolph Tanzi, PhD and Deepak Chopra, MD (Harmony, 2012). Below are some examples of whipping statements and redirecting statements.

a   On Your Case Whipping:

- How could I be so dumb?
- Don't I know better than this?
- I'm an idiot for doing that!
- Why didn't I start this sooner?
- I could have done a much better job!
- What's wrong with me?
- I should have known better!

b   On Your Side Redirection:

- Which parts of this performance went well?
- What didn't turn out the way I wanted?
- Is there anything I could have done differently?
- What will I have to do to accept this performance and not beat myself up?
- What can I learn from this performance?
- Is there any learning, training or help I need to improve my performance?
- What is my next step?

The redirecting statements are designed to elicit a tempered, thoughtful review that is compatible with the redirecting process of first acknowledging and then validating what went well. It's a way to build a healthier overall self-evaluation process and thus disrupt the "more, better, faster" whipping pattern.

Below is a chart that identifies key words in defining the differences between "being on your case" and "being on your side."

	On Your Case	*On Your Side*
Quality	Demanding	Respectful
	Damaging	Constructive
	Irrational	Rational
	Overgeneralized	Realistic
Results	Dissatisfied	Encouraged
	Less confident	Action plan for future
	Overwhelmed	Energized

Our strategies refer to this chart in further probing our clients and patients for additional insight. Examples of these probes include:

- Circle the terms you experienced because of your self-evaluation.
- How accurate do you believe your self-evaluation is?
- What %age of the time are you on your case on a scale of 1–100?
- How do you feel after you've been on your case?
- What are the consequences for you and others for "being on your case?"
- Do you treat others as harshly as yourself?
- Is "being on your case" an effective pattern for you to continue with?
- If you don't change this, what do you lose out on?
- Are you keeping track of the times you've stopped being on your case and in-stead redirected to being on your side?
- What is most difficult about being on your side?
- What helps you to "be on your side?"
- Keep track of what %age of the time you are on your side each day using a scale of 1–100.

Case Study: Medical-Healthcare Executive Dr. E.

Dr. E. was an executive in a healthcare system. She constantly fell behind in everything she did: emails went unanswered, voicemails were not returned, one-on-ones with staff were downgraded from being important to being inconvenient. She was harsh on herself and unforgiving despite many of the positive things that she had been initiating since she arrived in this position almost three years ago. So instead of feeling confident and projecting confidence, she often opened conversations at the office apologizing for something she had not gotten to and for not having done more to help, or taking blame for what was really another person's responsibility, or dwelling on what was so small it did not merit her added attention. But it was not just her own confidence that was affected. Her negative self-evaluations started to influence her co-workers too: *perhaps she wasn't as competent as they had thought when she was hired?*

In a session with her Coach, Dr. E. became aware that she had apologized three times within thirty minutes and was overly critical of herself. This led to further awareness of both how automatic her self-evaluation belief system was and that it was also likely an unreliable one. She became aware too of how pervasive this pattern was in all her daily interactions – with family, friends, patients, and even casual encounters – and how it undermined her instinctive drive for a meaningful life.

When asked, Dr. E. started out saying that she was on her case about 80 % of the time. Through awareness and ongoing mindful assessment, and an action plan with an executive coach, Dr. E. was able to reduce that number to about 40 % on her own case, while positively increasing being on her side 60 % within six months.

Though this was still challenging, Dr. E.'s progress taught her that while she could not altogether eliminate being on her own case, because self-sabotage is a human characteristic, she could still bring herself to a higher level of functioning at work and in her personal life. The objective of her plan was for her to mindfully become aware of triggers and harmful automatic responses, then redirect and reframe those responses to being more on her side over time. As a result of showing herself compassion and empathy, she also became less demanding of her staff, and more on their side.

This included helping them be more realistic about their own limitations which further highlighted a need for their own positive mindset and self-talk for better self-care. This also resulted in higher levels of overall life satisfaction and happiness for both Dr. E. and her associates. By the last session with her coach, Dr. E. had demonstrated that she was on her case about 30 % of the time, a substantial reduction from her 80 % at the outset, and she became more proficient at redirecting her attention to being more positively focused on her own side.

Further Strategies for Developing Happiness and Satisfaction

Through studies with our own clients, in particular using the tools associated with the "being on your case" versus "being on your side" behavioral model, as well as independent research, it is evident that the efficacy of self-evaluations can be clouded by culturally influenced biases, levels of self-esteem, and other emotional and psychological factors including shame, guilt, degrees of social support and fear of social ostracism (Zell, 2014).

Thus, during these periods of self-reflection, the questions themselves are as important as the answers they are intended to generate. Neutral, cogent questions devoid as much as possible of the self-contamination and unconscious predispositions as discussed yield a more accurate self-evaluation as does a deeply analytical approach to stating the goals that are hoped to be realized through these self-evaluations (Judge & Kammeyer-Mueller, 2011). Examples of these types of questions include:

- What goals would you be interested in working toward?
- What are your personal strengths?
- How could you build and broaden these strengths?
- How do you remain motivated?
- How do you reward yourself for doing well?

In more recent studies, the concept of PERMA, which steps through five elements essential to human flourishing: positive emotions, engagement, relationships, meaning, and achievement was introduced to help clients achieve "happiness". (Seligman, 2012) Coaching can utilize the concepts of PERMA. By asking questions to encourage and help increase the elements of PERMA, physicians' happiness and well-being, and with that, resilience, can markedly increase. The PERMA includes the psychosocial measures associated with a positive work environment for wellbeing in the workplace. Professor Martin Seligman, one of the world's leading researchers in positive psychology, suggested that we can cultivate personal wellbeing by ensuring PERMA in our lives through:

Positive Emotions – integrate and encompass hope, interest, joy, love, compassion, pride, amusement, and gratitude leading to improved thinking patterns, and a reduced impact of negative emotions in our daily lives. By increasing positive emotion, we can improve overall wellbeing by building the intellectual psychological and social resources to build our levels of resilience and create the conditions to thrive and flourish. How can we each build more positive emotions?

Spend more time with people we care about; do activities that we enjoy (hobbies or play); listen to uplifting, joyful, or inspirational music; reflect on things we are grateful for and what is going well in our daily lives.

Positive Engagement – Positive engagement or flow – the loss of self-consciousness and complete absorption in a focused activity. You are living in the present moment and focused entirely on the task in front of you. How can you build more positive engagement?

Participate in activities we really love, where we lose track of time when we do them; practice living in the moment, even during daily activities or mundane tasks; spend more time in nature, watching listening, and observing what happens around us.

Positive Relationships – Relationships encompass all the various interactions individuals have with partners, friends, family members, colleagues, mentors, supervisors, patients, and their community. It refers to feeling supported, loved, and valued by others. Some of the questions asked include:

How can you build more positive relationships? Positive, useful, and inspiring connections lead to more positive emotions enabling us to feel heard, seen and supported. How can you benefit from those relationships and increase them, enjoy them, and rely on them more?

Lastly, playing an active role within these relationships, by offering support, listening, and helping in return, will also lead to greater positive engagement. What are 2 or 3 steps the client can take to be an active participant?

Another approach to help with resilience is utilizing the concept of "Five Better Choices", developed by Dr. Stejskal. (Stejskal, 2023). By focusing on these five choices, the coach can help support the physicians through helping augment, magnify, or master each choice:

- **Vulnerability** – allowing inside selves to show outside – it's the cornerstone of resilience and empathy.
- **Productive perseverance** – pivoting in the face of lower returns.
- **Connection** – Knowing ourselves deeply to be able to connect intuition and navigating with others.
- **Graciosity** – combines gratitude and sharing the challenge generously.
- **Possibility** – navigating the paradox of risk of opportunity – but manage the inherent risks that emerge.

Resilience allows us to tell our story – but our story also creates vulnerability – because when we tell our story – we risk other's opinions or judgements of us. This may lead to not liking us, leaving us, or if we are able to evoke vulnerability in others through our genuine story, they may even love us. By starting with our resilience story, we can recall the steps we took that created our "bounce back" and reflect on how the lesson created a "bounce forward" with greater competence for autonomy and relatedness for achieving more as we focus on our purpose.

Conclusion

Results show that resilience is positively related to happiness, negatively related to stress, and moderates the relationship between mindfulness and happiness thus strengthening its role in deepening and inculcating how we experience happiness in all aspects of life. (Jan 10, 2022 www.frontiersin.org.articles). By becoming more resilient, physicians are automatically able to better manage all the things in their lives that create anxiety and stress. Being resilient doesn't prevent them from experiencing negative events: it helps them create a healthy mindset for coping with these events (www.forbes.co May 25th, 2023). The three C's of psychological resilience depend on levels of hardiness. Hardiness is how people interpret the world and make sense of their experiences within it. There are three components to an individual's hardiness: Challenge, Control, and Commitment (Ramos & Sharma, 2017).

The emergence of a distinct field of research into happiness and its counterpart resilience, is anticipated to progress as new studies reveal the neurobiological functioning behind emotions.

One of the most groundbreaking related discoveries is that the brain responds similarly to emotional pain as it does to physical pain. With physical pain, there are usually clear treatment protocols in place – take an aspirin, apply an icepack, undergo surgery, or other therapies as appropriate. With emotional pain though, the protocols have been less defined. A potential corollary to these findings involves research suggesting similarities in neural activity for both emotional pleasure and physical pleasure. Thus, a greater acceptance of, and subsequent application of evidence that supports self-awareness, self-expression, empathy, and other components of emotional intelligence offer hope for advances in understanding happiness and overall neuro-health.

Central to this scientific movement that builds on Goleman's emotional intelligence model is the value of "being on your side" versus "being on your case." The former can be arrived at first through self-awareness and then through cognitive reappraisals to redirect perspectives on misfortune and disappointment toward an outlook with a sense of greater wellbeing. In short, changing the narrative about the experience to the benefits of lessons learned in a full life despite the outcomes allows for a resilience effect, and bouncing forward. The alternative negative narrative is a cyclical pattern of "being on your case" that can self-injure and even self-traumatize with little to no readied resilience. True resilience results in learning experiences that enhance our human needs for autonomy, relatedness, competency, and purpose.

In terms of an enhanced quality of life, being kind, compassionate, and loving toward one's own self, or "being on your side," results in increased happiness as expressed through greater degrees of creativity, a stronger sense of closeness in relationships, better overall social skills, more readied resilience, sharper decision-making skills, and deeper stress tolerance levels.

References

Achor, S. (2010) *The Happiness Advantage: The seven principles of positive psychology that fuel success and performance at work.* Crown Business/Random House.

Baker, D., Greenberg, C.L., & Hemingway C. (2006) *What happy companies know: How the new science of happiness can change your company for the better.* Upper Saddle River, NJ: Pearson Education.

Baker, D., Greenberg, C.L., & Yalof, I. (2007) *What happy women know: How new findings in positive psychology can change women's lives for the better.* New York: Rodale Books.

Brickman, P., Coates, D., & Janoff-Bulman, R. (1978) Lottery winners and accident victims: Is happiness relative? *Journal of Personality and Social Psychology.* 36 (8):917–927.

Butler, A.C., Chapman, J.E., Forman, E.M., Beck, A.T. (2006) The empirical status of cognitive-behavioral therapy: a review of meta-analyses. *Clinical Psychological Review.* 26(1):17–31. doi:10.1016/j.cpr.2005.07.003. Epub 2005 Sep 30. PMID: 16199119.

Carmody, J., Baer, R.A. (2008) Relationships between mindfulness practice and levels of mindfulness, medical and psychological symptoms and well-being in a mindfulness-based stress reduction program. *Journal of Behavioral Medicine.* 31 (1):23–33. doi:10.1007/s10865-007-9130-7. Epub 2007 Sep 25. PMID: 17899351.

Cialdini, R. (2016) *Pre-suasion: A revolutionary way to influence and persuade.* New York: Simon & Schuster.

Connor K.M., Davidson J.R. (2003) Development of a new resilience scale: the Connor-Davidson Resilience Scale (CD-RISC). *Depression & Anxiety.* 18(2):76–82. doi:10.1002/da.10113. PMID: 12964174.

Cohn, M.A., Fredrickson, B.L., Brown, S.L., Mikels, J.A., Conway, A.M. (2009) Happiness unpacked: positive emotions increase life satisfaction by building resilience. *Emotion.* 361–368. doi:10.1037/a0015952. PMID: 19485613; PMCID: PMC3126102.

Csikszentmihalyi, M. (1990) *Flow: The psychology of optimal experience.* New York: HarperCollins.

Davies, W. *The happiness industry: How the government and big business sold us wellbeing.* New York: Verso.

Dunn E.W., Gilbert, D.T., & Wilson, T.D. (2011) If money doesn't make you happy, then you probably aren't spending it right. *Journal of consumer psychology.* 21(2):115–125.

Easterlin, R.A. (2005). Building a Better Theory of Well-Being, in Luigino Bruni, and Pier Luigi Porta (Eds), *Economics and Happiness, Framing the Analysis.* (Oxford, 2005; online edn, Oxford Academics, Feb 2006). doi:10.1093/0199286280.003.0002.

Eisenberger, N.I. (2012) The neural bases of social pain: evidence for shared representations with physical pain. *Psychosomatic Medicine.* 74(2):126–135. doi:10.1097/PSY.0b013e3182464dd1. Epub 2012 Jan 27. PMID: 22286852; PMCID: PMC3273616.

Eisenberger, N.I. (2015) Social pain and the brain: controversies, questions, and where to go from here. *Annual Review of Psychology.* 66:601–629. doi:10.1146/annurev-psych-010213-115146. Epub 2014 Sep 22. PMID: 25251482.

Ferguson, M.A., Nielsen, J.A., King, J.B., Dai, L., Giangrasso, D.M., Holman, R., Korenberg, J.R., Anderson, J.S. (2018) Reward, salience, and attentional networks are activated by religious experience in devout Mormons. *Social Neuroscience.* 13(1):104–116. doi:10.1080/17470919.2016.1257437. Epub 2016 Nov 29. PMID: 27834117; PMCID: PMC5478470.

Gilbert, D. (2007) *Stumbling on happiness.* New York: Knopf.

Goldsmith, M., Greenberg, C., Robertson, A., Hu-Chan, M. (2003) *Global leadership: The next generation*. New York: Pearson.

Goleman, D. (1995) *Emotional Intelligence*. New York: Bantam Books.

Goleman, D., Boyatzis, R. (2008) Social intelligence and the biology of leadership. *Harvard Business Review*. 86(9):74–81.

Greenberg, C.L. & North, T.C. (2014) *Fearless leaders: Sharpen your focus: How the new science of mindfulness can help you reclaim your confidence*. San Diego, CA: Waterfront.

Greenberg-Walt, C.L., Robertson, A.G. (2001) The evolving role of executive leadership. In W. Bennis, G.M. Spreitzer, T.G. Cummings (Eds.), *The Future of Leadership (P 139–157)*. San Francisco: Jossey Bass.

Greenberg, C., Nadler, R. (2020) *Emotional Brilliance: Living a stress less, fear less life*. Waterside Productions.

Haybron, D.M. (2008). Philosophy and the science of subjective well-being. In M. Eid & R.J. Larsen (Eds.), *The science of subjective well-being* (pp. 17–43). The Guilford Press.

Kahneman, D. (2011) *Thinking fast, and slow*. New York: Farrar, Straus and Giroux.

Krakauer, M., Ruscio, D., Froh, J., Bono, G. (2017) *Handbook of Australian school psychology: Integrating positive psychology and gratitude to work in schools* (pp. 691–706). Springer International Publishing, Gewerbestrasse, Switzerland.

Kushlev, K., Heintzelman, S., Lutes, L., Wirtz, D., Oishi, S., Diener, E. (2016) ENHANCE: Design and rationale of a randomized controlled trial for promoting enduring happiness & well-being. *Contemporary Clinical Trials*. 52. doi:10.1016/j.cct.2016.11.003.

Judge, T. A., Kammeyer-Mueller, J.D. (2011). Implications of core self-evaluations for a changing organizational context. *Human Resource Management Review*, 21(4):331–341. doi:10.1016/j.hrmr.2010.10.003.

Longe, O., Maratos, F.A., Gilbert, P., Evans, G., Volker, F., Rockliff, H., Rippon, G. (2010) Having a word with yourself: neural correlates of self-criticism and self-reassurance. *Neuroimage*. 49(2):1849–1856. doi:10.1016/j.neuroimage.2009.09.019. Epub 2009 Sep 18. PMID: 19770047.

Lyubomirsky, S. (2013) *The myths of happiness: What should make you happy but doesn't. what shouldn't make you happy but does*. New York: Penguin Press.

Martin, J.J., Byrd, B., Wooster, S., Kulik, N. (2017) Self Determination Theory: The role of the healthcare professional in promoting mindfulness and perceived competence. *Journal of Applied Behavioral Research*. 0(0):1–16.

Medline, A., Grissom, H., Guissé, N.F., Kravets, V., Hobson, S., Samora, J.B., Schenker, M. (2022) From Self-efficacy to Imposter Syndrome: The Intrapersonal Traits of Surgeons. *Journal of the Academic Orthopedic Surgeons: Global Research and Review*. 6(4):e22.00051. doi:10.5435/JAAOSGlobal-D-22-00051. PMID: 35412493; PMCID: PMC10566864.

Monti, D., Newber, A.B., Weil, A. (2018) *Behavioral Strategies for Happiness and Satisfaction* appeared as Chapter 6 in Integrative Psychiatry and Brain Health, 2nd Edition.

Neck, C. P., Houghton, J. D. (2006). Two decades of self-leadership theory and research: Past developments, present trends, and future possibilities. *Journal of Managerial Psychology*, 21(4):270–295.

Pryce-Jones, J. (2010). *Happiness at work: Maximizing your psychological capital for success*. Wiley Blackwell. doi:10.1002/9780470666845.

Quoidbach, J., Mikolajczak, M., Gross, J.J. (2015) Positive interventions: An emotion regulation perspective. *Psychological Bulletin*. 141(3):655–693. doi:10.1037/a0038648. Epub 2015 Jan 26. PMID: 25621978.

Ramos, J.A, Sharma, M. *Practical Stress Management: A Comprehensive Workbook*. Academic Press; 7th edition.

Rolnick, A., Oren, N.T., Bassett, D. (2016) Developing acceptance with the help of sensors-"Embracing the Me that I Can See". *Biofeedback*. 44(3):148–151.

Schnieder, S.M. (2016) Income inequality and subjective wellbeing: Trends, challenges, and research directions. *Journal of Happiness Studies*. 17:1719–1739.

Scoular, A., Scoular, I. (2019) The Leader as Coach. *Harvard Business Review*.

Seligman, M.E. (2012) *Flourish: A visionary new understanding of happiness and well-being*. Atria Paperback.

Seligman, M.E.P., Csikszentmihalyi, M. (2014). Positive Psychology: An Introduction. In: *Flow and the Foundations of Positive Psychology*. Springer, Dordrecht. doi:10.1007/978-94-017-9088-8_18.

Siegel, M.D. & Daniel J. (2012) *Pocket guide to interpersonal neurobiology. An integrative handbook of the mind*. (Norton series on interpersonal biology.) New York: W.W. Norton.

Stejskal, T.M. (2023) *The 5 Practices of Highly Resilient People: Why Some Flourish When Others Fold*. Hachette Go.

Turk, D.C., Swanson, K.S., Tunks, E.R. (2008) Psychological approaches in the treatment of chronic pain patients–when pills, scalpels, and needles are not enough. *Canadian journal of Psychiatry*. 53(4):213–223. doi:10.1177/070674370805300402. PMID: 18478824.

Tversky, A., & Kahneman, D. (1986). Rational Choice and the Framing of Decisions. *The Journal of Business*, 59(4):S251–S278. http://www.jstor.org/stable/2352759.

Tversky, A., Kahneman, D. (1992) Advances in prospect theory: Cumulative representation of uncertainty. *Journal of Risk Uncertainty*. 5:297–323. doi:10.1007/BF00122574.

Zell, E., Krizan, Z. (2014) Do People Have Insight into Their Abilities? A Meta-synthesis. *Perspectives on Psychological Science*. 9(2):111–125. doi:10.1177/1745691613518075. PMID: 26173249.

Zettle, R.D., Hocker, T.R., Mick, K.A., Scofield, B.E., Petersen, C.L., Song, H., & Sudarijanto, R.P. (2005). Differential strategies in coping with pain as a function of level of experiential avoidance. *The Psychological Record*, 55(4):511–524. doi:10.1007/BF03395524.

11 Truly Human-Centered Leadership

Coaching for Physician Leadership

Cathy Greenberg

Introduction and Literature Review

Physicians and healthcare workers are struggling. This crisis goes back years – even decades – but considerably worsened during the covid pandemic. In a 2015 study of nearly 7,000 doctors, 54% reported symptoms of burnout – a rate already roughly double that of the general population. That was pre-pandemic! Data published recently in the peer-reviewed journal Mayo Clinic Proceedings found that nearly two-thirds (63%) of physicians reported at least one symptom of burnout at the end of 2021 and the beginning of 2022. (Shanafelt et al., 2022). Only 30% felt satisfied with their work-life balance. (Miller, 2023 sixseconds.com). Leadership has been shown to be one of the control variables not just of burnout (Shanafelt et al., 2015), but of the overall health of the physician workforce and the healthcare industry.

There is more to focusing on the need for leadership among physicians than just burnout and their wellbeing. The literature has shown that the benefit of developing leadership skills among physicians include better patient outcomes, decreased mortality, increased financial rewards to the organization, decreased rates of burnout, healthier physicians, improved quality of care, and enhanced patient safety. (van de Riet et al., 2019; Rotenstein, Sadun & Jena, 2018; Satiani & Prakash, 2016).

To support and enable a more effective and balanced environment for physician leadership and growth and to complement the current needs of healthcare environments, this author proposes a "human-centered leadership approach" among the most effective leadership styles to advocate for physician coaching as a leadership model for success beyond 2024. A human-centered leadership approach (HCL) includes a focus on developing deep skills required for physician leaders as coach models to counterbalance the negative impacts of burnout and high emotional exhaustion-related consequences to close the gap between what exists and what is needed to be an inclusive, effective leader in today's clinical environments.

DOI: 10.4324/9781003452065-11

This chapter includes defining, highlighting, and developing essential leadership competency skills through coaching tools and awareness techniques to begin a journey toward developing *human-centered leadership* (HCL) strategies by applying *self-awareness and empathy for building psychological safety as a foundation among the eight domains outlined here. Human-centered leadership approaches are essential* in evolving organizational systems like *hybrid teams,* which require understanding the importance of modeling critical leadership attributes for *demonstrating vulnerability and self-care.* Combining these eight domains into 4 case studies for human-centered leadership (HCL) offers an opportunity for co-designing experiences by showcasing how to incorporate these eight domains for maximizing results. The case study examples here may support the evolving role of a physician as a human-centered leader (HCL) and a model coach in the process.

Key Concepts

- Leadership
- Coaching
- Human-Centered Leadership

Supporting Concepts

- GROW Model
- Hybrid Teams
- Coaching Tools

Introduction

On Becoming A Leader, initially published in 1989, is a timeless classic from a pioneer in leadership studies and, in this author's humble opinion, one of the only books you need to read on becoming an effective leader. Warren G. Bennis (WGB) (1925–2014) was a pioneer in leadership studies, a scholar who advised presidents and business executives alike on becoming successful leaders, and my mentor for almost two decades. Warren Bennis famously wrote in his book *On Becoming a Leader* that "a manager does things right, and leaders do the right thing."

He identified six personal qualities of effective leaders (referred to as influential leaders here) across industries: Integrity (Integrity means alignment of words and actions with inner values. You can find all six qualities of effective leaders in his book, Bennis,1989), dedication, magnanimity, humility, openness, and creativity.

While many of these concepts have remained on our leadership radar throughout the past decade and since his death, several unique leadership qualities have been on the rise, which Bennis would likely agree with.

Between the pandemic, inflation, political turmoil, and financial instability, employees and leaders are under immense pressure and related stress at work and home. For physicians, this is magnified by the increase in mental health issues that manifest in both their patient population and, to some extent, in their colleagues, primarily due to burnout. These issues impact regulations and policies that rely on risk avoidance rather than the underlying human-related need for remediation focused on stress tolerance that underscores human error.

The heightened levels of uncertainty and change through 2023 have given rise to the need for a different leadership style. While business-centered leadership and related competencies, such as strategic thinking and financial acumen, will always be cross-industry leadership essentials, the unique competency for *"human-centered"* leadership (HCL) skills is rising to the top of the list. Human-centered leadership is predicted to be one of the most essential leadership competencies in today's fast-paced, high-pressure cultures around the globe.

Considering the growing burnout rates for physicians, a human-centered approach to leadership, along with coaching strategies to support the exponential growth of these competencies, is paramount for sustaining physician resilience and well-being for leadership roles across healthcare providers. (Kennedy et al., 2021) Regardless of what you call *human-centered or employee-centered* leadership, according to author Josh Bersin, it refers to "Leaders who understand what makes people thrive, what drives creativity and problem-solving, and how to support people during times of change, stress, or disruption." (Bennet, 2022.)

Human-centered leadership is a powerful combination, especially in any healthcare environment, and essential for today's physician leaders. Below is a table by Niagara Institute on the distinctions between a typical existing workplace and a human-centered (or employee-centered) workplace. This model provides a foundation for a brief description of these leadership competencies and examples of how to coach them. While we could easily dedicate an entire text to this subject, due to the objective of this chapter on physician leadership, we'll offer a few coaching techniques to achieve a combination of these valuable leadership competencies in the context of a real-life case study.

Shame and Blame: People hide their errors in punitive environments

Healthcare providers are reluctant to report their errors in a system fraught with risk and blame that relies on tort law. Tort law is a civil wrong that causes a claimant to suffer loss or harm, resulting in financial liability for the person who commits the "tortious" act. Tort law differs from criminal law, which is punishable by the state through severe punitive actions such as jail time, loss of rights, and financial fines.

Such a major regulatory force has profound implications beyond the standard ethics for practicing medicine. One of the consequences of tort law as a significant regulatory force is that clinicians and healthcare delivery systems have become reluctant to report errors perpetuating risk levels and failing to integrate corrective feedback into the system. We often see the pervasive influence of legal implications across healthcare, significantly underscoring the foundations of a more controlling and directive *risk-averse leadership style* over time. This condition perpetuates shame and blame, where people hide their errors rather than become aware of when or how these errors may be more likely to occur. It's no surprise as humans endure "destress" (negative stress) over "eustress" (motivating stress), the incidence of error will likely increase without healthy opportunities for remediation built into the system as part of the feedback for peak performance over time.

Instead of focusing on the liability of human error, human-centered leadership, as a coaching model for physician success, can help rebalance medical cultures for a higher standard of care. Why? Greater Integrity through support systems allows awareness of and compassion for the self-reported remediation needs of physicians in high-risk environments. How? With a focus on the same empathy and self-awareness required for self-care in physicians, their teams, and support systems as they endeavor to apply to their patients.

Case Study Application

Our case study begins with my experience as a breast cancer patient starting in 2021 and ending in 2022. Fortunately, or unfortunately, my experience as a professional coach, leadership development consultant, and an actual member of the Western Regional Board of a Major Cancer Center opened my eyes to these issues firsthand. Having opened their doors in 1988, I was invited by their co-founders, CEO, COO, and President to attend their combined national board meeting, comprised of both senior leaders and board members across their existing regional hospitals (Illinois, Oklahoma, Pennsylvania, Arizona) as a leadership consultant. I joined the Western Regional Center board upon opening in 2008 and remained a regional board member until 2011, mentor, and coach until 2014 when they opened their Regional Center in Georgia. Unofficially, I remained a coach for various projects until they decided to relocate, and a certification partner for internal coaches on the use and application of emotional intelligence assessments until 2015.

Having been exposed to one of the most "human-centered" approaches to treating stage 3 stage 4 cancer patients between 2005–2015, receiving the advice and support of their breast cancer experts after my diagnosis in 2021 was a blessing.

I was honored to be invited as both a professional coach and an advisor to both senior and junior teams across the organization, providing an excellent coach and "participant-observer" experience. This unique window into the leadership styles of CEOs across several regional hospital facilities nationally and as a board member locally increased my under-standing, perspective, and confidence in the expertise of human-centered leadership as a coaching model long before its published acceptance as an accepted leadership practice. As a social scientist and professional coach, it was a firsthand scholarly view of how one of the most advanced and highest levels of patient care can be enabled and managed to successfully deliver a quality of life to terminally ill and vulnerable patients and their families. It was also a mesmerizing view of how unhealthy inter-collegial competition, unchecked egos, and the risk-averse blame, shame, and tra-ditional leadership style have no place in delivering innovative, integrative, and patient-centered care.

In this case, CEOs with a variety of fantastic track records in fields of medicine or related hospital industries were hired to implement a relatively new emerging "patient-centered" approach to cancer treatment, including a team of both traditional, alternative, and research physicians. They were required to combine medical experts with clinical strategies, including team collaboration from pharmaceutical, dietetic, and spiritual experts. This "integrated" approach was the cornerstone of a standard of care that idealized and customized patient care to include the caregiver and patient advocate community required for success. Many of these success stories were featured at the kickoff of every board meeting with a spotlight on the 3–5-year survivor's story, who, along with their families, added profound expressions of gratitude, where they each detailed the events that took them from utter despair to informed discovery and eventually to daily hope and grace for their condition and their loved ones.

Between 1990 and 2015, this was, by all accounts, the apparent beginnings of a truly "human-centered" (patient-centered) leadership approach for physicians treating a variety of cancers while consistently practicing across a nationally recognized spectrum of medical treatment in cancer care. It required an equally human-centered leadership (HCL) approach to the oversight, compassion, and administration needed for both the success of their patient population and, just as importantly, the success of their respective care associates (nurses and physicians), their hospital and business results, and their overall success as measured by quality of life, cancer remission or cure, and profitability.

While other examples of HCL have been published, this firsthand approach will provide some background for this chapter's case studies in applying the eight domains of a human-centered leadership approach (or the employee-centered model featured above).

These clinicians were hired to be highly team-centric and, therefore, would be more responsive to a culture that emphasizes safety and encourages learning over shaming. All medical specialty practices were often acquired and integrated into these regional systems with great care. These learning cultures replicated the work of similar facilities, with a focus on detecting and sharing errors, reflecting upon and understanding underlying causes, proactive involvement in professional life, and increased dedication to improving safety. (Hoff et al., 2003)

In such an ideal world, clinicians would speak openly about their mistakes. Senior staff would be viewed as role models, secure about reporting and learning from their errors. Asking for and receiving support would be encouraged and viewed as a strength rather than a weakness. Safety cultures would be strongly endorsed by top-down organizational policies and promoted by leaders as best practices. These are just a few positive outcomes of a human-centered leadership approach. The Niagara institute shared some of their outcomes where they would shift toward an employee-centric workplace by creating the following changes, and I quote:

- From oversight and process to empowerment and trust
- From telling to inspiring
- From department focus and silos to internal and external collaboration
- From employment to belonging
- From scheduled learning to agile learning and intellectual curiosity
- From financials to purpose
- From formality and hierarchy to genuine connections and empathy
- From employees to people
- From fear of failure to creativity, resilience, and growth
- From location-based best for the company to work from anywhere best for the individual

What do these human-centered leadership competencies look like? Here are the eight trial leadership competencies supervisors, managers, and senior leaders need to motivate, inspire, and connect with their people. (Bennett, 2023)

- Inspirational leadership communication. (Covery, 2022)
- Creating psychological safety (www.mckinsey.com)
- Fostering connections and trusting relationships (https://hbr.org/2019/02/the-3-elements-of-trust)
- Coaching and developing employees. (Greenberg & Nadler, 2020)
- Granting autonomy through delegation and accountability
- Adopting a growth mindset
- Being resilient and courageous (Greenberg & North, 2014)
- Demonstrating self-awareness (Nadler, 2011)

The following outlines three of these eight competencies for effective Physician Leadership now and into the future through coaching strategies to support them. (Adapted from https://www.niagarainstitute.com/blog/p sychological-safety-at-work)

Inspirational leadership communication

When everything seems in flux, employees need to leverage inspirational leadership communication where leaders bring purpose to work, reiterate the vision, and mobilize individuals to move past the chaos to take action. Developing competencies in storytelling and delivering inspiring and clear messages should be a central focus in 2023.

Creating psychological safety.

Unfortunately, psychological safety is still a work in progress for many. In 2022, 61 % of leaders with diversity-related titles said they were only "somewhat confident" that their employees felt a sense of belonging, inclusion, and psychological safety at work, while another 24% said they were "somewhat unconfident." (Trailent/www.WBR.org Research, 2023). Meanwhile, in a separate study by Ipsos, less than half /(45%) of American respondents said they felt safe sharing their opinions or thoughts in the workplace for fear of negative consequences. (https://prnewswire.com/news-releases/new-survey-that-nearly-half-of-american-workers-are-conside ring-leaving-their-current-place-of-employment-301466289.html.)

Amy Edmondson, a pioneer of psychological safety, defines it as "a belief that one will not be punished or humiliated for speaking up with ideas, questions, concerns or mistakes and that the team is safe for inter-personal risk-taking." Psychological safety within a team translates to groups who embrace change, are more creative and innovative, find solutions quickly, appreciate diversity, and accept unique perspectives. These are qualities we all benefit from.

However, despite the importance of psychological safety, a 2021 McKinsey Global Survey found that only a handful of leaders demonstrate the behaviors needed to create this environment. Undoubtedly, these concepts are quickly evolving with a focus on inspiring Physicians here.

Some good news: there appears to be a direct correlation between investing in leadership competency development and psychological safety. Employees who agree that their company invests in leadership development tend to agree that their team leaders frequently adopt consultative, supportive, and related leadership styles for better and safer "human-centered" approaches for peak performance. Moreover, those leaders are 64% more likely to be rated as inclusive by their employees, making the case even stronger for developing this key leadership competency in 2024 and beyond.

When coaching for "psychological safety," we want to emphasize the environment we need to create.

Fostering connections and trusting relationships

Creating connections and building trusting relationships with employees should be a major goal for all leaders. For example, a 2022 study by Zenger and Folkman, revealed: "When we analyzed data from more than 113,000 leaders to find the top behavior that helps effective leaders balance results with their concern for team members, the number one behavior that helped was Trust. When direct reports trusted their leader, they also assumed that the manager cared about them and was concerned about their well-being." (https://hbr.org/2022/08/quiet-quitting-is-about-bad-bosses-not-bad-employees).

What can leaders do to inspire others, build connections, and communicate Trust? Another article by Zenger and Folkman, in 2019, looked at this by analyzing over 87,000 360-degree reviews of leaders. As a result, they uncovered three commonalities of the behaviors and competencies of leaders genuinely trusted by their direct reports. (https://hbr.org/2019/02/the-3-elements-of-trust).

a   **Trust** was directly correlated to how leaders could foster connections and positive relationships with their people. The leaders with the highest levels of Trust had the skills and competencies to balance results with caring for the well-being of their direct reports, frequently touching base on employees' issues and concerns, promoting collaboration and cooperation, and resolving conflict.

b   **Sound judgment and expertise** followed leaders who generated high levels of Trust with their people. In practice, people perceive these leaders as good decision-makers. Associates seek out their ideas and opinions as thought leaders due to their depth of knowledge or expertise and, just as necessary, because they respond quickly to reported problems, translating Trust into sound judgment.

c   **Leading by example** and doing what they say they will do were leadership behaviors that employees rated among the highest. These leaders are seen to be role models who set a good example at work where their actions speak louder than their words, keeping their commitments and delivering on promises. They're willing to get their hands dirty or go above and beyond for others. Too many people have personal experience with a leader who says one thing but then does another. Someone who doesn't walk the talk or practice what they preach. This is one of the most frustrating workplace experiences anyone can have because it goes against what employees need, want, and expect from their leader. According to one survey of 500 American employees, it was found that: (Sesco Management Consultant)

- 90% say they want **honesty and Integrity.**
- 89% want **fairness** and to hold all employees accountable to the same standards.
- More than 86% want to **trust** and be trusted.
- 84% want to **respect** and be respected.
- 81% say they want **dependability** in those who lead or manage.

These leadership behaviors combined result in "human-centered" approaches to managing others in the workplace. They can translate to physicians through greater self-awareness, self-care, and empathy during uncertainty or stress. Here are a few tools and techniques to get started.

While a physician leadership candidate may not have all eight competencies for effective "human-centered" leadership in healthcare, we can acquire these competencies through coaching and assessment for these traits to leverage during the development of new competencies.

As Warren G. Bennis (WGB) once said: *"Effective leaders make a full commitment to be a learner, to keep increasing and nourishing their knowledge and wisdom."* I've shared some of his most famous leadership quotes to inspire your "inner leader" throughout this chapter on coaching for leadership.

- Visionary Leadership
- Bureaucratic Leadership
- Directing Leadership
- Paternal & Maternal Leaders
- Situational Leadership
- Participative Leadership
- Transformational Leader
- Transactional Leader
- Servant Leadership
- Autocratic Leadership
- Hands Off Leadership
- Democratic Leadership
- Coaching Leadership
- Strategic Leadership
- Laissez-Faire Leadership
- Charismatic Leadership
- Pacesetter Leadership

While I've provided this reference to the 17 models of Leadership Style to create awareness on this broad subject, our focus here is on improving physician leadership through coaching to the values inherent in a human-centered approach to leadership (HCL). Aspects of HCL may also be found in other leadership models, such as emotional intelligence; behaviors like empathy and impulse control for interpersonal and strategic skills; trust, and insight for decision-making. The HCL approach to physician leadership complements patient-centered approaches to medical treatment and patient-empowered care.

As you review the HCL case examples, remember that I have combined the eight domains of HCL into a smaller number of helpful coach approaches to achieve the same outcome. This should not preclude your review of these respective HCL domains for independent application as appropriate for a wide array of situations where all domains of the 8 HCL may be applicable. This is also true for a comprehensive review of the 17 Leadership Styles. While we don't have time to cover all these 17 styles in this chapter, we encourage your curiosity to ask questions that may help you better understand how or when to apply these styles for physicians over the evolution of their career as both leaders and team members supporting others.

Throughout any career, but especially in healthcare, we must learn to become flexible in applying leadership styles to address both the dynamic needs of the patient, the supporting staff and structures for their care, and the administration of the system in which we operate.

Professionals like physicians will experience and apply an array of leadership styles based on the tenure of their role, the familiarity with their environment, support staff, peers, specialists, and residents and interns operating within the organization or system they may be responsible for.

The 8 Domains for HCL have been combined in the case studies here based on my experiences and the experiences of the physicians interviewed. Together, they demonstrate powerful positive approaches to improving performance and are very useful as a complement to each other for success in the pairs outlined.

- Inspiring Communications and fostering Trust (with Integrity)
- Psychological Safety & Granting Autonomy and Delegating Accountability
- Adopting A Growth Mindset & Coaching and Developing Employees
- Being Resilient and Courageous and demonstrating Self-awareness.

Our case begins with two of the most important domains for HCL or any leadership style in today's BANI (brittle, anxious, negative, inconceivable) environment:

a   Inspiring Communication and Inclusion.

During my tenure in this hospital setting, both regionally and at a corporate level, we hired several experienced staff, including senior management, physicians, and support staff. I'll focus on the senior leadership roles I supported during my affiliation with this organization between 2005–2014. While Physicians were encouraged to operate in key leadership roles, their workload and research focus often exceeded capacity. However, we were highly impressed with several physicians who consistently performed above average with others and maintained excellent patient performance.

On closer examination, we noticed these physicians also performed better than their peers on overall patient satisfaction, peer reviews, and ratings from their subordinates. These physicians practiced inspiring, open, transparent, and inclusive communications regularly and more frequently than their peers. They invited 360 feedback and offered opportunities for observation from all team members on all patient matters regardless of expertise or tenure at the center. Whenever we met formally or informally, it was always refreshing to learn how much more effective they became because of the genuinely open communication and trusting collaboration on any subject as it applied to their patient's experience. After all, as a team approach was valued as the foundation for patient-centered care, so too was their focus on the entire team's responsibility for the success of an array of therapies and treatments for all types of patients. Therefore, regardless of their expertise, everyone was a valued contributor to the overall well-being of the patient and their family advocate.

This included an observation that many patients often suffered from loss of appetite due to treatments. Yet, there was good evidence that, as a team, they had a higher rate of success managing these issues when compared to other groups who did not apply the same communication strategies. Physician leaders who insisted that a smaller population of people were essentially the only people who needed to be informed or included in these patient-centered communications made a mistake that often led to critical care. They also recognized that "a one size fits all" approach to patient care was not only less effective but also provides less input to the patient's health. It also made the difference between a patient who would thrive after treatment and ultimately leave the hospital altogether.

In reflection, when coaching, try encouraging the physicians to use these three questions to determine who should be involved and how best to include them in their communications. This will help the physician determine who is on the team and needs to be involved:

- Who observes the patient in any 72 hours? (Include all patient caregivers, therapists, nurses, and technicians supporting those staff and attending family advocates.)
- Who needs the patient to help them through these times and between treatments? (All the above plus spiritual guidance, nutritional guidance, and related practitioners to their well-being such as alternative health professionals like acupuncturists or O.T.s)
- What does the patient love to eat or look forward to after treatment? (Ask all above, as they too may have some insight into a patient's life choices).

When leading a conversation about care for a team approach, always ask the questions to as broad a group as possible and remember other experts beyond medical experts may want to and need to be involved to make the difference for both the success of the treatment, the patient, and the delivery team. Too often, a physician leader who is not inclusive or supportive of various views may hinder progress throughout a patient's Journey. The greater the communication and the wider the relationships – the more likely we will find answers together.

a   The Case for Psychological Safety, Granting Autonomy, and Delegating Through Accountability (A formula for Trust with Integrity).

While many people treat these ideas as separate and independent from each other, new research suggests they are, in fact, interdependent (McQuaid & Williams, 2023). Psychological safety includes feeling like you can say something without feeling judged. It follows that trust and the ability of that trust to stand the test of time under any circumstance is a crucial factor underlying psychological safety. Granting autonomy and delegating through accountability provides a good structure for guiding and practicing steps for psychological security. This requires giving in to the idea of a central control of authority. The foundation for psychological safety is better once you adapt to a more flexible, distributed approach to managing results by creating autonomy with those who can own the accountability required for effective results. When supported by communication mechanisms such as teams' software (e.g., instant messaging for a group), it allows immediate sharing and access to information essential for reducing error while increasing team cohesion and patient results. Allowing everyone to exchange real-time information on behalf of the patient builds awareness of everyone's talents on the team. It demonstrates their autonomy in sharing, focusing on being accountable as a team member for the patient's benefit. This foundation is a critical step towards psychological safety, where everyone welcomes and embraces input, knowledge, experience, and collegial empathy for the patient's well-being. It also demonstrates the effectiveness of a patient-centered approach through teamwork.

Building on the case study above, when all team members are not only included but equally highly valued, the outcomes for both the patient and the team are maximized. It is extremely helpful when the physicians are coached to ask themselves these questions:

- Who needs to be included in group messaging to better acquire, understand, and integrate information requirements for effective patient treatment and cohesion of the team's approach to their care?

- What kind of information is essential, and how frequently should the team update the status of their contributions on behalf of the patient and the team?
- What software best suits the team to include viewable attachments such as charts and test results in photo and table format?
- How do I, as the leader, include others in these decisions?

a   Adopting A Growth Mindset & Coaching and Developing Employees

Carol Dwek's treatise on Growth Mindset has been adopted across every discipline as a principle for developing the capacity for new and different insights into all aspects of acquiring information for growth. This includes understanding a fixed mindset, a mindset with solid ideas that may be difficult to expand, or a growth mindset. A growth mindset usually allows for flexibility, adaptation to new ideas, or readily building on existing ones. When we combine the training and development of employees with coaching, we increase uptake by over 80%. As we examine our case study to include leveraging a growth mindset by using coaching and standard training and development for all team members in a human-centered leadership approach, we can expect even higher results with greater success outcomes for the patient. By educating the patient team to include the importance of distinguishing between growth or fixed mindset as a prerequisite with training and follow-up coaching, we increase the likelihood of success for everyone. We also provide a vehicle for a shared approach to growth through peer-to-peer coaching and developing accountability partners for continued team development and overall effectiveness of results beyond the existing team or patient focus. Through coaching, encourage the physician to ask these questions when thinking of the team:

- Based on the Growth Mindset Assessment provided, do you under-stand the difference between a fixed or growth mindset and how you have identified yourself?
- What measures must you take to increase your Growth Mindset or overcome your Fixed Mindset?
- How can you include this assessment to support these qualities in others?
- What steps can you take to promote these qualities as a leader in your team or organization?

a   Being Resilient and Courageous & Demonstrating Self Awareness

We expand on these ideas in Chapter 10. In summary, the first step is self-awareness to become a model for resilience and courage. We cre-ated the ARTE of Fearless Leading as a set of Principles to help anyone recognize and develop in our book, Fearless Leaders: Sharpen Your Focus (Greenberg and North, 2014). Use the model below and the worksheet provided to open the doors to the Fearless Leader in you. (we also suggest the use of an emotional intelligence assessment such as the EQI 2.0 as an excellent way to start any self-awareness journey in Relly Nadler's Chapter 5)

Act with inspiring courage.
Respond with resilience.
Think from a higher consciousness.
Engage with a mindset for success.

Once you have completed your Fearless Leader Assessment you may wish to apply the Team Assessment with your direct reports or network partners.

- Do you see how the ARTE of Fearless Leadership Principles can be applied in your environment and how it can create awareness in your team?
- Try this: STEP 1. When you take the Team Assessment, feel free to ask the group if they would like to share their answers in a working group session to help create more awareness for better group understanding and performance as a team.
- STEP 2. After taking the Fearless Individual and Team Assessments and comparing your findings, try retaking the assessments in about 30–60 days to see if there has been a change in the alignment of your answers.
- Check in again as a team and develop a team plan for applying the ARTE of Fearless Leadership Principles when interacting with all team members and supporting group-related members outside the unit.

a   Coaching Tool: Understanding Bias

Review this list of 5 Primary Biases to reveal how many biases you recognize may impact your decision-making or judgment. (neuroleadership. com)
Similarities: Is something like us or not like us?

a   Contributing biases:
b   Ingroup Bias – perceiving people who are like you more positively (examples: ethnicity, religion, age, gender, education, profession, socioeconomic.
c   Outgroup Bias – perceiving people who are different from you more negatively (for example, "We can't trust them; look where they grew up").

Experience: How do we see the world? We take our perceptions to be the objective truth.

Expedience: Is something easy or hard for you?

a   Contributing biases:
b   Belief bias: Relying on pre-existing beliefs.
c   Confirmation Bias – a tendency to look for information that is consistent with experiences or beliefs.
d   Availability Bias – a mental shortcut that relies on immediate examples that come to mind when evaluating a topic rather than going through all the information.
e   Anchoring Bias – a tendency to rely too much on the first piece of information or the first experience with that topic.

Distance: How do we relate to time and space?

a   Contributing biases:
b   Endowment effect – people tend to value items they own more highly than they would if they did not belong to them.
c   Affective forecasting – predicts how we will feel about future emotional events.
d   Temporal Discounting – a subjective reward loses its magnitude when delayed. We associate this with impulsivity because we would probably take $100 now rather than $150 in six months. (similar to "delayed gratification")

Safety: How do we process aversion to fear?

a   Contributing biases:
b   Loss Aversion – Making a risk-averse choice.
c   Framing Effect – Is it a gain or a loss rather than objective facts?
d   Sunk Cost – Having a hard time giving up on something once started.

Once you review these biases and how they may impact your decision making, you may begin to adjust them through self-awareness. According to HRO Today, a recent McKinsey study revealed that organizations with the most ethnically and culturally diverse boards were 40% more likely to have higher profits. (In contrast, low diversity across gender, culture, and ethnicity is 29% less likely to have above-average profitability). (hrotoday.com)

Coaching Tool: Emotional Audit for Connection and Interpersonal Effectiveness

• What am I thinking?
• What am I feeling?
• What do I want to have happen now?
• What am I doing that is getting in my way?

Coaching and Developing Employees

The snapshot of a human-centered leader is simply one who puts their employees first. Therefore, leaders who commit to employees by investing time and energy into coaching demonstrate their care and desire to put them first. In addition, in times of disruptive change that we're all facing, a leader who can coach their people through it is invaluable. (Reynolds, 2020)

Despite the need for leaders to be coaches, most leaders are not equipped with the competencies to do so. One study had leaders assess their coaching effectiveness, and then these assessments were paired against what their direct reports said. The results showed that 24% of leaders significantly overestimated their coaching abilities, rating themselves above average, while their people ranked them in the bottom third of the group. (Scoular, 2019)

To ensure all physician leaders are great coaches for their people, they need the opportunity to build their knowledge and skills to coach and develop all their people, which can be acquired through specialized training.

The GROW Model

One of the best ways to get better at *nondirective* is to try a dialogue using the GROW model, devised in the1980 by Sir John Whitmore and others. GROW involves four action steps, the first letters giving the model its name. It's easy to grasp conceptually but harder to practice than you might imagine because it requires training yourself to think in new ways about your role and value as a leader. (Whitmore, 1992)

Coaching Tool: The Four Action Steps for GROW

STEP 1. Goal

When discussing a topic with people you're coaching, establish exactly what they want to accomplish *right now*. Not what their goals are for the project, their job, or their role in the organization, but what they hope to get out of this exchange. People don't do this organically in most conversations and often need help. An excellent way to start is to ask, "What do you want when you walk out the door now?"

STEP 2. Reality

With the goal of your conversation established, ask questions rooted in *what, when, where,* and *who,* each of which forces people to come down out of the clouds and focus on specific facts. This makes the conversation real and constructive. You'll notice that we didn't include *why*. That's because asking why demands people explore reasons and motivations rather than facts. In doing that, it can carry overtones of judgment or trigger attempts at self-justification, both of which can be counterproductive.

During this stage, an excellent reality-focused question is, "What are the key things we need to know?" Attend carefully to how people respond. Are they missing something important? Are they talking about operational issues but forgetting the human side of the equation? Or the reverse? When you ask people to slow down and think this way, they often lose themselves in contemplation – and then a light comes on, and off they go, engaging with the problem on their own with new energy and a fresh perspective. This step is critical because it stops people from overlooking pertinent variables and leaping to conclusions. Your job here is to raise the right questions and get out of the way.

STEP 3. Options

When people come to you for coaching, they often feel stuck. "There's nothing I can do," they might tell you. Or "I have only one real option." Or "I'm torn between A and B."

At this point, your task is to help them think more broadly and deeply. To broaden the conversation, sometimes it's enough to ask something as simple as "If you had a magic wand, what would you do?" You'd be surprised how freeing many people find that question – and how quickly they start thinking in fresh, productive ways. Once they've broadened their perspective and discovered new options, your job is to prompt them to deepen their thinking, perhaps by encouraging them to explore the upside, the downside, and the risks of each option.

STEP 4. Will

This step also doesn't usually happen organically in conversations, so that most people will need help again. The action has two parts, each involving a different sense of the word *will*.

Part a.) In the first part, you ask, "What will you do?" This encourages people you're coaching to review the specific action plan that has emerged from your conversation. If the conversation has gone well, they'll have a clear sense of what that plan is. If they do not, you'll need to cycle back through the earlier steps of the GROW process and help them define how they'll attack the problem.

Part b.) The second part involves asking people about their will to act. "On a scale of one to 10," you might ask, "How likely is it that you will do this?" They're probably motivated enough to follow through if they respond with an eight or higher. If the answer is seven or less, they probably won't. In that case, you'll again need to cycle back through the earlier steps of the process to arrive at a solution they are more likely to act on.

Of course, workplace coaching usually takes place outside of formal coaching sessions. Most often, it happens in brief exchanges, when a manager might respond to a request for help by posing a single question, such as "What have you already thought of?" or "What matters here?" When more of those interactions occur – when you notice your managers growing increasingly inquisitive, asking good questions, and working from the premise that they don't have all the answers – you'll know you're on the right track.

Granting autonomy by delegating and accountability

At the root of the "hybrid workforce" is that all employees want autonomy and ownership over their work. A hybrid workforce comprises employees who work remotely and those who work from an office or central location. Gone are the days when they will accept a leader who uses a command-and-control leadership style. Today and beyond, human-centered leaders put their employee's needs first and develop competencies to lead in an environment that allows for greater flexibility and independence.

Building a flourishing environment that is both "self-directed" and "achievement-oriented" doesn't mean it's a free-for-all. Through delegation, assigning a project, task, or action, and applying accountability, holding someone responsible for their promise to deliver on their efforts is critical. Autonomy will not be successful without structure. What's measured gets results. You can't have independence and self-directed teamwork without accountability for the outcomes.

Therefore, building leadership attributes and competencies where leaders recognize what and how to delegate tasks and understand how to gain commitment for accountability from their team is essential for granting autonomy and leading.

Adopting a Growth Mindset

Leaders with a growth mindset can more readily adapt to change, which is critical in an environment of uncertainty. A growth mindset, simply put, is the belief that one can develop, learn, and grow. It is essential to embrace change and strive for continuous improvement. In addition, this mindset enables a leader to step up to increasing leadership and work through setbacks and obstacles, all of which are necessary for leading employees in 2023. There are multiple online tools to check for the kind of mindset one may have. It is a great tool that helps discover not only what type of mindset is someone's default, but for them to see how they use that mindset in certain scenarios. The opportunity for coaching is to help them understand how that particular mindset can be helpful (in which case, how do they do more), or harmful (how do they do less), and help them switch between the mindsets.

Being resilient and courageous

We took A DEEP dive into this in chapter 10. (briefly recapped here)

Employees want leaders who don't fold under pressure. They want to follow someone who can return stronger from setbacks (Stejskal, 2023), manage stress (NAME, Greenberg & Nadler, 2020), and resolve conflict with a positive edge. Despite the uncertainty, they need a courageous leader (Werner, 2023). Developing resilience and courage leadership competencies while navigating VUCA (volatility, uncertainty, complexity, and ambiguity) is a must beyond 2023.

Demonstrating self-awareness

Self-awareness is central to human-centered leadership and leading a team beyond 2023. These leaders understand their strengths and short-comings and understand authenticity is the key to everything they do. According to current trends in resilience (Stejskal, 2023) and designing transformative experiences for leaders (McClain, 2023), there are three central tenets to human-centered leadership models.

Empathy. Leaders who are self-aware of their biases and privileges enable them to listen and demonstrate compassion for others' perspectives and circumstances. They can show care and concern for people and understand life can get in the way. They demonstrate flexibility in their interpersonal relationships with both patients and colleagues.

Vulnerability. Self-aware leaders do not fear being vulnerable in front of their people. They take the time to self-reflect on their leadership, admit when they're wrong, and regularly seek feedback from their team. While they may share their decisions as "patient-centered care," they believe in "empowered patient care" and are willing to share decisions in uncertain times for the patients and the facility's best outcome. They were always balancing what was suitable for all impacted.

Humility. Humility and a growth mindset must go hand in hand. When leaders are self-aware of their knowledge and skills, they will gladly assume there is more to learn. Therefore, these leaders prioritize their development and encourage their people to do the same. They offer this growth mindset to their patients, encouraging curiosity for understanding and insight for their patients and colleagues. (Brene Brown, www.happify.com)

a   **Coaching Tool**: Building Empathy

Four steps to practicing empathy from Dr. Brene Brown:

- *Perspective Taking-* Empathy is about putting yourself in someone else's shoes and trying to see things from their perspective. Practice empathy by imagining a time you felt a similar way or had a similar experience. As you allow yourself to become vulnerable, you unlock your past experiences, and as a result, you can better relate to where the other person is coming from.

- *Staying Out of Judgement* – Falling into the trap of making quick judgments about someone is a common issue. Staying out of judgment means simply listening without jumping to conclusions. To practice empathy, we must listen and understand.
- *Recognizing Emotions Someone Else is Feeling* – As we listen, we try to acknowledge the emotion the other person is feeling. Is it hate, anger, frustration, sadness, happiness, or many different feelings? Pinpointing the emotion can help you better understand what they may be feeling.
- *Communicating That You Understand an Emotion* – As we identify and connect with someone else's perspective and emotions, let them know you understand. Conveying your understanding builds connections and helps you respond accordingly.

You can visit Brene Brown's YouTube channel for videos on these and other topics related to developing empathy for a "human-centered" leadership style.

a   **Coaching Tool:** Developing Vulnerability

Vulnerability is the "human dimension of disasters" resulting from economic, social, cultural, institutional, political, and psychological factors that shape our lives and the environment that we live in. For this exercise, we will focus on the psycho-social aspect of being unable to protect ourselves against significant harm or threat or being taken advantage of in the workplace. This may also include interactions with patients who may be young or elderly or those with mental illness-related issues, physical disabilities, learning disabilities, or gender-related issues.

With emotions being useful messages from ourselves to ourselves, it seems that we shouldn't ignore them as often as we do. It's as though we allow that feeling to escalate out of control by not sharing our feelings. The goal here is to become more aware of the emotions that have been designed to help us keep a state of homeostasis to survive. Understanding how emotions create messages related to our experiences for protection is a key to learning to heal inner wounds and help us connect on a deeper level with those closest to us. It may also help to stop building a wall between us and others and open us up to new experiences.

Research demonstrates that individuals who are more in touch with their own emotions and the emotions of others experience less stress and greater levels of well-being. They are better able to regulate their emotions overall. (Karimi, 2013)

Five Tips to be More Emotionally Vulnerable: (Kaiser, 2023)

Speak your truth. Learn how to verbalize what you think and feel.

A new graduate, a physical therapist, had anxiety about the need to perform for her co-workers to respect her. She was terrified of admitting what she didn't know about her profession. She developed a relationship with a co-worker, and once she opened up, she discovered she had put a lot of stressors on herself. Sharing with her co-worker allowed her to healthily deal with her emotions instead of nodding and acting like she knew what she was expected to do rather than being curious or eager to learn from her co-workers who had been on the job much longer and who were happy to help once she shared her genuine emotions.

Embrace all of your emotions

Part of being vulnerable with your emotions is allowing yourself to experience all your emotions, good and bad. If you don't embrace sadness or frustration, coping effectively will be more challenging when these emotions overwhelm you by surprise. Many people experience difficulty transitioning between roles over a lifetime, for example, from medical school to practicing medicine and from being a specialist to a hospitalist. These emotions can lead to heightened ones and, when left unchecked, can create depression or worse. Finding a way to check in on all your emotions helps to balance their relative impact and the attention you need to give them for both your short-term and long-term goals.

Create safe space

Developing a safe space for sharing your feelings is critical for healthy relationships. These can be as simple as a look to seek privacy on the job or an actual place to share emotions away from others, such as children or friends at home. It can be a little scary to tell someone how you're feeling, especially if you are overwhelmed or surprised by your reaction or someone else's. A safe space makes it easier to be emotionally "vulnerable" and may offer a place to feel whatever is essential for your well-being in that moment.

Write it all down

We can all learn to embrace emotions through communicating with a suitable medium, like putting it in writing. Not for a book or public media purposes, just to see what we are feeling in the moment. Seeing it in living words and color can help us digest the impact and rebalance our view of the situation. Getting it all out can also help us feel less emotional and find an end to the feelings so we can refocus, move on, and let our true selves shine. Once in a while, I've written a letter or two, and having seen it all out there, written down, I either stuck it in a drawer for final review later on or trashed it with great joy after ripping it up or squashing it in my fist. Either way, it was satisfying. I've learned to use this to create a safe space for my unpleasant emotions and generally never send the letter. It also lets me get on with my day instead of rehashing it.

Ask yourself questions

Often, when avoiding being vulnerable, we need to ask ourselves why. Or, more accurately, what am I afraid of or hiding from? Avoiding emotional confrontations with myself involves being embarrassed, ashamed, or guilty. While I'm the only one who will know about these ugly feelings, even I don't want to deal with them. The bigger question is, what do I risk by not sharing these feelings? Ultimately, we risk our well-being and happiness or, worse, a relationship we value with ourselves or others we care about. Once I have the patience and the courage to ask the question, it usually ends the cycle fairly quickly because the risks of covering up these emotions far outweigh the risks of getting them out.

Being emotionally vulnerable doesn't have to be an uncomfortable experience for long. It is, however, an essential step towards being a better leader and critical for a human-centered leader. Once we understand and embrace the array of emotions we feel and learn to communicate them with a little practice and "graciosity" (Stejskal, 2023), we remove the layers of emotional protection that allow us the freedom to be both fearless and happy both as a physician leader and an individual who can fully understand themselves. Over time, we can combine these strengths to be better contributors or leaders at work.

References

Bennett, M. (2023) Excerpts from Niagara Institute blog posts.

Bennis, W. (2009) *On becoming a leader*. Basic Books, 4th edition.

Covery, S.M.R (2022) *Trust and Inspire: How Truly Great Leaders Unleash Greatness in Others*. Simon & Schuster.

De Smet, A., Rubenstein, K., Schrah, G., Vierow, M., Edmondson, A. (2021) *Psychological safety and the critical role of leadership development*. Mckinsey & Company. https://www.mckinsey.com.

Dweck, Carol. *A Summary of The Two Mindsets (fs.blog)*.

Greenberg, C., Nadler, R. (2020) *Emotional Brilliance: Living a stress less, fear less life*. Waterside Productions.

Greenberg, C.L., North, T.C. (2014) *Fearless leaders: Sharpen your focus: How the new science of mindfulness can help you reclaim your confidence*. San Diego, CA: Waterfront.

Hoff, T., Pohl, H., Bartfield, J. (2003) Implementing Safety Cultures in Medicine: What We Learn by Watching Physicians. *Advances in Patient Safety*. 1:15–38.

https://www.hrotoday.com/market-intelligence/white-paper/have-you-accepted-your-sourcing-reality/.

Kaiser, A. (2023) 5 Tips to be More Emotionally Vulnerable (and Why It's So Important). www. trackinghappiness.com.

Karimi, L. (2013) Emotional rescue: the role of emotional intelligence and labor on well-being and job-stress among community nurses. *Journal of Advanced Nursing*. 70(1):176. doi:10.1111/jan.12185. email: l.karimi@latrobe.edu.au.

Kennedy, K., Leclerc, L., Campis, S. (2021) *Human-Centered Leadership in Healthcare: Evolution of a Revolution.* Morgan James Publishing, 1st edition.

Mclain, B. (2020) *Designing Transformative Experiences: A Toolkit for Leaders, Trainers, Teachers, and other Experience Designers.* Berrett-Koehler Publishers.

McQuaid, M. & Williams, P. (2023) *Your leadership blueprint: Fostering psychological safety at work.* 1.

Miller, M. (2023) *We're Facing a Global Human Energy Crisis.* www.sixseconds.com.

Nadler, R. (2011) *Leading with Emotional Intelligence: Hands on strategies for Building Confidant and Collaborative Star Performers*NY: McGraw-Hill.

Nine Things Employees Want From Their Managers | Free Online HR Resources from SESCO Management Consultants (sescomgt.com).

Reynolds, M. (2020) *Coach the person, not the problem. A Guide to Using Reflective Inquiry.* Berrett-Koehler Publishers; Illustrated edition.

Rotenstein, L.S., Sadun, R., Jena, A.B. (2018) Why doctors need leadership training. *Harvard Business Review.*

Satiani, B. & Prakash, S.H. (2016) It is time for more physicians and nursing representation on hospital boards in the US. *Journal of Hospital and Medical Management.* 2(16):1–5. https://api.semanticscholar.org/CorpusID:53074094.

Scoular A, & Scoular I. (2019) The Leader as Coach. *Harvard Business Review.*

Shanafelt, T.D., Gorringe, G., Menaker, R., Storz, K.A., Reeves, D., Buskirk, S.J., Sloan, J.A., Swensen, S.J. (2015) Impact of organizational leadership on physician burnout and satisfaction. *Mayo Clinic Proceedings.* 90(4):432–440. doi:10.1016/j.mayocp.2015.01.012. Epub 2015 Mar 18. PMID: 25796117.

Shanafelt, T.D., West, C.P., Dyrbye, L.N., Trockel, M., Tutty, M., Wang, H,. Carlasare, L.E., Sinsky, C. (2022) Changes in Burnout and Satisfaction with Work-Life Integration in Physicians During the First 2 Years of the COVID-19 Pandemic. *Mayo Clinic Proceedings.* 97(12):2248–2258. doi:10.1016/j.mayocp.2022.09.002. Epub 2022 Sep 14. PMID: 36229269; PMCID: PMC9472795.

Stejskal, T.M. (2023) *The 5 Practices of Highly Resilient People: Why Some Flourish When Others Fold.* Hachette Go.

The Best Definition of Empathy We've Heard – Brené Brown (happify.com)

TTPs to become truly "FEARLESS" with Matthew Werner Friday, December 22, 2023 (voiceamerica.com)

The 5 Biggest Biases That Affect Decision-Making (neuroleadership.com)https://www.mckinsey.com/capabilities/people-and-organizational-performance/Psychological safety and leadership development | McKinsey

van de Riet, M.C.P., Berghout, M.A., Buljac-Samardžić, M., van Exel, J., Hilders, C.G.J.M. (2019) What makes an ideal hospital-based medical leader? Three views of healthcare professionals and managers: A case study. *PLoS One.* 14(6): e0218095. doi:10.1371/journal.pone.0218095. PMID: 31185051; PMCID: PMC6559653.

Whitmore, J. (1992) *Coaching for Performance*. Nicholas Brealey.

Zenger, J., Folkman, J. (2019) The 3 elements of trust. *Harvard Business Review*. https://hbr.org/2019/02/the-3-elements-of-trust.

Zenger, J., Folkman, J. (2022) Quiet quitting is about bad bosses, not bad employees. *Harvard Business Review*. https://hbr.org/2022/08/quiet-quitting-is-about-bad-bosses-not-bad-employees.

12 Career Coaching for Physicians

Zeina Ghossoub

Introduction

The definition of "career" is "an occupation undertaken for a significant period of a person's life and with opportunities for progress." (From Dictionary.com) Now, anyone who wants to pursue a career in medicine is advised to ask around, inquire about what it means to be a doctor, about all the time and effort, sacrifices and rewards, personal and professional expectations, and outlook for the immediate and distant future. But one of the key requirements that is gaining more and more interest is the idea that one needs to know more about themselves first before they decide which medical career and specialty they want to focus on. But who has the insight and ability to look that far into the distant future? Or even the immediate one? And how do we understand the information we might be able to gather? And what is the information we need to find? Who can help? Up until the recent past, the quest for becoming a doctor was driven by a need to help others with the desire, will, and determination to dedicate one's life to the service of others. The concept of the "Career" was rather simple in its description and expectations, no matter how utterly difficult and demanding in practice and achievement. One was expected to study, train, and become proficient in the art and science of healing others while relying on the career that would provide the fulfillment, joy, and opportunity to gain experience, hone the skills, and be that much better in helping people. Further, the expectations from others, patients, friends, society, and the healthcare world, is that the doctor does just that and becomes that master of healing and conquering diseases and ailments. In the words of Sir William Osler:

> Medicine arose out of the primal sympathy of man with man; out of the desire to help those in sorrow, need and sickness.
>
> *Sir William Osler*

Fast forward into today's reality, and the practice of medicine, its demands, and expectations, have become so much more. Unfortunately,

DOI: 10.4324/9781003452065-12

the art and science of the practice make up only one of the multitude of responsibilities of this career. The problem is that medical education, training, and practice have not caught up with the new reality. Physicians are left to fend for themselves in learning how to deal with this reality and find the same joy and happiness they used to get from just being physicians.

While giving one of our presentations, we asked the audience, a group of about 100 physicians, if they remembered the day they got accepted into medical school. We asked them to express, in one word, their feelings. "Joy", "Happiness", "Relief", "Jubilation", "Disbelief", "Vindication", "Magnificence", and so on and so forth. The overwhelming theme was relief and happiness. When asked to describe their feelings about being doctors and practicing their profession and being in this career, words turned to "disgust", "angst", "remorse", "fatigue", "doubt", "regret", "anger", "sadness", "existential crisis". Is this an exaggeration? Was our sample representative of the entire work force of doctors, or did we just uncover the most miserable group on the planet?

Looking at the literature, you will find that a rather significant number of doctors want nothing more than to either change their careers or get out of medicine all together. The numbers vary, and the range is wide. Anywhere between 40 to 70 % of physicians would not recommend this career for their children. They would even go as far as opposing it! That is a sad, disheartening, and alarming reality! The numbers are even more after the pandemic.

This book has touched upon the reasons why this is happening. It has discussed burnout, the difficulties of the healthcare industry, the demands and their toll, the expectations and their impact, and the ever-increasing responsibilities. In every chapter, we have discussed coaching as a tool or approach to help physicians thrive. Is there a place for coaching to help physicians, or students who want to become physicians, decide on the best career options for them? Does career coaching help? And if so, when? Before medical school, during, during residency, after residency, during practice, when during practice? And how does it help? With what does it help? And why does it help?

Career coaching helps physicians no matter their stage of training or development or practice. That is emphatically and unequivocally true. Let us explore that reality.

Literature Review

Career coaching, as the name implies, is coaching someone to help them decide on their career choices and development. It helps people navigate their career challenges, develop the ability to master their career choices, and support them with decisions that can arise from their career choices. These can range from wanting to improve and climb the hierarchical ladder to the other end of the spectrum, leaving their career altogether and finding a new one. Career coaches help in work-life integration, reconnecting to purpose, leadership, and career development, combating burnout, shifting focus, and mastering the environment.

Coaching is coaching. The same tools and approaches and philosophies that have been discussed so far apply here. The focus of this chapter will be to look at the literature, discuss choices and the reasoning behind them, discuss the value and place of career coaching in the healthcare industry, discuss the assessments and other tools that are part and parcel of career coaching, and utilize an example or two for illustration purposes. There are several ways to approach this review. I will start by discussing some of the tools that can be used with career coaching. Then, I will discuss the stages of the medical profession where career coaching can be applied.

The assessment tools discussed are because of their validity and reliability in applicability, scientifically based theories, and practical usage. These tests are the MBTI, STRONG, and BIRKMAN.

MBTI Myers Briggs Type Indicator

According to the CPP website, which is the website that administers the MBTI assessment test, (www.themyersbriggs.com), MBTI

> helps individuals to identify, from self-report of easily recognized reactions, the basic preferences of people in regard to perception and judgment, so that the effects of each preference, singly and in combination, can be established by research and put into practical use.
>
> (https://www.cpp.com/products/mbti/index.aspx)

A great tool, and one of the most used in identifying personality types and utilizing information for career choices, the MBTI is a personality test assessment tool that divides us into 16 different personality types based on 4 scales. This is a non-judgmental self-assessment tool. It helps individuals identify their brain patterns and how they use them. Based on Carl Jung's theory, this test helps people identify their different thought patterns and helps group them into personality types with distinct observable mental functioning differences.

The four scales of the MBTI test are:

Table 12.1 MBTI Preference Scale

MBTI Preference Scale	Scale Description
Extraversion (E) or Introversion (I)	How do you direct your energy and attention?
Sensing (S) or Intuition (N)	How do you prefer to take in information?
Thinking (T) or Feeling (F)	How do you prefer to make decisions?
Judging (J) or Perceiving (P)	How do you orient to the outer world?

Each personality type is made of a different combination of these 4 letters yielding a total of 16 different personality possibilities. This tool is merely informative. It does not predict and is not used to prescribe anything about the client. It is merely a self-reflecting tool that allows the client and coach to better understand who the client is and what might fit best their personality, their tendencies, thought preferences, comfort areas, and strengths. During coaching the MBTI is used to help deepen and expand self-awareness. (Myers & Myers, 1995). Myers and Myers developed the MBTI for multiple uses, one of them being occupation and careers. This tool is also used to help the clients understand others and their tendencies. Whatever can be applied to the client can be applied to others (Kroeger et al., 2002).

It is beyond the scope of this chapter and book to go into detail about the MBTI and what each category means. The literature shows that some personalities fare well with some specialties, and vice versa. For example, introverts tend to gravitate or do better with specialties that require less interactions with patients, including radiology, pathology, and anesthesiology. Those who are extroverts usually find themselves better suited for psychiatry, internal and family medicine, and surgery. In 1977, there was an extensive study done on personality types and medical specialties. (McCaulley, 1977). This is a summary of the findings. (Table 1, personalities and specialties)

Others, (Jafrani et al., 2017) found that those who are ESFP preferred surgery, ESTJ chose medicine, ESFJ were linked to gynecology, ISFJ to pediatrics, ISTP to cardiology. It is evident that these studies are meant as a guideline, and they are not the last word on choosing a career or specialty in medicine.

Table 12.2 Personalities and Specialties

Personality type	Specialty
ISTJ (The organizer): Innately organized, preferring order and predictability, step by step instructions, are objective and reliable.	Dermatology, Obstetrics-gynecology, Family practice, Urology, Orthopedic surgery
ISFJ (The nurturer): Full of compassion, they use their reliability, follow through, and need to fulfill expectation to help others.	Anesthesiology, Ophthalmology, General practice, Family practice, Pediatrics
ISTP (The mechanic): A balance between being spontaneous and logical, they are adaptable, rational, flexible, independent, and analytical.	Otolaryngology, Anesthesiology, Radiology, Ophthalmology, General practice
ISFP (The adventurer): Inherently creative and original, they love change, do not like monotonous environments, and are hands-on.	Anesthesiology, Urology, Family practice, Thoracic surgery, General practice

Personality type	Specialty
INFJ (The protector): Our of the box thinkers exploring multiple options, strictly professional and private, are able to read other people's emotions and help them.	Psychiatry, Internal medicine, Thoracic surgery, General surgery, Pathology
ESTJ (The supervisor): Natural leaders who value organization and structure. They love traditions and love to follow guidelines. They are logical and stick to facts.	Obstetrics-gynecology, General practice, General surgery, Orthopedic surgery, Pediatrics
ESFJ (The caregiver): Social butterflies with a desire to help and take care of others, including patients and staff. They value teamwork and make others feel comfortable.	Pediatrics, Orthopedic surgery, Otolaryngology, General practice, Internal medicine
ENFP (The inspirer) Great people skills, creative, enthusiastic, and idealistic. Loves new ideas, and loves to help people and support them.	Psychiatry, Dermatology, Otolaryngology, Pediatrics
INTJ (The scientist): Extremely independent, great leaders, make plans happen, are determined and analytical, love challenges, and maintain high standards.	Psychiatry, Pathology, Neurology, Internal medicine, Anesthesiology
INFP (The idealist): Love to understand and help others. They are adaptable, laid back, love to connect with their patients and seeing possibilities.	Psychiatry, Cardiology, Neurology, Dermatology, Pathology
INTP (The thinker): Philosophers at heart, reserved and quiet, they love to think. Proficient in problem solving, they prefer being alone.	Neurology, Pathology, Psychiatry, Cardiology, Thoracic surgery
ESTP (The doer): With great people skills, they love to get immediate results. They have high energy, process quickly and produce immediate solutions.	Orthopedic surgery, Dermatology, Family practice, Radiology, General surgery
ESFP (The performer): Social butterflies, they love the spotlight. Can speak well and relate to everyone. Considered practical, they prefer actions, not theories.	Ophthalmology, Thoracic surgery, Obstetrics-gynecology, Orthopedic surgery, General surgery
ENTP (The visionary): Resourceful and quick on their feet. Generally outspoken and assertive. They enjoy challenges, are good company, and apply logic to situations.	Otolaryngology, Psychiatry, Radiology, Pediatrics, Pathology
ENTJ (The executive): Driven to lead, they are outspoken and assertive. They have little tolerance of inefficiency and disorganization and love knowledge and competence.	Neurology, Cardiology, Urology, Thoracic surgery, Internal medicine
ENFJ (The giver): Very sensitive and usually popular. They are not loners, are focused on others, view life through personal humane lenses, and are interested in serving others.	Thoracic surgery, Dermatology, Psychiatry, Ophthalmology, Radiology

Birkman Personality Assessment Test

This test focuses on behavior and psychological characteristics. It is commonly used by companies in different industries to assess college students for hiring and career choice purposes. The test measures strengths and weaknesses in motivation, communication, behavior, and teamwork. There are four perspectives in the Birkman personality testing: Motivation, self-perception, social perception, and mindset. With 40 different possible reports, it takes mastery and proficiency in administering the Birkman, understanding it and using it career coaching.

The results are formulated within a chart called the Birkman Map. It has four quadrants. Right and left quadrants highlight task-oriented versus people-oriented. The top and bottom quadrants show one's ability to work with direct involvement/communication versus indirect involvement/communication. Within each quadrant there are four colors-blue, yellow, red and green. Colors represent personality characteristics. The last results in the chart are four symbols: Diamond to represent what someone's usual style is, asterisk to show where interests lie, circle that detail where needs lie, and square that highlight stress behaviors.

Briefly, the colors represent the following:

Table 12.3 Birkman's Personality Colors

Red	*Focus on solving problems, achieving real results and working in the physical world/realm. Usually decisive with good management abilities and expeditious actions.*
Blue	Focus is on creativity, ideas, intuition and planning. Their approach is unusual or creative new ways while maintaining a broad focus.
Green	Focus is on communication, counseling, motivating, and persuading. They prefer working in social spaces while having flexible and supportive behaviors.
Yellow	Focus is on procedures, rules and regulations. They are "numbers" people, process oriented and detail driven.

A detailed review of the literature found no reference for the use of Birkman personality testing in the healthcare industry except among a group of pharmacy students.

Strong Interest Inventory

This inventory (Harmon, 2004) measures a person's interest based on the psychological theories of John Holland. Interest is divided into 6 major categories: Realistic, Investigative, Artistic, Social, Enterprising, and

Conventional (RIASEC). RIASEC is then broken down into further categories, Basic Interest Scales which are related to fields of study, leisure activities, and careers.

Realistic (The doers)	Active, hands on, and adventurous
Investigative (The thinkers)	Analytical, theoretical, and inquisitive
Artistic (The creators)	Expressive, imaginative, and free-spirited
Social (The helpers)	Caring, collaborative, and supportive
Enterprising (The persuaders)	Influential, ambitious, and risk takers
Conventional (The organizers)	Practical, orderly, and efficient

The use of this inventory has not yet found its way in the healthcare industry. Specifically, it has not been used to help physicians or nurses identify which specialty they may want to venture into. However, most physicians, and nurses, will seek to change their careers at some point in their lives, or supplement their medical careers with other interests. In helping the clients determine what might suit their personality or help answer their questions about whether they will be able to pursue their dreams and be successful in their aspirations, career coaching benefits from these assessment tests. These tests require the coach to be certified in their use and applications. These certifications are usually done through a third-party vendor, usually the owners or the administers of the different assessment tests.

Medical students

In 2016, Hur, Y. discussed an interesting concept. The author divided the three stages of medical students into pre-med (crystallization period), first 2 years of medical school (specification period), and the final 2 years (implementation period). The author noted that a significant number of students who choose medicine do so because of their aptitude test scores, academic performance, parent's recommendations, socioeconomic status, and employment outlook. (Hur, 2016). The argument is made that the students are ill prepared to face the challenges of their career choice. If one of the core values of medicine is professionalism and balancing work and life, it is important that students understand their career choice and learn how to master it as soon as they make that career choice. The author provides a very useful diagram to approach career coaching. (Adapted from Hur, Y. 2016)

Rather than think of these categories as distinct, they are best approached as a continuum through career coaching. The author emphasizes a point that is well documented throughout literature: When coaching someone for their careers, it is important to start with them and who they are to help them develop self-awareness. Being able to identify what best fits the person's character, strengths, and weaknesses creates the best opportunity to help. Other than the coaching sessions, there are a multitude of assessment tools that can be used. The personality tests that have been discussed will help the client/student and the coach determine a person's strengths and weaknesses, interests and abilities, as well as helping the client determine what will best fit their personalities by raising their self-awareness and helping them understand what career choice has the best chance of resonating with them.

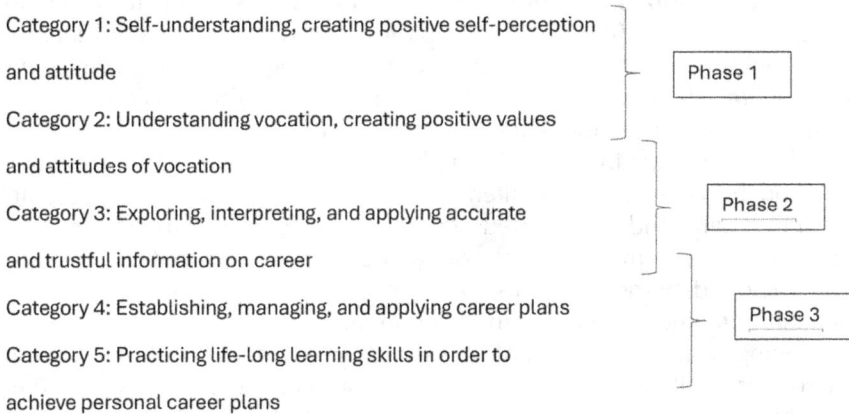

Category 1: Self-understanding, creating positive self-perception

and attitude ⎤ Phase 1

Category 2: Understanding vocation, creating positive values

and attitudes of vocation

Category 3: Exploring, interpreting, and applying accurate ⎤ Phase 2

and trustful information on career

Category 4: Establishing, managing, and applying career plans ⎤ Phase 3

Category 5: Practicing life-long learning skills in order to

achieve personal career plans

Figure 12.1 Career Competencies Map

Residency and fellowship

Data on residency and fellowship career coaching is extremely limited. In theory, career coaching will be extremely beneficial for the same reasons it is for professionals in other fields. Again, the same basic rules and assumptions apply. Helping someone to identify what they want to focus on or specialize in based on their own personalities and other attributes would likely be a positive predictable outcome from career coaching. Cheesebrough et al. in 2020 showed that three career coaching sessions were very beneficial for fellows in their career trajectories and was received extremely well and deemed highly beneficial by the fellows.

In 2020, the Coalition for Physician Accountability's Undergraduate Medical Education-Graduate Medical Education Review Committee (UGRC), released the following statement regarding coaching while students transition from undergraduate (UME) to graduate medical education (GME) was made.

Targeted coaching by qualified educators should begin in UME and continue during GME, focused on professional identity formation and moving from a performance to a growth mindset for effective lifelong learning as a physician. Educators should be astute to the needs of the learner and be equipped to provide assistance to all backgrounds.

Even though the statement does not specifically discuss careers, it refers to helping physicians in training transition from a transactional mindset to a transformational mindset that allows for growth.

Physicians in the clinical and academic setting

There is a plethora of studies that highlight the impact of coaching to help physicians master their careers or professions. Even though a majority have focused on helping in burnout and dealing with stress, there are some which discuss career growth within the specialty, outside the specialty, and outside of medicine. The overall arching theme is the recommendation of coaching in any and all of these scenarios.

Through his review of the literature, Smith in 2020 summed up the literature nicely and highlighted the relevance and positive impact of coaching on the many aspects of surgeons/physicians in their careers. This included burnout and its management, physician wellness, facing difficult outcomes, dealing with litigation, enhancing a technique or skill, advancing in the career, training, sustaining, and mastering the surgical career, as well as juggling the many priorities in the surgeon's life. Coaching also helped in patient outcomes and optimization of the practice. (Gwathmey & Miller, 2023).

When it comes to changing one's profession and incorporating a nonclinical part to it, or leaving medicine altogether, physicians now have so much more opportunities and avenues than 20 or 30 years ago. Some of these include pharmaceutical work, executive leadership work, consulting expert work, health insurance and utilization management, medical technology and informatics, education, public health, expert witnesses, and, yes, coaching. The reasons for this transition range from lack of fulfillment in the clinical work to burnout to an entrepreneurial spirit to seeking new challenges to supplementing income to finding a better fit for their personality.

Case studies

Transitioning to leadership: Doctor A had been a masterful surgeon for the past ten years. She specialized in bariatric surgery and had one of the best clinical outcomes in the nation. When the opening for chair of the surgical department opened, she was nominated to lead a robust faculty of 20 full time surgeons. She was intrigued by the idea and felt leadership was natural for her as she knows how to lead her operating theater. Dr. A accepted the offer. It took around 3 to 4 months before the staff and the executive team noticed that complaints were increasing, both in the surgical theater and among the department physicians. Dr. A's complaints included being temperamental, arrogant, withdrawn, "bossy", almost "bullying" in her approach, and unapproachable. Even her patients started complaining. Several discussions ensued and Dr. A was referred for coaching.

Through coaching, Dr. A. initially was extremely resistant. She felt everyone was being unfair and she was being forced to undergo coaching for someone else's mistakes or incompetence. Once she understood that the coaching sessions were purely for her sake, and that she is the one that determines the goals and what she would like to achieve, she felt a bit calmer in that she is not following someone else's agenda.

The sessions started with developing an understanding of why she was referred. After much questioning, she acknowledged that she has changed since she took on the leadership role. Admittedly, she felt that her natural leadership skills in the operating room would carry over to the department level. Further questioning revealed why she was successful in the operating room and why she was a good leader there. She identified the following as keys to her calmness, communication abilities, and management of the situation in the operating room, no matter how difficult it could be: Competence of her supporting staff, knowledge of her staff, knowledge of her operating room and equipment, the ability to anticipate, having her expectations being met, being in control, minimizing surprises, orders being followed without questioning as she was "the expert", and a track record of proven outcomes. When she focused on her role as a leader at the department level, she realized she had almost none of the above keys. The lack of knowledge of her fellow physicians, the inability to predict, the lack of response to her demands, the fact that she "was not the expert", and the lack of her proven track record, along with the volatility of the environment and the ever-changing demands and challenges created an anxiety in her and the development of an imposter syndrome.

After much discussion, Dr. A. wanted to take on the challenge of leadership as she had her eye on "bigger and greater things" to have a more profound impact on the practice of surgery at the administrative and policy development level. Dr. A. underwent the MBTI and the EQi testing and assessments. Finding out her type of personality, along with her strengths and blind spots in her EQi helped her focus on enhancing those which specifically helped her in her leadership role, such as communication skills, flexibility, empathy, assertiveness, and optimism. Coaching helped her develop leadership skills outside the operating room and helped her propel her career forward in the direction she had desired.

Becoming a coach: Dr. B. has been an internist and a program director for around 7 years. He loved his job and loved to teach. However, Dr. B. felt that he can help his interns, residents and fellows, as well as his staff, more than what he was doing. He felt that his ability to convey messages and to help people grow around him were limited by his lack of knowledge and expertise in that area. Dr. B. explored coaching after he heard from his friend who had recently become a coach.

Dr. B. met with me for an introductory session. In the first session, there was a discussion on what coaching is, its potential impact in general, and how he can benefit from it in his realm of work. Dr. B. was very interested in pursuing a career in coaching. He agreed to do the MBTI and EQi to learn about his personality type, as well as his strengths and weaknesses.

It took around 8 sessions for Dr. B. to set clear goals on how he wants to help his staff and trainees. He also was able to develop a program that he can incorporate into his residency and fellowship training and would like to pilot new ideas and approaches. His greater goal was to be able to spread his approach on a national level. For Dr. B., he understood that becoming a coach was essential for him to apply his model, and to train others locally and nationally. He has enrolled to become a coach.

Summary and Conclusion

- Career coaching can happen at any level of training. It can start at the medical school level, even before, and continue throughout the life of the doctor.
- Career coaching can be applied to help the physician determine which specialty to choose, and how to best excel in the specialty clinically and professionally.
- Career coaching can help physicians master their profession and all its challenges while maintaining health and well-being and avoiding burnout.
- Career coaching can help physicians take on different clinical and non-clinical roles in medicine.
- Career coaching can utilize several assessment tests such as the MBTI, STRONG, and Birkman.
- Career coaching has been shown to help individuals and organizations tackle and thrive in the challenges of healthcare. Some may argue that without career coaching, such mastery of the healthcare industry may not be possible.

It is said that sometimes, a career chooses us rather than the other way around. Whether that is true or not, the reality is that having a wonderful prosperous and fulfilling career necessitates mastery of oneself and one's abilities, one's career requirements and challenges, and maintaining an eye on the now and the future to achieve purpose. In Lebanon, there is an expression: "No one is born knowledgeable". When we embark on a career, we seek to gain experience and become knowledgeable. We do not enter it as masters, but rather as newborns. The expectation in medicine is that physicians do enter as masters. To navigate one of the most demanding careers and professions, and to help prepare for it, career coaching maybe the missing link between the nuance of theory and the mastery of practice with all its demands.

References

Chang, Y.C., Tseng, H.M., Xiao, X., Ngerng, R.Y.L., Wu, C.L., Chaou, C.H. (2019) Examining the association of career stage and medical specialty with personality preferences – a cross-sectional survey of junior doctors and attending physicians from various specialties. *BMC Medical Education*. 19(1):363. doi:10.1186/s12909-019-1789-2. PMID: 31547826; PMCID: PMC6757380.

Cheesebrough, K.R., Bronzert, J., Frazier-De La Torre, E. (2020) Leadership, academia, and the role of career coaching. *TranTranslational Behavioral Medicine*. 10(4):870–872. doi:10.1093/tbm/ibaa057. PMID: 32667034.

Fink, S.B., Capparelly, S. (2013) *The Birkman Method: Your personality at work*. Jossey-Bass; 1st edition.

Gwathmey, F.W., Miller, M.D. (2023) Coaching in Sports Medicine. *Clinical Sports Medicine*. 325–333. doi:10.1016/j.csm.2022.12.005. PMID: 36907630.

Harmon, L. (2004) *Strong interest inventory manual revised*. Consulting Psycholgistss.

Hur, Y. (2016) Development of a career coaching model for medical students. *Korean J Medical Education*. 28(1):127–136. doi:10.3946/kjme.2016.19. Epub 2016 Jan 27. PMID: 26867586; PMCID: PMC4926935.

Jafrani, S., Zehra, N., Zehra, M., Abuzar Ali, S.M., Abubakar Mohsin, S.A., Azhar, R. (2017) Assessment of personality type and medical specialty choice among medical students from Karachi; using Myers-Briggs Type Indicator (MBTI) tool. *The Journal of the Pakistan Medical Association*. 67(4):520–526. PMID: 28420908.

Kroeger, O., Thuesen, J. M., & Rutledge, H. (2002). *Type talk at work: How the 16 personality types determine your success on the job*. Revised Edition. New York: Dell Trade Paperback.

McCaulley, M.H. (1977) *The Myers Longitudinal Medical Study (Monograph II)*. Gainesville, Fla: Center for Applications of Psychological Type.

Myers, I. B., & Myers, P. B. (1995). *Gifts differing: Understanding personality type. Mountain View*. CA: CPP, Inc.

Smith, J.M. (2020) Surgeon Coaching: Why and How. *Journal of Pediatric Orthopedics*. Suppl 1:S33–S37. doi:10.1097/BPO.0000000000001541. PMID: 32502069.

Talha, K.A., Hasan, M.F., Selina, F., Ahmad, H., Kaiser, F.R., Erica, K.T. (2022) Myers-Briggs Type Indicator Personality Types of Female Intern Doctors and Their Specialty Preference. *Mymensingh Medical Journal*. 31(3):806–811. PMID: 35780367.

The Coalition for Physician Accountability's Undergraduate Medical Education-Graduate Medical Education Review Committee. https://physicianaccountability.org/.

13 Female Physicians

Unique Challenges and Coaching Approaches

Zeina Ghossoub

Introduction and Literature Review

At the time of writing this chapter, the literature on coaching physicians and healthcare providers has focused mostly on those who identify as males or females. So, why dedicate a chapter on female physicians? The answer is easy: Female physicians, whereas they share the pathophysiology with their male counterparts, have unique internal and external characteristics/variables that warrant this chapter.

Literature shows that female physicians are 60% more at risk to be burned out than male physicians. (Dyrbye et al., 2017). Men score higher on depersonalization while women score higher on emotional exhaustion. (Purvanova et al., 2010) The reasons for these discrepancies include their childbearing roles, their pay discrepancies, family needs responsibilities, lack of opportunities for leadership, infertility, very little mentorship, and inadequate recognition. (Yeluru et al., 2022). In general, the literature lists four factors that impact careers or status of women in medicine (Hastie et al., 2022): Motivational, environmental, situational, and structural. Factors identified as situational include dependent care obligations, frequently shared unevenly and heavily relying on the women. This is detrimental to their careers and became more evident during the covid era. Institutional resources, such as absence of role models and sponsorship, along with a persistent paygap, represent the structural factors. Motivational factors are represented by an interest and a drive for leadership. And finally, the work culture and its impact, such as gender biases, round up the environmental factors.

In academic medicine (Hastie et al., 2022), female physicians deal with 4 misconceptions. The first is that women need more mentorship. The truth is that women need more sponsorship, not mentorship. There is a clear difference between the two and the solution proposed by the literature is that women should seek more sponsorship, not mentorship, and not settle for anything less. The second misconception is that the pay gap ceases to exist in leadership positions. More often than not, the issue in the pay gap is at a structural and institutional level, not an individual

DOI: 10.4324/9781003452065-13

level. The third misconception refers to the lack of leadership self-efficacy among women. There are several reasons for this misconception. Early literature described women as having internal psychological barriers which resulted in self-limiting beliefs and behaviors that impeded career progression and advancement. Women tend to minimize their achievements in past leadership and think less of themselves and believe less in their ability to lead in the future. Simply stating, women were believed to have lower self-efficacy than their men counterparts. This belief has been challenged successfully. Rather than self-efficacy being an internal issue, it appears that self-efficacy is impacted by external factors, such as failure to recognize these female physicians, gender biases, and a general sense of lack of ambition due to the toxic nature of the environment. In essence, "why try when the environment is not conducive?". This has created a belief among women that their abilities are not as good or important as their male counterparts. Therefore, intrinsic motivation is dampened, and perhaps at times, eliminated. Another factor that impacts women's views about themselves and their abilities, both clinically and managerially, is what is known as vertical gender bias. In contrast to horizontal gender bias/segregation where females are underrepresented across certain specialties, vertical bias/segregation refers to underrepresentation in leadership and managerial positions. These create what is known as stereotype threats that impact not only how women perform, but also how well they think of themselves, or their self-efficacy! The fourth and last misconception is that women are less likely to be in leadership roles due to their less than effective leadership style. It seems that women in leadership roles are stuck between a rock and a hard place. Leadership, in the eyes of many, necessitates having the qualities of decisiveness, competence, and assertiveness. However, these characteristics among women are perceived as arrogant, impulsive, and difficult to work with. Women are expected to be more diplomatic and communal. Being likeable as leaders deems them less effective, and being unlikeable makes them less accepted as leaders.

The pressure and stereotype stress also comes from patients. Female physicians are viewed differently and face different expectations from their patients. (Linzer and Harwood, 2018). Female physicians are expected to be more empathetic, provide more empathetic care, spend more time with their patients, and expected to listen to clinical and psychological concerns. However, female physicians are not afforded the time or the space to do so. This leads to poorer reviews when the patients do not get what they expect. This impacted burnout rates among female physicians for several reasons: Expectations of patients, misconceptions about clinical styles, lack of satisfaction among physicians, having more demands on female physicians without the time and space to meet them leaving them with a sense of incompetence or failure, having more bad reviews, and having more pressure on them.

Another area of difference between female and male physicians is their coping mechanisms. Female physicians tend to use more self-blame as a coping mechanism which leads to higher rates of burnout. (Spataro et al., 2016) This pervasive thought process can carry them into the Imposter Syndrome. It is known that this syndrome is more prevalent among female physicians and younger physicians. This was discussed in chapter 10. (Medline et al., 2022).

Summarizing what the literature mentions, target areas for coaching intervention become more evident. These include, but not limited to: Career satisfaction, managing expectations of self and others, work-life integration, changing culture, self-efficacy, coping mechanisms, leadership skills, burnout, and personal as well as professional satisfaction.

Coaching Literature

A review of the literature reveals that coaching has its impact, both on an individual level and a group level. Palamara et al. (2022) reviewed the literature on the impact of coaching on different residents across five hospitals. Their conclusions showed that coaching programs need to be tailored to physicians whose well-being is impacted by race and or gender.

In 2022, Fainstad et al. conducted a randomized controlled study that demonstrated the impact of on-line group coaching on female resident physicians. Their experimental group experienced significant reductions in imposter syndrome and emotional exhaustion and an increase in self-compassion scores compared to the control group. Mann et al. (2023), studied the impact of coaching female physicians through a 4-month web-based group coaching program. Their results showed a positive impact and a decrease in imposter syndrome, emotional exhaustion, depersonalization, and moral injury. There was an increase in self-compassion and flourishing.

Coaching Applications

Although each one of the above stated targets of intervention has been discussed in various chapters of this book, it is worth nothing that some coaching approaches may work better than others given the situation and the target population. The literature and data on coaching female physicians are at its infancy stage.

Coaching works. This is not where the questions lie. Rather, they are directed at which approach applies to whom, when, how, and where? What are the target goals? What is the true impact? Are they reproducible, feasible, and cost effective? How long are the interventions? And as we seek to answer some of those questions in the last 2 chapters, we can look at suggestions for answering the rest.

The most obvious answer is that the best coaching approach depends on the coachee, her goal, and the coach. Given the possible areas of coaching interventions, perhaps it is best to illustrate through a few examples/case studies.

Summary and Recommendations

a   Along with having the same challenges of their male counterparts in the healthcare environment, female physicians face unique challenges of their own that are purely the byproduct of their gender.
b   The impact of the healthcare environment can be even more detrimental on female physicians in certain areas.
c   Coaching has been shown to have extremely positive results on helping female physicians manage their lives and deal with their unique situations.
d   Coaching helps female physicians with career satisfaction, managing expectations of self and others, work-life integration, changing culture, self-efficacy, coping mechanisms, leadership skills, burnout, and personal as well as professional satisfaction.

Case studies

While conducting a coaching intervention for female physicians, I had the privilege to work with 3 outstanding ladies from different walks of life and specialties. The group of physicians faced several challenges that mirrored the industry's issues. Of particular interest was the one related to their work-life balance and expressing a strong desire for change. A pivotal concern was the need to establish better boundaries between their professional and personal lives.

One physician, at the age of 52, aimed for a significant shift towards a more balanced work-life equilibrium, emphasizing the importance of having dedicated personal time.

Another physician lamented a recent period of intense work without a single day off, highlighting the absence of time for self-care and expressing a longing to prioritize health and well-being. This sentiment echoed in the acknowledgment that despite early morning gym sessions, insufficient sleep hindered a consistent routine. The challenges extended to the ability to make significant decisions and find time for meditation.

One physician, recognizing the importance of connection, highlighted the positive impact of affiliating with professional organizations such as the American Academy of Neurology, which contributed to a sense of purpose and belonging.

In response to these multifaceted challenges, group coaching and individual coaching were employed to address specific needs and foster a holistic approach to well-being. The interventions focused on creating actionable strategies, setting realistic time commitments for self-care activities, and emphasizing the significance of maintaining connections within their professional community.

Assessment Tools

1   Emotional Intelligence (EQ) Assessments

- Purpose: To enhance self-awareness, interpersonal skills, and stress management.
- Method: Physicians underwent EQ assessments, providing valuable insights into their emotional strengths and areas for improvement.
- Application: Results were utilized to tailor coaching strategies, fostering emotional well-being within the professional setting.

2   Maslach Burnout Inventory (MBI) Assessments

- Purpose: To identify burnout-related factors and guide targeted interventions.
- Method: Physicians participated in MBI assessments, allowing for a comprehensive evaluation of burnout levels.
- Application: MBI results informed coaching sessions, focusing on addressing burnout factors and fostering resilience.

3   Strengths Tests

- Purpose: To uncover individual strengths and talents.
- Method: Physicians underwent strengths tests, highlighting their unique capabilities and potential areas of excellence.
- Application: Strengths were incorporated into coaching strategies, empowering physicians to leverage their positive attributes in both personal and professional spheres.

4   Positive Intelligence Tests

- Purpose: To assess positive mental fitness and resilience.
- Method: Physicians took Positive Intelligence tests, providing a measure of their ability to navigate challenges with a positive mindset.
- Application: Positive Intelligence results guided coaching sessions, promoting mental resilience and enhancing the physicians' capacity to manage stress.

Coaching Strategies

The coaching sessions focused on creating actionable strategies tailored to each physician's unique combination of emotional intelligence, burnout factors, strengths, and positive intelligence. Group coaching sessions provided a collaborative space for shared experiences and collective growth.

Individual coaching sessions allowed for a more personalized approach, addressing specific needs and concerns. Strategies included the establishment of effective boundaries, realistic time commitments for self-care activities, and the emphasis on maintaining connections within their professional community.

Results and Outcomes

Participants reported positive outcomes from the coaching interventions. They felt empowered to address their challenges and experienced a positive shift towards a more balanced work-life equilibrium. Strategies implemented improved decision-making skills, integrated mindfulness practices into their daily routines, and fostered a sense of connection within their professional community.

References

Dyrbye, L.N., Shanafelt, T.D., Sinsky, C.A., Cipriano, P.F., Bhatt, J., Ommaya, A., West, C.P., Meyers, D. (2017) Burnout among health care professionals: a call to explore and address this underrecognized threat to safe, high-quality care. *NAM Perspectives*. 1–11. doi:10.31478/201707b.

Fainstad, T., Mann, A., Suresh, K., Shah, P., Dieujuste, N., Thurmon, K., Jones, C.D. (2022) Effect of a Novel Online Group-Coaching Program to Reduce Burnout in Female Resident Physicians: A Randomized Clinical Trial. *JAMA*. 5(5):e2210752. doi:10.1001/jamanetworkopen.2022.10752. Erratum in: JAMA Netw Open. 2022 Jun 1;5(6):e2220348. PMID: 35522281; PMCID: PMC9077483.

Hastie, M.J., Lee, A., Siddiqui, S., Oakes, D., Wong, C.A. (2022) Misconceptions about women in leadership in academic medicine. Ide´es rec̦ues concernant les femmes en position de leadership en me´decine universitaire. *Canadian Journal of Anesthesiology*. 1–7.

Linzer, M., Harwood, E. (2018) Gendered Expectations: Do They Contribute to High Burnout Among Female Physicians? *Journal of General Internal Medicine*. 33(6):963–965. doi:10.1007/s11606-018-4330-0. Epub 2018 Feb 12. PMID: 29435727; PMCID: PMC5975148.

Mann, A., Shah, A.N., Thibodeau, P.S., Dyrbye, L., Syed, A., Woodward, M.A., Thurmon, K., Jones, C.D., Dunbar, K.S., Fainstad, T. (2023) Online Well-Being Group Coaching Program for Women Physician Trainees: A Randomized Clinical Trial. *JAMA Netw Open*. 6(10):e2335541. doi:10.1001/jamanetworkopen.2023.35541. PMID: 37792378; PMCID: PMC10551770.

Medline, A., Grissom, H., Guissé, N.F., Kravets, V., Hobson, S., Samora, J.B., Schenker, M. (2022) From Self-efficacy to Imposter Syndrome: The Intrapersonal Traits of Surgeons. *Journal of the Academic Orthopedic Surgeons: Global Research and Review*. 6(4):e22.00051. doi:10.5435/JAAOSGlobal-D-22-00051. PMID: 35412493; PMCID: PMC10566864.

Palamara. K., Chu, J.T., Chang, Y., Yu, L., Cosco, D., Higgins, S., Tulsky, A., Mourad, R., Singh, S., Steinhauser, K., Donelan, K. (2022) Who Benefits Most? A Multisite Study of Coaching and Resident Well-being. *Journal of General Internal Medicine*. 37(3):539–547. doi:10.1007/s11606-021-06903-5. Epub 2021 Jun 7. PMID: 34100238; PMCID: PMC8858365.

Purvanova, R.K., Muros, J.P. (2010) Gender differences in burnout: a meta-analysis. *Journal of Vocational Behavior*. 77:168–185. doi:10.1016/j.jvb.2010.04.006.

Spataro, B.M., Tilstra, S.A., Rubio, D.M., McNeil, M.A. (2016) The Toxicity of Self-Blame: Sex Differences in Burnout and Coping in Internal Medicine Trainees. *Journal of Women's Health*. 25(11):1147–1152. doi:10.1089/jwh.2015.5604. Epub 2016 Oct 12. PMID: 27732118.

Yeluru, H., Newton, H.L., Kapoor, R. (2022) Physician Burnout Through the Female Lens: A Silent Crisis. *Front Public Health*. 10:880061. doi:10.3389/fpubh.2022.880061. PMID: 35685758; PMCID: PMC9171323.

14 Legalities, Ethics, and the Business of Coaching

Zeina Ghossoub

Introduction and Literature Review

The definition of ethics, depending on the source, refers to principles that govern a person's behavior or action based on moral guidelines.

The definition of a profession alludes to a paid occupation that undergoes significant training and education.

Coaching is a profession that deals with human beings. Much like healthcare, it is governed by a code of ethics that serves as its moral compass. Most coaches rely on the International Coaching Federation (ICF) code of ethics to help guide the standards of their practice. In some instances, if not all of them, the code of ethics serves as the only guideline and governing rules and regulations for coaching.

Unlike other professions, coaching is not a regulated industry. There are no rules or regulations on a local, state, and federal or country level. Coaches will operate strictly within their moral conscience and within the guidelines of the code of ethics.

The other issue with the coaching industry is that there are no norms, no set guidelines, no standards of practice that are well defined or need to be met. When dealing with physicians who operate in one of the most regulated industries, this may be problematic. Doctors depend on rules, regulations, guidelines, algorithms, and direction. They hold themselves to their professional standards, they hold others to them, and the public and the industry hold them to these standards. Coaching, for as great of an impact it can have, is almost the exact opposite. Ethical standards and professionalism can sometimes be an issue in this industry. It is the responsibility of the coaches to hold themselves to the highest and strictest of ethical, moral, and professional standards.

The ICF Code of Ethics serves to uphold the integrity of ICF and the global coaching profession by setting standards of conduct consistent with ICF core values and ethical principles, and guiding ethical reflection, education, and decision-making. This code of ethics describes the core values of the ICF, ethical principles, and ethical standards of behavior for all ICF Professionals. (ICF Code of Ethics).

DOI: 10.4324/9781003452065-14

The code discusses the ethical standards that coaches are held to with respect to the following: Responsibility towards the client, the coaching profession, communication, honesty, coaching and the professional relationship with the client, agreements and contracts, stake holders, record keeping and confidentiality, transparency, accountability, declaring any conflict of interests, a commitment to excellence by maintenance of certification and education, self-limitation recognition, conflict resolution, accurate representation, no false advertisement, and adherence to the code of ethics.

The other two main coaching associations are the European Mentoring and Coaching Council (EMCC) and the Association for Coaching (AC). They, too, have their code of ethics. They are very similar to the ICF. They emphasize 5 major points:

- Keep your focus the welfare of the clients and act in ways to promote that.
- Do no harm, to you and your clients.
- Practice within your scope of competency.
- The interests of the client should be respected.
- Be cognizant and respectful of the laws and regulations of where you are practicing.

An important part of the coaching experience is communication. Some suggestions for setting expectations, communicating clearly, and creating a safe and predictable environment, which would resonate with the physicians, are:

- Clarity of communication: Leave no ambiguity, discuss freely and clearly, and make sure your client's questions are answered and concerns addressed. This can be an ongoing process with frequent "check ins" to gauge your client.
- Make things visible. Make sure that certain points are highlighted and are hanging or visible in your practice space for your clients to see them. As there are no state regulations or standards, clients will feel much better if they see what your professional, ethical, and moral standards are. Make sure the clients know what to expect in terms of treatment, confidentiality, interactions, and ethical guidelines.
- Have the code of ethics, no matter the source, be available. Make copies and give them to your client, if need be, or give them the website to download it through their email. Make them aware and it never hurts to go over these guidelines with them.
- Make sure they know what steps to take and what options they have if there are conflicts that may arise. Conflicts can arise from the coaching process itself, from the coach, the coachee, the topic, the

feedback process, the boundaries, the goals, and the action plans. To identify the source of conflict, the coach needs to make sure that the conflict does not exist and if it does, to listen and question intently, without prejudice, and keeping the best interest of the client and the coach. The conflict sometimes arises with or from the coach due to the same processes or the client's behavior. It is the responsibility of the coach to address the conflict swiftly, thoroughly, and decisively. Some of the steps the coach can take are:

a   Identify the conflict and its origin.
b   Acknowledge the conflict and the emotions that go with it, for the client and coach.
c   Validate those emotions and thoughts.
d   Co-create solutions while exploring if they are available.
e   Maintain open communication, trust, and support. This can be challenging with difficult clients.
f   Actively listen, with intent, curiosity, and sincerity.
g   Make sure your non-verbal communication is sending the right message. Soften the voice, make sure your posture is non-threatening or defensive, your facial expressions convey empathy and understanding, and your gestures are warm and welcoming.
h   Own up to the points your coachee is mentioning if they are valid.
i   Do not pacify.
j   Confront and handle the topic or situation, not the client.
k   Legal considerations

Not being a regulated industry, and not having any state or country or legal obligations does not protect coaches from being sued. There are some points to consider that help protect you from being sued.

• Know the laws of where you are practicing. Not every country or state are the same.
• Sign a contract with your client. In the contract, outline your roles and responsibilities, as well as the client's roles and responsibilities.
• Stay within the scope of your practice. If you are specializing in life coaching, and this is what you advertise, practicing in the executive lane may cause problems and may get you sued for misrepresentation.
• Avoid tort: Negligence, causing emotional distress, and fraud. One of the key issues with coaching is not giving advice. Sometimes, the lines between counselling and coaching get blurry. Often, more often than not, especially with physicians, they may ask for advice because that is what they know how to do. They may put it on your plate to help them resolve their issues, especially if you as a coach are a

physician as well. Be very cognizant of this when it happens. Document it if you have to in your notes that at that moment, you were asked for advice and you clarified the situation, the advice, and the content. Some coaches record their sessions. If you get permission from your client to do so, while of course assuring the privacy of the conversation, these recordings may act as your "coaching records", or proof of the session should you be sued.

- Do not give any medical or counselling advice or therapy advice.
- You can purchase malpractice insurance to help ease your concerns.

The Business of Coaching

As coaching in healthcare gains traction, it will be imperative that you identify your expertise and your niche, and perhaps even more importantly, announce or market them. Coaching doctors and other healthcare professionals will be part and parcel of the industry. Further, being able to train, educate, and develop physicians and healthcare professionals as coaches may be paramount to the growth and sustainability of this ever-changing demanding landscape.

a   Why have a niche?

"Designing a presentation without an audience in mind is like writing a love letter and addressing it 'to whom it may concern'" *Ken Haemer, former AT&T presentation research manager.*

If coaching in the healthcare industry is your passion and you want it as your niche, make sure you let everyone know. Think about who will benefit from you coaching a physician? The target audience includes, but not limited to:

- Healthcare institutions
- Physicians and other healthcare professionals
- Physician groups
- Medical associations
- Coaching associations
- Risk management groups
- Malpractice insurance carriers
- Anyone else you may think of

  a   Understand your client: Hopefully, by now, you have a much better understanding of your client.
  b   When in doubt, ask for help. There are plenty of resources by ICF or online that can support you. Decide what your infrastructure will be. How do you want to structure your business or practice. As a corporation, sole practice... Do you want to form a group,

join a group, be independent, be part of an organization... Find out what works for you.

c   Be ready, be prepared: This is a young industry in the healthcare profession. Knowing your craft and knowing how to apply it through proper training and education is paramount to starting strong, maintaining momentum, and growing the business. News travels fast, and your best advertisement is word of mouth.

d   Identify your core message and theme. Make sure it is articulated and communicated well.

e   Market, market, market.

Marketing Your Business

Because of the novelty of this profession, your clients, doctors, will want to know so much about you and the industry before they entrust you with their lives. The more information, data, and scientific research you can display, the more you can make the profession and you understood and seen, the more the potential clients. The most obvious need is a well-designed website that clearly states who you are, your mission statement, your clients, your focus, your approach, and your specialty. This is an investment that can make or break you. Your website is your introduction to this group of clients who hold everything to certain standards of perfection, presentation, validity, reliability, and professionalism.

a   What should be on your website?

- Put your audience first.
- Speak your target audience's language.
- Write in your brand voice.
- Craft compelling headlines.
- Use images and videos.
- Write well-structured, easy-to-read posts.
- Post regularly.
- Keep your posts personal.

b   Create a blog.

- A blog post is any article, news piece, that's published in the blog section of a website.
- It typically covers a specific topic or query.
- It is educational in nature.
- It ranges from 600 to 2,000+ words, and contains other media types such as images, videos, infographics, and interactive charts.
- It helps drive traffic to your website.
- You can repurpose blog content for social media.
- It helps convert traffic into leads (use call-to-action).

- It drives long-term results by answering common questions your clients have.

c   How to start a blog?

- Understand your audience. Ask questions like:

d   What do they want to know about?
e   What will resonate with them?

- Check out your competition.
- Look at popular, highly reviewed blogs.
- Look at visuals, writing styles and topics.
- Determine what topics you'll cover. Ask yourself:

f   Who do I want to write to?
g   How well do I understand this topic?
h   Is this topic relevant?

There are several ways to market your business and yourself.

a   Social media. It can be great for:

- Building awareness of your business
- Letting people know how they can benefit from your services, *and*
- Staying connected with your customers and your competitors.
- Reaching a broader client base
- Creating and maintaining your brand
- Understanding your audience better
- Increasing customer loyalty
- Building better relationships with clients
- Some of the examples include, other than your website: Twitter, Facebook, LinkedIn, Pinterest, Instagram, YouTube
- Doctors prefer professional platforms. The more you can be visible on those platforms, the better your chances of gaining clients.
- Referrals/ Word of mouth.
- Networking.
- Public speaking and seminars.
- Partnerships: Have partnerships with coaches providing complementary services to yours.
- Joining an association (like ICF).
- Cross-promoting your business.
- Create a customer avatar: Bring together the facts you've gathered about your niche.
- Demographics – age, sex, marital status etc.
- Social and cultural environment.
- Their values.

- Their experiences and expertise.
- How do they feel about life right now?
- How do they want to feel about life in the future?
- What do they fear?
- What fills them with hope?
- How do they like to access information?
- How do they like to learn?
- Who inspires them?
- How familiar are they with the ideas you want to share?

b Answer these customer questions:

- What does this person want or need right now?
- What resources or learning would best serve their interests?
- What are 3 ways or places I can connect with this person? Where can I find them and how could I talk to them?
- What are 3 channels to this person? Their HR person, their group, their leadership.
- What's the one thing that if this person could hear it from me they would want to hear? what would they Google?

Conclusions and Recommendations

There are no rules or regulations that govern the industry of coaching. However, there are ethical, moral, and professional guidelines that help ensure the best possible coaching relationship. Problems can arise in any one of those guidelines through the coach, the coachee, or the coaching process. One of the best ways to avoid that is to make sure that roles, responsibilities, and expectations are clearly defined. It is worthwhile and worth every effort to make sure that adequate time is spent identifying, clarifying, delineating, and answering all questions and concerns regarding those guidelines. Coaching is a relatively new professional arena in the healthcare industry. Knowing this profession, this industry, and the business models and how to market and advertise helps the coach develop and maintain a successful business.

Summary and Key Points

a The coaching industry, until now, is not a regulated industry.
b Ethical, moral, and professional guidelines on a local, national, and international level
c Coaches need to know the laws and regulations that govern the profession of coaching where they practice.
d Coaches can be liable to legal action for misrepresentation, for unprofessional conduct, and for practicing counselling or giving unsolicited and sometimes solicited advice.

e   Malpractice insurance could be bought for coaches.
f   Communication, setting expectations, and knowing boundaries and limits for the coach and the coachee goes a long way in mitigating misunderstandings and potential legal, ethical, and professional downfalls.
g   Coaching is a business. It is a relatively young business in the healthcare industry. Knowing your clients, and knowing how to market to them will help you create and maintain a successful business.

References

ICF Code of Ethics – International Coaching Federation.
The EMCC and AC signed code of ethics.

15 Challenges of Coaching in the Healthcare Industry

Naim El-Aswad MD, FACP, ACC

Introduction and Literature Review

The challenges that face implementing coaching in the healthcare industry come at multiple levels. From a system's level, challenges include financial, time, application, documented impact, and relevance. From an institutional level, financial, feasibility, documented impact, relevance, and return on investment. From an individual level, financial, time, feasibility, documented impact, return on investment, purpose, and self-fulfillment.

The cost of certain medications can be prohibitive. However, when weighed against their impact on quality and quantity of life, cost seems almost an afterthought. The reason for that is the documented benefit of the medication. No one would deny their loved ones or themselves the gift of such a medication or an intervention if it is known to help. But to arrive at that conclusion, a few things must happen:

1 Identifying the disease
2 Understanding its pathophysiology
3 Developing a medication/protocol/algorithm/approach for treatment
4 Researching the approach/medication
5 Documenting efficacy of the approach/medication while accepting the risks of treatment
6 Assigning the cost to the approach/medication
7 Accepting the approach/medication as scientifically sound
8 Accepting the medication/approach ethically, morally, legally
9 Application of the medication/approach with documented results
10 Continuous evaluation and assessment with improvement and change as necessary to enhance the impact.

We have seen this model play out in the business world with respect to coaching, and in the healthcare industry, albeit for a disease process. In the 1980's and 1990's, a new disease emerged, and it was known for its most striking of symptoms. So much so, we named it after its two most prominent presentations: Kaposi's Sarcoma/Pneumocystis carinii. At the

DOI: 10.4324/9781003452065-15

time, we did not know that a virus was the cause although there was a suspicion. Once discovered, the HIV virus, and its potentially fatal sequalae, AIDS, came the taboo of having the disease. It took years to manufacture the first treatment, get the treatment accepted, and then expand on that treatment. Before medication targeting HIV, we were merely trying to help the body fight the other diseases and their manifestations and symptoms. Fast forward to today, and we hardly ever see those same symptoms. Today, we target the virus, and we have managed to effectively treat and control HIV, almost to the point where we do not see AIDS anymore.

If we are to follow that example, we are currently in the "treating the symptoms" phase or trying to. We have yet to address, in earnest, the "virus" or true cause. There was a time when we thought that HIV was too smart as a virus that we may not be able to do anything substantial about it. Thankfully, we proved ourselves wrong.

The healthcare industry seems as complex. Every single one of these steps is a challenge or can be a challenge to introducing coaching as a modality/approach for help with burnout, life-work integration, leadership, self-care, and wellbeing, enhancing the patient experience, minimizing errors, decreasing turnover, decreasing cost, addressing organizational needs, managing change, being efficient, and increasing revenue.

If you are to pause for a second and reflect, how would you rate yourself in terms of proficiency in each of the above fields/categories? On a scale of 1 to 10, which number would you give yourself? After you are done, how confident are you with your abilities to not only "float" in those fields/challenges, but to master them? On top of all these demands, one needs to add the challenge of the cost of coaching and its programs, as well as the time investment for its application.

The healthcare industry is just that, an industry. It is a dynamic field that is extremely demanding and ever changing. As of 2021, there are over 22 million workers in the healthcare industry in the USA. (www. census.gov). There are around 30 million workers in the health and social industry in Europe as of 2023 (www.statista.com) India and China combine for around 20 million workers. One can only imagine the numbers in the rest of the world, as the data varies. It is safe to say that there are over 80 million workers in the healthcare industry, if not more.

How do you "treat" them all? How do you help them "master" their environment?

Why coaching?

Trying to convince the healthcare industry in general, and CEO's and CFOs in particular, of the benefits of coaching sometimes may feel like pulling "tusks", not teeth! The following are some of the arguments and data that may help in convincing them of the need for it.

Anticipating why stake holders and people in the decision-making spaces may refuse coaching, its application, its approach, and its impact, will help you pave the way for convincing them to turn their "no's" into "yes's". As mentioned before, people will pay and reach for their medication if it is worth it. Using a scale, on the one side of the scale, there are the real and the perceived deterrents of coaching:

- Real Deterrents: Cost, time, lack of proven benefits, resistance among the physicians, focus on "fixing" the system, not the person, and coaching is not enough, so why try it?
- Perceived deterrents: Coaching is complicated and demanding, managing burnout is complicated, coaching is for "fixing" problem physicians, if it did work, then others would have done it, and physicians are not ready for coaching.

No matter the type of deterrent, most, if not all of them, come from a place of lack of knowledge, lack of courage, and lack of resources.

On the other side of the scale, there are the "proven" or "shown" benefits: Efficient, impactful beyond any other measure of intervention on a personal level, diverse and dynamic, cost-effective with a high return on investment, applies to physicians regardless of their fields of practice, their culture, their ethnicity, their religion, their workplace and environment, or their specialty. Further, there is proven impact in other industries and in the healthcare industry, sustainable results, validated and reliable results, measurable outcomes, impacting the person, the institution, the system, and the industry. It is applicable to almost all aspects of physicians personal and professional lives, through its processes, and through its tools and their applications. (As has been demonstrated in other chapters such as emotional intelligence...)

Literature demonstrates that helping individuals, teams, and groups with professional development, communication, collaboration, and team building helps support them and enables them to master their environment.

"Communication is the cornerstone of healthcare". (Merlino, 2017) Effective communication from clinical, administrative, and interpersonal perspectives, depend on being accurate, thorough, clear, open, honest, and compassionate.

Communication needs to be horizontal and vertical in both directions. Effective teams and communications not only protect patients from risks and improve outcomes—they also create a more positive, engaging, and resilient workplace... with lower rates of injuries, burnout, presenteeism and absenteeism (Rosen et al., 2018).

There has been a lack of investment in management and leadership in the healthcare industry. The mistake that most programs and organizations make lies in the assumption that successful clinicians will make great leaders. One of the main problems in this approach is that physicians get promoted based on their clinical expertise and success into roles that require a totally different set of abilities, desires, and expertise (Quinn & Perelli, 2016).

There is a need to develop physician leaders. (Stoller et al., 2018) The challenges to do so are:

- Health-care organizations are made up of many professional work forces and "silos", making them complex structures to manage.
- Physicians' characteristics emphasized during their training.
- Not enough time or opportunities during academic training.
- The presence of several urgent challenges with respect to quality, access, and affordability: Leadership from within the organization, the external environment, new technologies with their own challenges and evolving structure, and the difficulty of managing the professional workforce while operating in multiple and potentially competing goals of service

Developing physicians' skills as leaders and communicators has been shown to result in (Rotenstein et al., 2017; van de Riet et al., 2019): Better patient outcomes, decreased mortality, increased financial rewards to the organization, decreased rates of burnout, healthier physicians, improved quality of care, and enhanced patient safety.

In 2018, Kane and Cyr surveyed physicians who identified the following as important competencies for them in their roles as managers and leaders. As you read through them, you can identify those skills that would benefit from coaching: Financial literacy, strategic thinking, change leadership, organizational awareness, analytic thinking, collaboration, communication, self-development, project management, and performance management

"Professional coaching has been associated with improved retention, interpersonal relationships, job satisfaction, organizational commitment, ability to manage complexity, and communication skills." (Dyrbye et al., 2019). "Coaching helps provide leadership 'language' and 'identity'. It appears to 'name' clients as 'leaders' and challenges 'imposter phenomenon'. Coaching provided bespoke, deep, experiential learning, with transferable benefits not otherwise available in the Specialty Training programme" (Harte & McGlade, 2018).

> For all participants, executive coaching appeared to positively impact their personal and professional development…The added professional development tool of executive coaching for specialist physicians may have a significant role in supporting productivity, increasing workplace engagement and transforming the culture of medical practice.
>
> (Kirk, Kania-Richmond, and Chaput, 2019)

One of the gurus discussing the personal, professional, and financial impact of burnout is Tait Shanafelt, MD. His body of work has helped solidify the importance of investing in physicians' well-being and abilities for themselves, their patients, and their institutions. In 2015, he outlined 9 organizational steps necessary for developing physician leaders with all the benefits. Of those 9 steps, he emphasized the need to harness the power of leadership, cultivate community at work, align values and strengthen culture, and promote flexibility and work-life integration.

> On a national scale, the conservative base-case model estimates that approximately $4.6 billion in costs related to physician turnover and reduced clinical hours is attributable to burnout each year in the United States.
> This estimate ranged from $2.6 billion to $6.3 billion in multi-variate probabilistic sensitivity analyses. At an organizational level, the annual economic cost associated with burnout related to turnover and reduced clinical hours is approximately $7600 per employed physician each year.
>
> (Hahn Shasha et al., 2019)

In another study published by Shanafelt in 2017, the cost of burnout was calculated through physician turnover. National data showed it costs anywhere between 500,000 to 1,500,000 USD to replace one physician. Direct costs resulted from recruiting, onboarding, and reaching maximum efficiency. Indirect cost came from burnout among other team members, disruption of the department processes/flows, added burnout and stress among other team members. Patients get better and cheaper care by their long-term physician than their replacements. With turnover, there is decreased productivity, much higher loss of revenue for the healthcare organization (felt across employed and non-employed models, academic and non-academic programs). Other costs are related to decreased patient satisfaction, increased staff turnover, worse patient outcomes, increased readmission rates, decreased quality of post-hospital care, and worse mal-practice cases.

In 2022, we published an article on the impact of peer coaching has on physician turnover, and consequently, on the bottom line in dollars. (El-Aswad et al., 2022). 92 physicians were referred for coaching for being "problem physicians". Our company trained a certain number of physicians to become coaches. Their initial investment: 20,000 USD. Through coaching, the projected terminations which were 45.4 were reduced to 7. The ROI from their investment ended up equaling 5.376 million dollars. Not only were there more retention, but the physicians also ended up becoming "star" physicians with extremely positive feed-back from patients and staff alike.

20,000 USD investment returned 5.376 million USD. Show me a CEO who would turn that down.

Of the available solutions for targeting these challenges, very few are maybe as effective in time and cost as coaching. Thankfully, the coaching world has gathered enough data and proof of concept in various industries. Even more impressive is that the impact of coaching in these industries can be transferred to healthcare because coaching targets the same human and industrial challenges.

Let us focus on a resource that is more valuable than money. Time! This is frequently one of the largest and most difficult hurdles you will face. Stating it simply, no one has time! Not the executive, not the physician, not the manager, not the institution… no one. So, how do we convince the people that time is not only a non-issue, but could also be a positive and a facilitator, not a hurdle?

The following serves as a guideline. Each case is different.

- Ask, ask, ask: Ask the powers that be what their issue with time is? Or are?
- Inquire what they know about the whole process of coaching.
- Inquire about their expectations from coaching.
- Ask them to give you their three best time-efficient interventions.
- Inquire about what they believe a cost-effective use of time looks like. (Cannot argue or make your case unless you know what the expectations are. If the expectations are unrealistic, ask them about a practical approach they have used to justify their expectations)
- Ask about what they have tried so far. What has worked, what has not and why.
- Ask them to inquire about coaching and for you to be able to answer all their questions.
- Do not promise anything you are not able to deliver… or anyone else for that matter.
- Provide some information about coaching and time:
    - How long would a session last.
    - How many sessions to expect.
    - The potential impact of completing sessions vis a vis the targeted outcomes.
    - Compare the time of coaching to other interventions, not just through quantity of time spent, but quality of outcomes. In terms of impact, coaching is and remains to be one of the most impactful interventions whether on an individual, group, or company level.

It seems, hopefully by now, that coaching is a vital "medication" or approach to help achieve these goals of self-care, leadership, productivity, efficiency, decreased errors, decreased burnout, increased engagement, and "mastering" one's environment. But what can we do to convince others of this potential?

Changing minds... and hearts

Here are a few steps that will help you convince others that your services and expertise are not only justified, but are necessary and vital, just as that "costly" medication. This simple algorithm can be used as a baseline approach. You can modify it, change its order of steps, add to it, remove from it, or use it as is. There is no literature to back this model up. It does not come from any source. Where it comes from is years of experience in this field and its successful implementation across different states and countries and continents.

Step 1: Announce yourself as an expert in the field of coaching:

- To your friends and colleagues
- To c-suite, HR, and anyone else who is a decision maker. This applies to either your company, if you are employed in a physician-lead company, physician staffing company, or physician-based companies, or to other entities such as hospitals, healthcare institutions, mal-practice insurance companies, risk management companies, or any company that deals directly or indirectly with physicians.
- To physicians, individually, or groups
- To societies.
- To medical schools and residency programs.
- To anyone you perceive, know, or think needs to know.
- Online through website and social media.

Step 2: Once you do, it is important to talk about coaching and show its impact. This can be done either through initial pro-bono work or through paid work. Presentations and lectures, demonstrations, seminars, round-table discussions, workshops, publications, coaching sessions, poster-presentations, and university/educational curricula.

Step 3: Have an identity, a brand, way, or philosophy of approach. Focus on targeted goals. Be ready to identify, discuss, elaborate, and defend the how, where, when, what, and why you want to help physicians.

Step 4: Be confident, relentless, fearless, and motivated. Remember why you are doing this. If you do not believe in coaching, you will falter, you will give up, and you will neglect. Whether you are a coach by trade, or a physician turned coach, this industry will test your resolve, your sense of worth, your sense of belief, your commitment, and your why. You are not gifted the benefit of the doubt that you experience as a coach in other industries or as a physician in the practice of medicine. People do not know what you do. They are sometimes on the other end of the spectrum and can be downright hostile! Dig deep and remember why you are doing this. One life changed is worth it; worth it for that life, and worth it for all the lives it will touch. I have been a physician for over 25 years, and by my modest estimation, I have seen over 150 thousand patients. I wish I knew then what I know now. I can only imagine the impact this knowledge would have had on me and my patients. You do not need to imagine. Just know: Coaching works, it works marvelously, and it is worth it!

Step 5: Know your challenges. To get people to use your services and trust in you and in coaching, you need to identify what your challenges are. That happens by gathering information. Do not assume anything. Instead, focus on identifying all the reasons why you cannot, should not, and must not be hired, and go after them systematically, scientifically, and methodically. This chapter has listed some of your most common scenarios. But each entity has its own challenges and thoughts. Once you identify them through asking the decision makers and the physicians, target them with an open mind, a focused approach, and a scientifically sound argument. The literature is now much better and supportive than what it was five years ago vis a vis coaching. Some of the arguments, as you have seen, are already made for you. Others you will need to make. The beautiful part is that new data is coming out almost every day, and the announcement of coaching as a viable and real option in the health-care industry has been made and is being reenforced. People are getting exposed to the knowledge of this "wonder drug or medication" more frequently, more intensely, and more emphatically. What a wonderful time for you to be the one who is the expert in that field!

Step 6: Know your ROI! At some point in the conversation, money will be a topic of discussion. How much will this cost? What is the projected ROI? How can you prove it? One of the best ways you can answer these questions is by asking the client for their outcomes or goals.

Case Study

Contracting with a hospital in Texas, I asked the hospital Medical/Executive committee to list their targeted goals and expectations. They had four, for nurses and physicians:

- Decrease burnout and increase engagement.
- Increase retention and decrease turnover.
- Decrease medical errors.
- Enhance patient satisfaction scores.

I then asked them how they would measure these outcomes, and what is their target goal. One physician per year, three nurses per department, patient satisfaction scores instruments, etc. Then I asked what they had done so far? What steps have they taken, and how much has it cost them? Finally, I asked how much they are willing to pay, and what is their expected ROI.

Once you make your proposal, tailor it around their expected measurable outcomes. I cannot emphasize enough the importance of focusing on measurable outcomes. This provides clarity for you and the client. As much as possible, keep the measures as objective as possible. Keep the expectations reasonable and clear. You are not going to "fix" all the problems. You are, however, going to potentially impact positively their stated goals. Make sure you quantify your "impact". For example: Increase the patient satisfaction scores by a certain number or delta change. Decrease physician turnover by 1 or 2 per year. Once you identify the sources for medical errors, analyze and identify your potential impact. If errors are due to resource management, that is beyond your control. If errors are due to communication and collaboration, that is something you can impact. Make sure you put it in measurable words and actions: Quantity and quality of communications. Help them create a measuring tool if they do not have one. Help them create their own metrics for communication and collaboration if they do not have one. And finally, have them translate those changes in dollar signs. What will it mean for them to retain one or two physicians? How will it translate to decrease medical errors? This step can be tedious and time consuming. Sometimes, it can be frustrating. I cannot stress enough its importance to help you not only show your impact but justify your cost. Remember, you are serving the current client, and auditioning for the next one, while building the case for your services.

Another frequently discussed issue is the availability of human resources, or humans as resources. Acting as consultants or supporting institutions can be done in two major ways:

- Train the trainer program: In this scenario, you are hired to develop an in-house wellness officer/committee by providing the training in: work-life integration, leadership, coaching, team coaching, collaboration and communication, resilience, well-being, and any other institute specific demand/need. Although this makes financial sense sometimes by training in-house professionals and utilizing them as paid or reimbursed employees instead of continuously paying a third-party vendor, the problems that most face are availability of their employees, and their retention. Investing in their selected group requires that they take time from their clinical responsibilities, and that they remain with the institution for a considerable amount of time to justify the investment of time, money, and expertise in them by the institute.
- Third party vendors: In this approach, the institute hires you to be a third-party vendor. You would be responsible for implementing and managing the program while you help develop some stake holders and some levels and once goals are achieved, be a resource for the institution as a consultant.

People in the healthcare industry genuinely do not know or know very little about the ROI of coaching. There are not set rates or standards to rely on or use as reference. And without any guideline, you will face extreme hesitation, trepidation, and doubt. The following numbers are approximate numbers. They come from personal experiences and rates from other industries. They depend and fluctuate depending on your level of expertise and training, the size of the institution, the number of clients, and the goals of the job.

You set your own cost. Just make sure it is within reason for you and them. What frequently happens is that once you propose a fee for services, a financial department will study the Fair Market Value (FMV) of your proposal. The industry does not have any known benchmarks. So, you need to make the argument that your rates are reasonable by citing your expertise, the impact of coaching in this industry and other industries, and by a potential ROI.

- 200 to 400 USD per coaching session per physician. (Average of at least 6 sessions. Can be up to 12 or 24 sessions or even ongoing)
- 750–1500 USD per presentation.
- 5000 to 10000 USD per workshop day. (Max twenty participants per workshop) (To allow for optimum participation)
- 2500–5000 USD per half a day of workshop. (Max twenty per workshop)
- 500–1000 USD per group coaching session. (Maximum ten per group)

Outcomes are measured by whatever has been decided on in your prior conversations. I gave the example of the company that invested 20,000 USD and saved 5.376 million dollars. If the literature cites that replacing a physician costs anywhere between 500,000 to 1,500,000 USD, then spending anywhere between 1200 USD and 10000 USD seems to not only be a smart move, but really a relative drop in the bucket.

Summary and Conclusion

We are at a crossroad. A world and an industry exist that is ailing and demanding a new medication/approach for help. In some ways, it has given rise to this ailment, perpetuates its existence, and is looking for outside help or internal resources to mitigate and manage this festering reality. In other ways, it holds the key to its own healing approach.

The timeline is set. The symptoms have been identified. The causes have been outlined, and the afflicted population highlighted. The "client", the healthcare industry, is suffering from economic challenges, resource constraints, unrealistic expectations, a growing population in numbers and demands/needs, while relying on a workforce that is tired, burnt out, overworked, practicing in hostile environments, driven by purpose and need that are continuously challenged and eroded, and lacking in certain skills and abilities that are necessary and vital to not only survive, but thrive on an individual basis and a healthcare industry level. The expectations are to do so much more with so much less.

An approach "medication" is available. The healthcare industry is an industry, a business, with its financial, political, ethical, legal, and social rules and regulations. At its heart, and brain, are people. It is people who drive it, manage it, master it, direct it, grow it, protect it, enrich it, dedicate it, and support it. It is our "why" to help protect and nourish these people. This workforce in general, and physicians in particular, need and deserve our support and help. And while some efforts are directed at making the healthcare industry more "friendly" to its workforce, too many are suffering now and cannot afford to wait for the potential impact and outcome of these efforts.

Coaching, a scientifically proven practice, can help physicians and the healthcare industry on multiple levels. Through its impact on the personal and professional lives of physicians, on leadership and self-care, on burnout and engagement, on systems and individuals, coaching has proven and continues to prove its worth and its impact, both immediate and long term.

In the next chapter, I will be talking about what the literature suggests needs to happen in the healthcare industry. So why am I mentioning it here? I think this chapter is a summary and a conclusion by itself!

References

Dyrbye, L.N., Shanafelt, T.D., Gill, P.R., Satele, D.V., West, C.P. (2019) Effect of a Professional Coaching Intervention on the Well-being and Distress of Physicians: A Pilot Randomized Clinical Trial. *JAMA Intern Med.* 179(10):1406–1414. doi:10.1001/jamainternmed.2019.2425.

El-Aswad, N., Ghossoub, Z., Nadler, R., Olsen, K. M., Sigler, S., Simmons, S. (2022). Impact of intensive peer coaching on physician performance. *Management in Healthcare: A Peer-Reviewed Journal.* 6(4):369–378.

Han, S., Shanafelt, T.D., Sinsky, C.A., Awad, K.M., Dyrbye, L.N., Fiscus, L.C., Trockel, M., Goh, J. (2019) Estimating the Attributable Cost of Physician Burnout in the United States. *Annals of Internal Medicine.* 170(11):784–790. doi:10.7326/M18-1422. Epub 2019 May 28. PMID: 31132791.

Harte, S., McGlade, K. (2018) Developing excellent leaders – the role of Executive Coaching for GP specialty trainees. *Education for Primary Care.* 29(5):286–292. doi:10.1080/14739879.2018.1501770. Epub 2018 Aug 21. PMID: 30129393.

Kane, N., Cyr, L.A. (2018) Physician Leader Training: The Value, Impact, and Challenges. *NEJM Catalyst Innovations in Care Delivery.*

Kirk, V.G., Kania-Richmond, A., Chaput, K. (2019) Executive Coaching for Leadership Development: Experience of Academic Physician Leaders. *Healthcare Quarterly.* 22(1):54–59. doi:10.12927/hcq.2019.25835. PMID: 31244469.

Merlino, J. (2017) Communication: A critical healthcare competency. *Patient Safety and Quality Healthcare.*

Quinn, J.F., Perelli, S. (2016) First and foremost, physicians: the clinical versus leadership identities of physician leaders. *Journal of Health Organization and Management.* 30(4):711–728. doi:10.1108/JHOM-05-2015-0079. PMID: 27296888.

Rosen, M.A., DiazGranados, D., Dietz, A.S., Benishek, L.E., Thompson, D., Pronovost, P.J., Weaver, S.J. (2018) Teamwork in healthcare: Key discoveries enabling safer, high-quality care. *American Psychology.* 73(4):433–450. doi:10.1037/amp0000298. PMID: 29792459; PMCID: PMC6361117.

Rotenstein, L.S, Sadun R., Jena A.B. (2017) Why doctors need leadership training. *Harvard Business Review.*

Shanafelt, T.D., Gorringe, G., Menaker, R., Storz, K.A., Reeves, D., Buskirk, S.J., Sloan, J.A., Swensen, S.J. (2015) Impact of organizational leadership on physician burnout and satisfaction. *Mayo Clinic Proceedings.* 90(4):432–440. doi:10.1016/j.mayocp.2015.01.012. Epub 2015 Mar 18. PMID: 25796117.

Shanafelt, T., Goh, J., Sinsky, C. (2017) The Business Case for Investing in Physician Well-being. *JAMA Intern Med.* 177(12):1826–1832. doi:10.1001/jamainternmed.2017.4340.

Stoller, J.K. (2018) Developing Physician Leaders: A Perspective on Rationale, Current Experience, and Needs. *Chest.* 154(1):16–20. doi:10.1016/j.2017.12.014. PMID: 30044730.

van de Riet, M.C.P., Berghout, M.A., Buljac-Samardžić, M., van Exel, J., Hilders, C. G.J.M. (2019) What makes an ideal hospital-based medical leader? Three views of healthcare professionals and managers: A case study. *PLoS One.* 14(6):e0218095. doi:10.1371/journal.pone.0218095. PMID: 31185051; PMCID: PMC6559653.

16 Coaching for Change in the Healthcare Industry

Naim El-Aswad MD, FACP, ACC

Goals! Everyone has them. This whole book is predicated on that word. No matter the level of intervention, leadership, work, profession, or even just existence, we all have goals. In fact, some might argue that the very definition of life itself is the constant achievement of goals. Put in another light, it is the process of change, of movement, on all levels. Some would argue that death is the cessation of change. That once any organism, ceases to change and achieve different goals, it essentially "dies". This is not meant to be a philosophical conversation. More so a practical one. Inherent in this formula of life, change, and achieving goals is the question of "how"? There are, for sure, other questions that help clarify the "how"? The why, the what, the when, and the where are all essential for the process of change and goal achievement. The very basis of medicine is the discovery of what is, the determination of what and where it should be by understanding the "why", and the emphasis on the "when". What is almost more often missed is the question that is at the heart of failure for achievement of goals.

"How" is where people, institutions, intentions, dreams, and goals falter. To minimize that failure, medicine came up with recommendations that seemed ubiquitous to all patients: Low cholesterol, normal blood pressure, controlled blood sugar, appendectomy, weight loss, and so on and so forth. It was the complexity of the treatment and the high rates of failure that prompted the practice of medicine to realize that "not one glove fits all". That is so true. But ask a physician or a nurse or a healthcare provider or executive, how do they personalize that approach/goal to their patients/clients, and you often see a blank stare. That blank stare gets more accentuated if you ever ask the providers to try and apply their recommendations to themselves, then envision their patients and clients to do the same.

The past 15 chapters have discussed some of the issues in healthcare. They have also discussed goals, and helping people achieve their goals by coaching them and their "how". If we are to apply the concept of "one glove does not fit all", of "goals", and of the need for change, can anyone see a more pressing need to rely on coaching in the healthcare industry to help trailblaze that needed change?

DOI: 10.4324/9781003452065-16

Read any recommendation about dealing with burnout, no matter the level of intervention. Dissect the conversations on work-life integration. Analyze leadership guidance tools and advice. Look up needed applications of changes to the industry. What is inherent in all of these are "goals", and the need for "change". Some will even give the "how" on an industry and institutional stage by suggesting algorithms of steps. The literature will provide detailed approaches to combating burnout, decreasing cost, enhancing physician well-being, reducing turnover, optimizing performance, minimizing medical errors, and improving the quality of life for patients. One needs to develop a wellness committee, align values, change culture, discuss with leadership, develop leadership...

Relying on a single reference to reflect this is not wise, is not advisable, nor is it adequate to state one's case. Some would argue that relying on one source may weaken the argument. That could very well be true. However, the quotes and ideas or recommendations taken from this one source serve only to reflect those same ideas and recommendations from multiple sources and not meant to serve as the only reference. It is merely used as an illustration to emphasize the point of coaching needs in the healthcare industry.

It is perhaps best served if it is directly quoted. The source, "Strategies to Reduce Burnout: 12 Actions to Create the Ideal Workplace", is a beautifully written, methodically, and meticulously articulate, and insightfully revealing book on developing and implementing strategies to reduce burnout. (Swensen & Shanafelt, 2020) I would consider this book a vital reference for any recommended change on a micro and macro level in the healthcare industry to try and reduce burnout and help with physician well-being. There are other books that discuss work-life integration, and almost every other "goal" outlined above. Let me quote some of the recommendations as an illustration. They are not in any particular order.

- "A Losada ratio of 6:1", or 6 positive comments or events to 1 negative event or comment, "is highly correlated with superior team performance".
- "The eight ideal work elements: Trust and respect, community at work and camaraderie, control and flexibility, fairness and equity, intrinsic motivation and rewards, professional development and mentorship, safety, and partnership."
- "Ultimately, creating an environment of well-being for healthcare professionals is about culture change."
- "The most important determinant of value in health care organization is an intangible asset called social capital".
- "For professionals to flourish and patients to receive the best care, attention to organizational culture and a balance between independence and standardization in work must be achieved."
- "The root of the tree is trust". That tree refers to workplace culture as quoted from Michael Bush. "The key to having people feel trusted is respect".

Take a moment and look at these recommendations. Analyze their demands and their goals. Then, ask yourself: How do I achieve them? How do I get others to do so?

I can go on and on citing the different recommendations from this resource, and a multitude of others. No doubt they are based on sound scientific data that is valid, reliable, and effective. Again, it is necessary that these recommendations be applied adequately, correctly, efficiently, thoroughly, and repeatedly. Which again begs the question: How?

One of the oldest methods of teaching in the medical field is: See one, do one, teach one. In 2017, at one of the conferences for AHME (Association for Hospital Medical Education), I presented a poster showing the blind leading the blind. Recommendations were being made left and right. The problem: No one knew or knows "how" to apply them. Very few, if any, could lead by example. There was a collective agreement that some "goals" need to be met. Yet, where implementation fell short is the actual "how". No different than when we recommend to patients that they need to lose weight, buy certain foods, take their medications, exercise… and frequently they fall short because of not being able to, and not knowing how.

In 2009, the ICF published the potential impact of coaching in the healthcare industry. These were wonderfully summarized by Stephany et al in 2023. The areas that are positively impacted by coaching in the healthcare industry include (quoted directly from the article):

Table 16.1 Impact Areas of Coaching

Individual level	*Interpersonal relationship skills, Communication skills, Work performance and efficiency, Time management, Career strategies, Work/life alignment or balance, Human well-being and resilience, Perspective taking, Imposter phenomenon, Personal accountability, Development of a service orientation, Development of a learning and growth mindset, Individual-level support in times of stress, duress or trauma*
Organizational level	Leadership skills, Organizational perspective taking, Stakeholder engagement, Employee engagement and retention, Team effectiveness, Development of a positive organizational culture, Organization-level support in times of stress, duress or trauma.

In 2024, Miller-Kuhlmann et al published an article that gave an outline as well as a detailed approach on "how" to build a coaching program in medical education. Without going into its specifics, they discussed 12 steps, or "tips" as they referred to them. These steps have been discussed throughout the book. This approach can help make the argument to the healthcare industry in general, and to the medical education world in particular, on why, where, when, and how to apply coaching. These steps can easily be applied to any residency program, any departmental, institutional, or even system wide intervention. These tips are quoted from the source:

> Identify "the why" or reasons a coaching program is needed; learn from established programs and prior literature; conduct a needs assessment of key stakeholders; identify and obtain resources needed; outline program goals and objectives; design programmatic approach; gather, adapt, or design tools for coaching; recruit coaches; design and implement faculty development for coaches; create and implement an orientation for learners; gather feedback on the program to assess feasibility and acceptability and to guide program improvement; collect program outcome data to demonstrate programmatic impact.

Conclusion

There are a few truths to be emphasized.

The healthcare industry is filled with recommendations for change while asserting the need for individuality of approaches.

The healthcare industry, and its professionals, do not provide a way for their patients, and their workforce, to achieve their set goals.

The healthcare industry, and it's professionals, have yet to fully embrace the profession of coaching, and still question, at times, its relevance, validity, and applications.

It is our responsibility to bring coaching to the healthcare industry. It is our privilege, and pleasure.

Over the past ten years, as I have presented and discussed burnout and the challenges of the healthcare industry that face physicians and other professionals, I am often met with an applause that is an acknowledgement of the truths that I share. Overwhelmingly, my audience agrees with the material, and the recommendations. Over 95 % agree to the necessity of change. Where they stumble and falter is their "how".

I challenge physicians, professionals, executives, and anyone who serves in the healthcare industry to state a recommendation and then, more importantly, show me their "how". No matter the level, the task, the goal, the change, the destination, I love to hear their "how".

How will they:

- Be a leader?
- Evoke trust?
- Integrate their work and life?
- Decrease their burnout?
- Enhance their productivity?
- Become more engaged?

- Connect to purpose and need?
- Change the culture?
- Adapt?
- Evolve?
- Create?
- Support their family?
- Support themselves?
- Be well?
- Apply?

There is an intersection of the healthcare industry and the coaching industry. That intersection did not occur haphazardly. On the one side, there is an industry, with its workers in general, and physicians in particular, that are being driven and are consequently suffering, on a personal and professional level, to the point of sometimes paying the ultimate price: Life itself. This industry, that serves humanity, is suffering. It is burdened with more demands, less supplies, more expectations, less margins of error, more responsibilities, and less resources, to produce better, cheaper, more efficient, and more universal outcomes.

On the other side, there is coaching, an industry that is predicated on scientific premises, proven approaches, evolving data, and applicable knowledge that provides the approach and methodology to help people, institutions, and industries not only meet their challenges, but thrive.

By focusing on the individual, the group, and the collective good; by becoming experts, yes experts, in eliciting the possible best in any and all of us, and providing the environment, tools, and blueprints to help; by having the ability to be at the center of any change, or life itself; and by helping to answer the "how", coaching presents itself not only as a viable way, but I dare say, a necessity.

One question left to answer: What are we still waiting for?

References

Miller-Kuhlmann, R., Sasnal, M., Gold, C.A., Nassar, A.K., Korndorffer, J.R.Jr, Van Schaik, S., Marmor, A., Williams, S., Blankenburg, R., Rassbach, C.E. (2024) Tips for developing a coaching program in medical education. *Medical Education Online.* 202429(1):2289262. doi:10.1080/10872981.2023.2289262. Epub 2023 Dec 5. PMID: 38051864; PMCID: PMC10783821.

Sensen, J.S., Shanafelt, T.D. (2020) *Maro Clinic Strategies to Reduce Burnout: 12 Actions to Create the Ideal Workplace.* Oxford University Press.

Stephany, A.M., Archuleta, P., Sharma, P., Hull, S.K. (2023) Professional coaching in medicine and healthcare. *Clinical Sports Medicine.* 42:195–208 doi:10.1016/j.csm.2022.11.001.

Index

Note: **Bold** and *Italic* page numbers refer to **tables** and *figures*.

Abi-Jaoudé, J.G. 104
academic medicine 180
accountability 26, 56, 84, 149, 155,
    161, 188
Accreditation Council for Graduate
    Medical Education (ACGME)
    109, 112
active listening 85
agreements: establishing and main-
    taining 84
Alexander, Graham 6
Anderson, T. 104
anxiety 24, 33, 91, 122, 131, 139,
    164, 177
appreciative inquiry 2
Arendt, Hannah 76
Arora, S. 109
assertiveness 41, 112, 116, 177, 181
assessments 97, 170
attention management 119, 120, 127,
    129–130
attention mismanagement 119,
    129, 130
autocratic coaching 21
autonomy, relatedness, and
    competence (ARC) 120
autopilot 64, 74, 126
awareness 97; evoking 85
awareness-based coaching 78

Babiker, A. 80
Barber, K. 104
Bar-On, Dr. Reuven 102
Barron, Fr. Robert 32
behavioral disconnect 35–36;
    collaborative work, case study
    36–37; focus, coaching 36

being on your case 120, 135–137, 140
being on your side 120, 135–137, 140
Better Up 58
Binns, Jeremy 51
Blessingwhite 64
blind spots 62, 63, 106, 111, 177
Boet, S. 57
Borenstein, D. 120
bouncing forward 120
*Bouncing Forward: Why "Resilience"
    Is Important and Needs a Definition*
    (Borenstein) 120
Bourke, L. 104
Boyatzis, Dr. Richard 60, 65, 110
Breso, E. 105
Brown, M.T. 17
bureaucratic coaching 26
burned-out brain 96, 98, 99
burnout 33, 34, 37, 40, 44, 49, 57,
    90–101, 105, 106, 144, 199, 208,
    210; case study 100–101; coaching
    for 96–98
business: of coaching 187, 189–191,
    193; marketing your 191–193

career coaching 21, 168–179; Birkman
    personality assessment test 173,
    173; case studies 176–178; clinical
    and academic setting, physicians
    176; MBTI Myers Briggs type
    indicator **170**, 170–171; residency
    and fellowship 175–176; strong
    interest inventory 173–174
careers 14, 153, 168, 169, 171, 174,
    176–180; choices 169, 170, 174,
    175; growth 20, 176; satisfaction
    182, 183

case studies, healthcare: approach 28; presentation 27–28; process 29; results 29; situation 28
case study 77–78; scary cardiac surgeon, Dr. T 66–67
Castillo, F. G. 81
Cavanaugh, K. 48
challenges 48–52
challenge-specific coaching 39–40
Cheesebrough, K.R. 175
chronic stress 91
chronic uncontrolled stress 49
Cialdini, Robert 128
CID-CLEAR coaching model 82
circle of concern 52, *52*
circle of focus 52, *52*
circle of influence 52, *52*
clarity 108
client-coach relationship/alliance 26
client growth facilitation 85
Clutterbuck, D. 83
coach, word meaning 1
coachability 46–49, 54
coach-client relationship 27
coaching, defined 1
coaching approaches 10, 13, 19, 20, 23, 24, 27, 41–44, 90, 92, 180, 182
coaching interventions 68, 129, 182, 183, 185
coaching sessions 6, 8, 10, 40, 41, 78, 79, 94, 97, 98, 100, 175, 177, 184, 185
coaching tools 61, 124, 145, 157–159, 162, 163
code of ethics 187, 188
cognitive scarcity 35
communication 34, 58, 59, 61, 63, 66, 81, 82, 85, 88, 154, 155, 188, 197, 198, 203; skills 21, 40, 53, 58, 100, 108, 109, 177, 198
competence/competencies 63, 64, 83, 109–112, 114, 116, 119–121, 123, 139, 146, 150–152, 159, 161, 177, 181
components, coach 56
conscious attentional deployment 128–130
constructive development 2
contract 9, 10, 188, 189
conversation 9, 12, 14, 36, 39, 59, 64, 65, 68, 74, 76, 77, 100, 159, 160
costs 18, 103, 104, 195–197, 199, 200, 202–204
Covey, Stephen 52

critical thinking 75, 134
Cronkite, Walter 32
crushing identity crisis (CIC) 107
C-suite 38
cynicism 107
Cyr, L.A. 198

decision fatigue 108
decision-making cluster 113
Deiorio, N.M. 1
Dembkowski, S. 12
democratic (participative) coaching 20–21
depression 33, 91, 106, 119, 122, 126, 164
derailer detector 63, 66
developmental coaching 25–26, 28
Dewey, John 74, 75
dial down clues 72
dial up behaviors 72
disillusionment 107
Dwek, Carol 156

Edmondson, Amy 150
effective leaders 144, 145, 152
effective leadership styles 144, 181
Eisenberger, Naomi I. 129
El-Aswad, N. 58, 107, 109
Eldridge, F. 12
Emotional Brilliance: Living A Stress Less, Fear Less Life (Lyubomirsky) 128
emotional competence inventory (ECI) 110
emotional connection 34; focus, coaching 34–35
emotional exhaustion 58, 101, 106, 180, 182
emotional expression 112
emotional intelligence 2, 34, 40–41, 98, 100, 102–105, 107–110, 184; action plan 114; balance 110; case study 114; dissatisfied and overwhelmed 116; interventions 108–109; measuring 110; in medicine 102–116; pillars of 109; poor decision making 114–115
Emotional Intelligence (Goleman) 102
emotional intelligence tools 69; success in excess 69–72
emotional pain 129, 140
emotional pleasure 126, 140
emotional quotient 102
emotional regulation 76, 106
emotional self-awareness 111, 116

emotional thermostat 65, 107
emotions 10, 11, 23, 24, 34, 35, 102, 111–113, 128, 163–165, 189
empathy 33, 108, 112
employee-centered leadership 146
engagement: coaching as 92–96
environmental factors 107, 180
ethical practice 84
ethics 97, 187–189, 191, 193
Eurich, Tara 62
executive coaches 60, 63, 66, 106, 137
executive coaching 1, 57, 59, 198
executive leadership 41
"expert model approach" 5
expert *versus* coach's approach **15**
extrinsic motivation 18, 25

Fainstad, T. 182
fast *versus* slow thinking **62**
fatal flaws 63
Fearless Leader Assessment 157
female physicians 180–185; assessment tools 184; case studies 183–184; coaching applications 182–183; coaching literature 182; coaching strategies 184–185; outcomes, coaching interventions 185
financial implications 104
Fine, Alan 6
flexibility 113
flow theory 2
focusing, physician 78–79
Folkman, J. 151
Fordyce Emotions Questionnaire 125, 134
foundational principles 59–61
Frames of Mind (Gardner) 102
Frankl, Viktor 49
Franklin, Benjamin 111
Friedland, Dr. Daniel 96
FUEL Coaching Model 12

Gallup 107
Gallwey, Tim 56
Gardner, Howard 102
Gawande, Atul 46
gender biases 180, 181
Gestalt Therapy 62
Ghossoub, Z. 107, 109
Gilbert, Andrew 8
Gilbert, Daniel 130, 131
goal-reality-options-will (GROW) process 6–8, 10, 12, 124, 145, 159, 160

goal-reality-options-will (GROW) process 122–125
Goethe 36
Goldsmith, Marshall 63, 106
Goleman, Dr. Daniel 102, 110
Gordon, Thomas 4
Grant, Dr. Anthony 65, 66
Greenberg, C. 130
group coaching 37, 183
growth mindset 149, 156, 161, 162, 176

Hackman, J. R. 81
H.A.P.I.E. model 130
happiness 119, 120, 125–127, 129–132, 134, 135, 137–139, 169
Harvey, S.B. 33
Hawkins, Peter 9, 82
healthcare 14, 15, 17–23, 27, 29, 80, 81, 85, 86, 105, 126, 127; environment 32–44, 144, 146, 183; team, coaching 80–88
healthcare industry: case study 202–204; challenges of coaching 195–205; changing minds and hearts 201–202; coaching for change in 207–211; perceived deterrents 197; real deterrents 197; refuse coaching 197
health-care organizations 198
healthcare professionals 34, 43, 44, 49, 104, 190, 208
healthcare workers 18, 34, 69, 116, 144
health coaching 18
Hella, J.R. 104
Helping People Change (Boyatzis, Smith and van Oosten) 65
Hippocrates 27, 41, 91
holistic coaching 22–23
Holland, John 173
How We Think (Dewey) 75
human-centered approaches 146, 147, 150, 152
human-centered leadership approach (HCL) 144–165; ask questions 165; case study application 147–150; coaching and developing employees 159; coaching tool, understanding bias 157–158; communication and inclusion 153–155; empathy 162–163; fostering connections and trusting relationships 151–159; granting autonomy and delegating through

accountability 155–156, 161; GROW model 159–161; growth mindset, adopting 161–164; humility 162; inspirational leadership communication 150; perspective taking 162; psychological safety 150–151, 155–156; punitive environments 146–147; putting it in writing, emotions 164–165; resilient and courageous 162; safe space 164; self-awareness 162; shame and blame 146–147; vulnerability 162, 163–164
human needs 37; focus, coaching 37–38
Hur, Y. 174

ICF Code of Ethics 187–188
imposter syndrome 57, 177, 182
impulse control 113
Influence: The Psychology of Persuasion (Cialdini) 128
insight 108
Insight (Eurich) 62
inspirational leadership communication 149, 150
institutional resources 180
internal medicine 96
International Association of Coaching (IAC) 1
International Coaching Federation (ICF) 1, 56, 60, 83, 187, 188, 190, 192, 209
internet based coaching 18
interpersonal cluster 112
interpersonal neurobiology 127
interpersonal relationships 112, 127, 162, 198
interpersonal skills 112, 184
interventions 33, 34, 54, 81, 109, 110, 182–184, 195, 197, 200, 207, 208, 210
intrinsic motivation 2, 18, 26, 181, 208
intuitive coaching 24
investment 60, 132, 191, 195, 197, 199

Jung, Carl 170

Kabat-Zinn, Jon 23, 96, 131
Kahneman, Daniel 61
Kane, N. 198
Keltner, Dacher 65
Kimieck, Jay 2

Kirkpatrick, H. 104
knowledge 14, 22, 38, 108, 120–122, 151, 152, 155, 159, 162, 177, 178, 202
Korn, F. 62

Lacerenza, C.N. 86
lack of control 44, 49, 50, 90
laissez-faire (leave alone) coaching 22
laissez-faire leadership 152
leadership 22, 40, 41, 61–64, 127, 144, 152, 176, 180, 181, 198, 208; coaching 57; development 126, 130, 150; focus, coaching 41; legacy 66; models 144, 152; skills 58, 105, 109, 177, 182, 183; styles 146, 148, 150, 152, 153; training 57, 86, 126
legal obligations 189
Leonard, Thomas 1, 56
life coaching 1, 18, 19, 26, 57, 189; defined 19
life skills 19
locus of control 50, *50*
Long, O. 134
Longstaff, Professor Patricia 120
long-term goals 25, 119, 164
loss of control 51
Lyubomirsky, Sonya 128

malpractice insurance 194
Mann, A. 182
Maslach, Christina 33
Mayer, J. D. 102
Mayer-Salovey-Caruso Emotional Intelligence Test (MSCEIT) 110
MBTI 170, 171, 177, 178
McLeod, Dr. Angus 10
McNulty, J.P. 104
medical education 169, 175, 209
medical errors 106, 202, 203
medical training 34–35, 109
medication 17, 19, 91, 195–197, 200, 205, 209; adherence 17
medicine 4, 5, 19, 33–35, 102, 104, 105, 109, 168, 171, 174, 176, 207
mental health 33, 37, 90–101, 127; problems 33
Miller-Kuhlmann, R. 209
mindfulness 23, 56, 96, 130–132, 134, 135, 139; coaching 23–24; defined 96
mindset 25, 39, 46–47, 53, 54, 84, 121, 124, 156, 157, 161, 173

mindset intervention coaching 38
misconceptions 37, 180, 181
modern healthcare 35, 36
Morgeson, Frederick 40
motivational interviewing 2

Nadler, R. 107
neural circuitry 119, 126, 129
Nietzsche, Frederick 18
nonviolent communication 2, 18

Obhi, Sukhvinder 65
observant-self theory 135
O Castell, Dr. Donald 96
On Becoming a Leader (Bennis) 145
"one glove fits all" approach 20
online coaching program 57
optimism 113, 116, 127, 177
OSCAR Coaching Model 8
Osler, Sir William 168
Oxford Happiness Inventory 134

Palamara, K. 182
patient care 112, 148, 154
patient-centered approaches 148,
    153, 155
patient-centered care 148, 154, 162
patient satisfaction 36, 154
peer coaching 58, 199
perceived deterrents 197
performance coaching 57
Perls, Fritz 62
PERMA 138
personal coaching 1, 57
personalities 98, 171, 174–177
personality types 48, 98, 170,
    171, 178
personal life 56, 93, 137
perspective coaching 26
physical pain 129, 140
physician burnout 106, 107, 110
physician leadership 36, 144–165
physician-patient relationship 34
physician training 85, 107
physician turnover 199, 203
Politis, Y. 104
Positive and Negative Affect Scale
    (PANAS) 134
positive emotional attractor (PEA) 60,
    65, 69
positive emotions 4, 125, 138, 139
positive engagement 138, 139
positive psychology 2, 15, 18, 56,
    130, 138

positive relationships 105, 138, 139, 151
potential coaching approaches 33
power 23, 27, 48, 65, 104, 199, 200;
    paradox 65
practice of medicine 4, 19, 34, 168,
    201, 207
prefrontal cortex 24, 32, 34–35, 43,
    49, 90, 91
presence, maintaining 84–85
pressure 42–43, 106; focus,
    coaching 43
*Pre-Suasion: A Revolutionary Way to
    Influence and Persuade* (Cialdini) 128
prevention: coaching as 91–92
primal sympathy 33–34, 168
problem solving 113
Prochaska, James 2
professional community 184, 185
professional development 20, 80, 108,
    197, 198, 208
professionalism 174, 187, 191
professional life 38, 100, 149
professional satisfaction 40, 182, 183
psychological motivations 120, 121
psychological safety 78, 81, 123, 145,
    149–151, 155
purpose, psychological need 120, 121

realistic time commitments 184, 185
reality testing 113
reflective inquiry 75–76
Reimers-Hild, C. 24
remote coaching 18
residency 20, 34, 91, 104, 106, 107,
    169, 175, 178
resilience 119–140, 184; being on
    your side *versus* being on your case
    132–134; case study 136–137;
    conscious attentional deployment
    128–130; emotional and
    physiological responses 119;
    happiness 125–128, 130–132;
    happiness and satisfaction, strategies
    137–139; medical-healthcare
    executive Dr. E. 136–137; return on
    investment 132; strategies 107,
    120–130; supporting concepts 120;
    tools to encourage being on your
    side 134–136
return on investment 132, 195
Rickard, M.J.F.X. 104
risk-averse leadership style 147
Roosevelt, Theodore 3
Rotter's theory 50

safety 84
Salas, E. 81
Salovey, P. 102
Sanchez-Gomez, M. 105
Satisfaction with Life Scale 134
scary cardiac surgeon, Dr. T:
   background 66–67; coaching
   activities 68; coaching interventions
   68; examples 67–68; result 68–69;
   situation 67
science of coaching 2; ACHIEVE
   coaching model 12; CLEAR
   coaching model 9–10; coaching
   models 5; FUEL coaching model 12;
   GROW model 6–8; mechanisms
   3–4; methods of delivery 5; OSCAR
   coaching model 8–9; outcomes 2–3;
   STEPPA coaching model 10–11;
   TIBA coaching model 12–14; tools
   4–5
self-actualization 25, 69, 111, 116
self-awareness 3, 62–63, 103,
   120–122, 127, 128, 140, 147, 149,
   152, 153, 156, 162, 175
self-care 33, 41, 42, 126, 127, 145,
   147, 152, 196, 200, 205; focus,
   coaching 42
self-compassion 42, 57, 105, 128, 129,
   134, 182
self-criticalness 133
self-determination 14
self-determination theory (SDT) 2, 15,
   18, 37, 120, 121
self-efficacy 18, 22, 24, 50, 181–183
self-empowerment 18
self-evaluations 136–138
self-expression cluster 112
self-fulfillment 14
self-knowledge 3
self-leadership 20, 40, 126
self-management 22, 62
self-perception cluster 111
self-regard 111
Seligman, Professor Martin 138
sense of control 21, 36, 49, 50, 53, 54
Shanafelt, Tait 40, 199
Sharp, G. 104
short-term goals 25, 27
Six Seconds.org 103, 104
skill set 36
slow thinking 59, 61, 66
SMART goals 4, 11
SMART goals (Specific, Measurable,
   Actionable, Realistic, Time-bound) 4

Smith, J.M. 176
Smith, Melvin 65
SOAP approach (Subjective,
   Objective, Assessment,
   plan) 97
social cognitive theory 2
social intelligence 102, 126, 130
social media 191, 192, 201
social pain 129
social responsibility 68, 112
social skills 102, 140
solution-focused coaching 78
specialties, coaching 57
Stejskal, Marie Taryn 127
Stephany, A.M. 209
STEPPA Coaching Model 10
Stinnet, Kathleen 12
strengths tests 184
stress 24; response 49; tolerance 113
stress management 109, 110, 184;
   cluster 113
Subjective Happiness Scale 125, 134
Sumner, L. W. 131
sympathy 33

Taylor 86
team approach 80, 154, 155
team building 81, 84, 86, 197
team coaching 80–88; case study
   86–88; discovery, diagnosis, and
   design 82–86
team development 80, 81, 85, 156
team effectiveness 81
team training 84, 86
Tee, D. 47
telephone coaching 5, 18
Thinking: Fast and Slow (Kahneman) 61
thinking partner 74–76
Thorndike, Edward 102
TIBA coaching model 12
Tomorrow's Leaders Today
   (Blessingwhite) 64
tort law 146
transactional coaching 25
transactional leadership 21
transformational coaching 26
truly human-centered leadership
   144–165
trust 84
truths 19, 32, 38, 76, 86, 164,
   180, 210

uniqueness, physicians 46–54; case
   study 52–53

van Oosten, Ellen 65
vertical gender bias 181
vision coaching 27
VIVID tool 61, **61**
Vogel, M. 104
VUCA environment 108
vulnerability 48, 132, 139, 145, 162, 163

Wageman, R. 81
Warren G. Bennis (WGB) 145, 152
Wasfie, T. 104
weaknesses 2, 3, 5, 19, 108–110, 173, 175, 178
wellbeing 24, 69, 97, 120, 124, 126, 127, 131, 138, 140, 144, 164
wellness 20, 33, 41, 42, 44, 54, 56, 57, 90, 120, 131; focus, coaching 42

Whitmore, Sir John 6, 159
Whittleworth, Karen 8
Wise, H. 80
women 180, 181
work environment 54, 87
workers 23, 24, 49, 105, 124, 196, 211
workforce 204, 205, 210
Working with Emotional Intelligence (Goleman) 102
work-life balance 39, 144, 183
work-life integration 92, 170, 182, 183, 199, 203, 208
workplace 106, 124, 127, 128, 132, 138, 146, 150, 152, 163, 197
workshops 37, 40, 51, 81, 86, 132, 201, 204

Zenger, John 12, 151

For Product Safety Concerns and Information please contact our EU
representative GPSR@taylorandfrancis.com
Taylor & Francis Verlag GmbH, Kaufingerstraße 24, 80331 München, Germany

www.ingramcontent.com/pod-product-compliance
Lightning Source LLC
Chambersburg PA
CBHW050643280326
41932CB00015B/2755

9 781032 589039